YO-CBT-212

Research and Education Reform

Roles for the Office of Educational Research and Improvement

Richard C. Atkinson and Gregg B. Jackson, *Editors*

Committee on the Federal Role in Education Research
Commission on Behavioral and Social Sciences and Education
National Research Council

National Academy Press
Washington, D.C.   1992

NOTICE: The project that is the subject of this report was approved by the Governing Board of the National Research Council, whose members are drawn from the councils of the National Academy of Sciences, the National Academy of Engineering, and the Institute of Medicine. The members of the committee responsible for the report were chosen for their special competences and with regard for appropriate balance.

This report has been reviewed by a group other than the authors according to procedures approved by a Report Review Committee consisting of members of the National Academy of Sciences, the National Academy of Engineering, and the Institute of Medicine.

The National Academy of Sciences is a private, nonprofit, self-perpetuating society of distinguished scholars engaged in scientific and engineering research, dedicated to the furtherance of science and technology and to their use for the general welfare. Upon the authority of the charter granted to it by the Congress in 1863, the Academy has a mandate that requires it to advise the federal government on scientific and technical matters. Dr. Frank Press is president of the National Academy of Sciences.

The National Academy of Engineering was established in 1964, under the charter of the National Academy of Sciences, as a parallel organization of outstanding engineers. It is autonomous in its administration and in the selection of its members, sharing with the National Academy of Sciences the responsibility for advising the federal government. The National Academy of Engineering also sponsors engineering programs aimed at meeting national needs, encourages education and research, and recognizes the superior achievements of engineers. Dr. Robert M. White is president of the National Academy of Engineering.

The Institute of Medicine was established in 1970 by the National Academy of Sciences to secure the services of eminent members of appropriate professions in the examination of policy matters pertaining to the health of the public. The Institute acts under the responsibility given to the National Academy of Sciences by its congressional charter to be an adviser to the federal government and, upon its own initiative, to identify issues of medical care, research, and education. Dr. Kenneth I. Shine is president of the Institute of Medicine.

The National Research Council was organized by the National Academy of Sciences in 1916 to associate the broad community of science and technology with the Academy's purposes of furthering knowledge and advising the federal government. Functioning in accordance with general policies determined by the Academy, the Council has become the principal operating agency of both the National Academy of Sciences and the National Academy of Engineering in providing services to the government, the public, and the scientific and engineering communities. The Council is administered jointly by both Academies and the Institute of Medicine. Dr. Frank Press and Dr. Robert M. White are chairman and vice chairman, respectively, of the National Research Council.

This project was supported by the U.S. Department of Education

Library of Congress Catalog Card No. 92-80848
International Standard Book Number 0-309-04729-3

Additional copies of this report are available from:

National Academy Press   First Printing, May 1992
2101 Constitution Avenue N.W.   Second Printing, August 1992
Washington, D.C. 20418

S583

Printed in the United States of America

COMMITTEE ON THE FEDERAL ROLE
IN EDUCATION RESEARCH

RICHARD C. ATKINSON (*Chair*), University of California, San Diego

LAWRENCE J. BADAR, Mathematics and Natural Science, Case Western Reserve University

G. CARL BALL, George J. Ball, Inc., West Chicago, Ill.

JAMES A. BANKS, Center for Multicultural Education, University of Washington, Seattle

KATHERINE L. BICK, USA Centro SMID, Washington, D.C.

C. LARRY HUTCHINS, Mid-continent Regional Laboratory, Aurora, Colo.

BEVERLY L. JIMENEZ, The Achievement Council, San Francisco, Calif.

CHARLES F. MANSKI, Institute for Research on Poverty, University of Wisconsin

PAUL E. PETERSON, Department of Government, Harvard University

ANDREW C. PORTER, Wisconsin Center for Education Research, University of Wisconsin

ALBERT H. QUIE, Minnetonka, Minn.

MARILEE C. RIST, National School Boards Association, Alexandria, Va.

CAROL H. WEISS, Graduate School of Education, Harvard University

KENNETH G. WILSON, Department of Physics, Ohio State University

GREGG B. JACKSON, *Study Director*

ANNE S. MAVOR, *Senior Research Associate*

SUSAN M. ROGERS, *Research Associate*

CINDY S. PRINCE, *Project Assistant*

Contents

Preface

The Office of Educational Research and Improvement (OERI) in the Department of Education is responsible for a broad range of research, development, and dissemination activities. Over the years, OERI and its predecessor agencies have been subject to widespread criticism: researchers have often claimed that support for education research has been insufficient, misguided, and poorly managed; teachers and principals have often been unaware of the office or claimed it hasn't done much to improve their schools; and members of Congress have often expressed dissatisfaction and frustration—as much with their votes as with their words.

With these historic problems in mind, with heightened national attention on educational issues, and with the scheduled reauthorization of OERI approaching, the agency asked the National Academy of Sciences to consider how federally supported education research can better contribute to improving the nation's education. The Academy, through its National Research Council, convened 15 distinguished experts to conduct the study. The Committee on the Federal Role in Education Research includes members from the physical, biomedical, and social sciences; a businessman and a former congressman and governor who have long involvements with research; several leading education researchers; a former teacher and a former principal, both currently working with practitioners; and an editor of education journals. (Brief biographies of the committee members and staff appear in the Appendix.)

The committee was given a broad charge. It was asked to evaluate the structure, operations, and functioning of OERI and the organizations it supports; to examine other federal agencies with research missions to ascertain if they might provide useful models for OERI; and to review the nation's overall educational research enterprise to identify unmet needs, duplication of effort, and appropriate activities for OERI. In the course of its deliberations, the committee determined that consideration of these issues would benefit from appraisals of how education research is used and how schools change, and both of these topics were added to the study.

The committee did not deliberate the substantive topics on which OERI's research and development efforts should focus because another major study, started a year earlier, was considering this matter. The report of that study is now available (National Academy of Education, 1991).

This is not the first occasion on which the National Research Council (NRC) has addressed issues related to education research. In a 1958 report, *A Proposed Organization for Research in Education*, it recommended the establishment of an "Organization for Research in Education" to contribute to the improvement and advancement of education. In 1977, *Fundamental Research and the Process of Education* concluded that government agencies were focusing on quick solutions to poorly understood problems and that more basic research on education was needed. A 1986 report, *Creating a Center for Education Statistics: A Time for Action*, found serious problems in the National Center for Education Statistics (NCES) and recommended either a major overhaul or elimination of the agency.

Those three reports are related to this current one by more than their common heritage. The first helped induce the federal government to become involved in education research. The second appears to have had a limited though brief impact on a problem that still exists and is examined again in this report. The third helped precipitate a major effort to restore NCES, and this report briefly reviews some of the outcomes of that effort.

Our committee met six times between February 4, 1991, and January 21, 1992. This was a complex and difficult study with a daunting schedule, but the committee members handled their tasks with unflagging enthusiasm, commitment, and goodwill. Our meetings were filled not only with discussions and debates, but also with teaching and learning, as each of us shared unique expertise and learned from our colleagues.

The committee has been generously assisted by many persons and organizations. Information and suggestions were solicited widely and received from approximately 200 people and organizations, including researchers, teachers, and principals; directors of research in large school districts; governors and chief state school officers; education writers; professional organizations; business organizations; foundations; and administrators and staff of federal research agencies. A few of their comments are quoted in the report; because we promised confidentiality, those quotes are without attribution.

The study would not have been undertaken without the foresight of Christopher Cross, who served as the Assistant Secretary of OERI from 1989 to 1991. In the summer of 1991, Diane Ravitch assumed that position and continued the full cooperation of the agency. The OERI project liaison, Tommy Tomlinson, did a superb job of handling our steady stream of requests for briefings, data, documents, and other assistance. At least three dozen people in the agency responded to those requests, with the heaviest burden falling on Tom Brown, Joseph Conaty, John Egermeier, Linda Jones, and Dawn Nelson.

The committee's deliberations have benefited substantially from work that was commissioned for this study. Carl Kaestle interviewed many of the key figures in federal education research and development and synthesized their views on the history of that enterprise. Brenda Turnbull prepared a review of the literature on the uses of research knowledge in school improvement efforts and contributed to the drafting of Chapter 1.

The committee also wishes to acknowledge the many contributions of Cindy Snellings Prince, who provided excellent administrative support; Janet Ewing, NRC reference librarian, who helped on numerous occasions; Anne Mavor and Sue Rogers, who served capably as research associates and helped draft parts of the report; Eugenia Grohman, associate director for reports, who provided invaluable editorial consultation and rehabilitation; and Alexandra Wigdor, director of the Division on Education, Training, and Employment, who generously provided the committee with advice and feedback.

Richard C. Atkinson, *Chair*
Gregg B. Jackson, *Study Director*
Committee on the Federal Role
in Education Research

Executive Summary

The National Research Council of the National Academy of Sciences was asked to examine how federally sponsored education research might better contribute to improving education throughout the nation. A multidisciplinary committee of 15 distinguished scientists and education experts was assembled to undertake the study.

The committee was asked to evaluate the Office of Educational Research and Improvement (OERI), explore other federal research agencies that might provide models for OERI; and briefly review the nation's entire education research enterprise. In the course of its deliberations the committee also undertook examinations of how education research is used and how schools change.

The United States is currently committed to major education reform. This commitment has resulted from evidence that substantial proportions of the nation's students appear headed for school failure while the academic and intellectual demands of the workplace are expanding and international economic competition is increasing. At the same time, the ratio of workers to retired persons is decreasing. The current goal for school reform is the most ambitious in the history of the country: it aims to provide virtually all students with in-depth understanding of subject matter and strong problem-solving skills. Although there is considerable enthusiasm for these ambitions, it is important to note that the country has a long history of launching education reforms that are soon abandoned.

Education reform is a difficult, complex, and lengthy process. Authentic and sustained school reform requires not only the contributions of research, but also coordinated improvements in the preparation of teachers, in the curriculum and instruction for all subject areas and grade levels, in the structure and administration of schools, in the opportunities for teachers to learn throughout their careers, in parental understanding and community support, in federal and state policies, and in the resources available to support these changes.

Education research has been used far more than is commonly believed. One example is basic research in cognitive science, conducted by scholars in psychology, linguistics, sociology, and neuroscience, some at OERI's centers and laboratories. It has dramatically expanded understanding of how people learn and apply their knowledge and skills. Several of these findings have been incorporated into innovative programs that have shown considerable promise for increasing student performance.

The contributions of research, however, are not well known because they find their way into practice by circuitous and obscure routes. For instance, it took a decade of work in cognitive science before the findings began to be incorporated into innovative curriculum materials and instructional approaches, and even now most teachers who use the products are unaware of their research origins.

OERI is the federal government's lead agency for education research and development. It undertakes a broad range of research, development, demonstration, dissemination, and technical assistance work. There are other offices in the Department of Education and other federal agencies that have some responsibilities for education R&D, but each has a much narrower mandate. This report presents our evaluation of OERI and our recommendations for its future.

CONCLUSIONS

Our examination of OERI found an agency that has been challenged by several external difficulties over which it has little control, as well as several internal problems. The external problems begin with never-ending conflicts about education, which spill over into controversies about the appropriate roles for federal education research and development (R&D). There have been attempts to make OERI serve political purposes, and the agency has been given marginal discretion over new initiatives. The agency has also been inadequately funded, with the R&D budgets of OERI (and its predecessor, the National Institute of Education [NIE]) spiralling downward over most of their history.

Between 1973 and 1989, the R&D budgets of NIE and OERI declined by 82 percent (in constant dollars). These funding declines extracted a heavy toll on the agency: directors were quickly criticized and became demoralized; long-term agenda setting undertaken in the early years of NIE became difficult and then futile; "quick fixes" replaced thoughtful investments; resources were spread so thinly that mediocrity was almost assured. Only a few lines of research have been sustained for the time needed to bring them to fruition. There has rarely been support for the successive iterations of research, development, and testing that are needed in any field to develop marketable innovations. Individual investigators doing field-initiated (extramural) research have been almost squeezed out: only 2 percent of OERI's R&D budget supports this work; the comparable percentages at the National Institutes of Health (NIH) and National Science Foundation (NSF) are 56 and 94 percent, respectively. And basic research, aimed at discovering new phenomena, receives only 5.5 percent of OERI's R&D budget: it receives 60 and 94 percent, respectively, of the R&D budgets of NIH and NSF.

The funding declines for OERI and NIE do not appear to have been offset by funding increases from other federal agencies or other sources. In 1973 the entire federal government spent $1.1 billion (in 1990 constant dollars) on education research and development; in 1991 it spent between $310 and $364 million. Limited information suggests there have been small increases in the funding of education R&D by states, school districts, foundations, professional education associations, and business organizations, but the total of these increases is probably considerably less than the declines in federal funding.

OERI is also faced with several internal problems. It has a weak advisory council and frequent turnover in the top administrative positions. There is limited coordination among the various offices in OERI and the institutions that it funds. Few efforts are undertaken to synthesize and publicize what the agency has learned and accomplished. Quality control is uneven, and the agency rarely attempts to resolve debates on important issues of education research.

The committee concludes that OERI needs to be rebuilt. Our recommendations are aimed both at strengthening OERI's capacity to support the traditional roles of education research and to encourage and foster learning communities of researchers, practitioners, and policy makers who are involved in the improvement of education. These communities would collaborate in the use of what is already known from research and experience to develop new theories and approaches and to test their efficacy.

RECOMMENDATIONS

The committee's recommendations are organized into four groups: governance, organization and functions, operations, and funding. We first present key highlights of the recommendations and then the full text. Additional substantive details of the recommendations are included in Chapter 5.

The committee recommends strengthening the governance of OERI in several ways:

• A policy-making board should be established and charged with responsibilities for monitoring the needs and accomplishments of federal education research and guiding the agenda-setting process of OERI;

• OERI should have a director appointed for a 6-year term to permit stable leadership;

• OERI should be required to support a balanced portfolio of research, development, and dissemination; this would require substantially expanding support for field-initiated research, basic research, and sustained R&D activities.

The committee also recommends restructuring the agency to better focus and coordinate its efforts:

• Several R&D directorates should be established, each targeting a specific problem area with a sustained program of research and development that includes field-initiated efforts, institutionally based R&D, and special projects;

• A Reform Assistance Directorate should be established to coordinate reform assistance efforts, including the work of the laboratories, the Program Effectiveness Panel and the National Diffusion Network, the FIRST office programs supporting local school-based reforms, and a new electronic network linking persons concerned about research and education;

• The electronic network should incorporate an enhanced Educational Resources Information Center (ERIC);

• The National Center for Educational Statistics (NCES) should remain as it is organizationally, but its staff should be substantially increased to be commensurate with the additional responsibilities it has been given over the past 5 years; and

• OERI should help researchers, practitioners, and policy makers forge learning community partnerships in the quest for education reform.

Finally, the committee recommends changes in several aspects of OERI's operations:

• The agency should have independent authority for staffing, contracts and grants, and reporting—the first and second to improve service and the third to minimize opportunities for political pressure;

• OERI's procedures for its contract and grant peer-review panels should assure that research merit and programmatic merit of proposals are judged only by those with the appropriate expertise;

• OERI should take steps to attract high-quality personnel to the field of education research, particularly scholars from other disciplines and underrepresented minorities; and

• OERI should recruit highly qualified personnel from various disciplines for the agency's staff and create an intellectually stimulating environment for its staff.

It should be noted that no two or three of the recommendations, by themselves, are likely to substantially improve OERI. A comprehensive rebuilding of the agency is needed. These recommendations will require more funding and staff for the agency—much more. The total of our rough estimates for all the recommendations is an additional $267 million annually in program funds after a 6-year phase-in period. We also estimate that 214 new program staff will be needed. During the phase-in of these resources, the agency should engage in strategic planning that identifies the subsequent needs and opportunities for education research.

Some people will say the nation cannot afford this expense, but the committee sees it as a critical investment. With the nation beginning to spend billions of dollars on school reform efforts, better understanding is needed of how to make best use of those expenditures. OERI's role is pivotal because it is the only federal agency with responsibility for education R&D that spans all grade levels and content areas of instruction.

If the increased resources are not provided, we recommend that the mission of OERI be substantially narrowed. It is currently trying to do far more than can be done well with the available funding and staffing.

Mission, Governance, and Agenda

A-1 The mission of OERI should be to provide leadership in:

- expanding fundamental knowledge and understanding of education;
- promoting excellence and equity in education; and
- monitoring the state of education.

The mission should be accomplished in collaboration with researchers, teachers, school administrators, parents, students, employers, and policy makers.

A-2 OERI should support a balanced portfolio of activities: basic research, applied research, statistics, development, evaluation, dissemination, and technical assistance; field-initiated and institutionally based R&D; and long-term sustained efforts and responses to newly identified needs and opportunities. To do so, OERI must substantially expand support for basic research, field-initiated research, and sustained R&D activities.

A-3 OERI should have a director appointed by the President, in consultation with the agency's board and with the advice and consent of the Senate, for a 6-year renewable term.

A-4 OERI's agenda setting should be guided by a 24-member policy-making board. At least one-third of the membership should be distinguished researchers who have done work on education issues, complemented by a balanced representation of practitioners, parents, employers, policy makers, and others who have made noteworthy contributions to excellence in education.

A-5 The OERI board should establish a process to develop priorities for OERI's agenda. The process should involve active participation of the various groups concerned with education. These priorities should be set so as to maintain the continuity, stability, and flexibility needed to conduct high quality research and to effect educational change.

A-6 The OERI board should publish a biennial report on federally funded education R&D that describes its accomplishments, summarizes the programmatic activities and funding levels throughout the federal government, identifies unmet needs, and makes recommendations for future directions.

A-7 The Office of Management and Budget (OMB), the National Science Foundation (NSF), or the Federal Coordinating Committee for Science Engineering and Technology (FCCSET) should extend data collection programs, in consultation with OERI, to provide annual data on federal agencies' program activities and expenditures for education R&D.

Organization and Functions

B-1 OERI's research and development activities should be organized under several R&D directorates. Direct support for school change should be organized under a single Reform Assistance Directorate. Organization and management practices should forge appropriate linkages and coordination among the all the directorates and the field.

B-2 Each of OERI's R&D directorates should allocate substantial resources to support field-initiated research for both basic and applied work.

B-3 Each R&D directorate should support national R&D centers for pursuing coherent and sustained programs of basic research, applied research, and development.

B-4 OERI's regionally governed laboratories should be administered by the Reform Assistance Directorate and converted to Reform Assistance Laboratories (RALs) with liaison and assistance staff assigned to each state in their respective regions.

B-5 The Reform Assistance Directorate should support the research-based refinement and rigorous evaluation of innovative programs and processes that have the greatest potential for use in school reform and help schools in using these programs and processes. This recommendation represents an expansion of the functions currently carried out by the Program Effectiveness Panel (PEP) and the National Diffusion Network (NDN).

B-6 The Fund for the Improvement and Reform of Schools and Teaching (FIRST) programs that support local school-based reforms should be administered by the Reform Assistance Directorate, should be modified to require utilization of research in development of the improvements, should involve teachers and principals in the development process, and should provide sustained support for these efforts.

B-7 The Reform Assistance Directorate should foster development of a national electronic network that allows all concerned with education to access research and exemplary practice information. The system should incorporate an enhanced ERIC.

B-8 The National Center for Educational Statistics (NCES) should remain as a separate office in OERI with careful attention to preserving its scientific independence. Staffing levels should be approximately doubled as soon as practical to be commensurate with the expanded responsibilities NCES has been given over the past 5 years.

B-9 OERI should work with teacher and administrator education programs, state agencies, and local districts to help practitioners and researchers create learning communities that use research findings, practitioners' craft wisdom, and pursue new inquiry in the quest for educational reform.

B-10 OERI should develop research, training, and fellowship programs to attract high-quality personnel into education research, with particular efforts to recruit underrepresented minorities and scholars in disciplines other than education.

Operations

C-1   OERI should have independent authority for staffing, contracts, grants, and reporting.

C-2   OERI should actively recruit highly qualified personnel from various disciplines for OERI staff positions and should create an intellectually stimulating working environment.

C-3   OERI's contract and grant application review process should provide an appropriate balance between expertise in research and in practice for all proposals, with technical research merit judged by research experts and programmatic relevance judged by program experts.

C-4   OERI should implement a consensus development process involving distinguished experts to review and report on the quality and implications of potentially important bodies of research and evaluations that appear to have unclear or conflicting results.

Funding

D-1   To implement the committee's recommendations, OERI should be given substantial, phased-in, increases in its budgets and staffing levels.

D-2   Unless OERI's budget is substantially increased in the near future, the mission and activities of the agency should be significantly narrowed.

1

Introduction

As a nation, the United States has high expectations for its education system. From the earliest days of the common school to the present struggle to meet the needs of an increasingly diverse population, the country has expected that education will equip citizens for economic survival and growth; strengthen the bonds among people from different racial, ethnic, cultural, and social class groups; and sustain the nation's democratic institutions. If schools are to do their part in contributing to fulfilling these expectations, they need to be extraordinarily resilient and resourceful. This report addresses ways in which federally supported education research and development can contribute to understanding and improving education.

We argue for a new view of the contributions of research to education. We do not consider research the handmaiden of any single reform effort in education, nor does it necessarily deliver tools that have immediate utility to teachers. Instead, we take a longer and broader view. We urge policy makers to support research that will outlive the reforms of the moment and will sustain and extend the capacity for learning in schools, school districts, institutions of teacher preparation, families, and communities.

THE CHALLENGE OF EDUCATION REFORM

In the past decade, hundreds of reports have identified major inadequacies of U.S. education, and there have been numerous efforts to reform schools in this country. Every state has proclaimed initiatives for reform, and countless local programs and alliances have tried to bring about change and improvement. Intense pressures have built up nationally for renewed attention to education, as indicated by the call for national education goals (National Education Goals Panel, 1991), the congressionally mandated rapid growth of the Education and Human Resources Directorate at the National Science Foundation, and the President's AMERICA 2000 proposal for improving education (Alexander, 1991).

An earlier generation looked to the schools to assimilate the tides of immigrants who swelled the population, to teach newcomers American ways and the privileges and rights of citizenship and democracy. More recently, the movement to fully extend equal opportunity to African Americans, Hispanics, and other minorities has been closely linked to education reform.

There is no question about the significance of the challenges now facing U.S. education. Part of the imperative for today's reforms comes from increasing academic and intellectual demands of the workplace. Part of it comes from low educational attainments of a significant proportion of youth in the United States, particularly those in low-income families and those of color. And part of it comes form shifts in the age distribution of the country's population.

Workforce 2000 (Johnston and Packer, 1987) focused public attention on the many changes that have occurred in the nature of work over the past several decades. Although there is scholarly debate about the finer details of Johnston and Packer's portrait of a yawning gap between the skills of workers and the technological requirements of an increasing number of jobs, the general trend toward more technical jobs seems inescapable. From 1900 to 1990, the "laborers" category of workers shrank from 30 to 6 percent of the total work force, while "professionals" expanded from 10 to 26 percent. In the past decade, jobs requiring high-level skills or training grew at three times the rate of those requiring low-level skills or training, and projections for the next decade indicate that more than one-half of all jobs will require education beyond high school. These developments have led many people to the conclusion that in the future, more and more jobs will involve judgment, problem solving, and self-regulation (Banks, 1982).

In the business sector, the need for a stronger education system has become an article of faith as corporate leaders contemplate the challenges facing them. Competitors are no longer in the next county or state—they are increasingly apt to be in another country. Employers in the United States will not confine their searches for skilled workers within national boundaries, and as a consequence this country's workers will have to compete with skilled workers throughout the world.

According to Harold Hodgkinson (1991): About one-third of preschool children are in some danger of school failure because of poverty, neglect, sickness, handicapping conditions, and lack of adult protection and nurturance. Most of the trends in the prevalence of these conditions are negative. For example, between 1970 and 1986 the proportion of children under 18 living in poverty increased from 15 to 20 percent (Peterson, 1991); many of these are in single-parent families. Between 1970 and 1987 the percentage of female-headed families increased rapidly—from 8 to 13 percent among whites and from 28 to 42 percent among African Americans (Jencks, 1991). Fortunately, not all the trends are negative: maternal education has increased, and the average number of siblings has decreased (Robert Hauser, personal communication).

The net impact of these trends and the effects of immigration are as follows: the high school completion rate for African Americans has risen over the years, by 1989 25 percent of those in the 19- to 20-year-old age group had not completed high school. The data for Hispanics in the same age group shows that 41 percent had not completed high school (National Center for Educational Statistics, 1991a). Although some dropouts subsequently complete their secondary education through the General Equivalency Diploma and other special programs, the immigration of poorly educated adults appears to have had an offsetting effect in the Hispanic population. For the 24- and 25-year-old age group in 1989, 15 percent of African Americans and 41 percent of Hispanics had not completed high school. It is very difficult for youths who drop out of school or who experience academic failure to become self-sustaining and productive participants in a postindustrial, technologically advanced society.

To further complicate the picture, the United States has an aging population, with proportionately fewer workers to support retirees. Observers argue that if education does not improve, many of the people needed to contribute to the incomes of retirees will not in fact be productive members of the work force.

These numbers and their implications are increasingly familiar to educators, business people, and policy makers. In response, many people have called on schools to renew their efforts to impart advanced skills to the future work force. In its simplest form, the new goal can be characterized as "hard content" for all students (Porter et al., 1991): that education is not just a matter of facts and numbers, but must also promote conceptual understanding, problem solving, and the ability to apply knowledge and skills in new contexts and to real-world problems. To achieve that goal, the school curriculum in all subjects and for all students would need to place much greater emphasis on nurturing higher order thinking and the intellectual adaptability called for by the complexities of modern life.

The ambitious nature of this new goal can be compared with the goals of past curriculum reforms in the United States. In the early 1960s, when the United States was in a race to the moon with the Soviet Union, the goal was to provide an intellectually enriching education for the academically gifted because more scientists, mathematicians, and engineers were needed. Gradually, this goal was replaced by the vision of a Great Society in the late 1960s and early 1970s—a vision of providing all students with mastery of basic academic skills.

Today's goal combines the most challenging aspects of both previous reforms: all students are to learn how to think, solve difficult problems, and have in-depth understanding of subject matter. Not only is this new goal for education unprecedentedly ambitious, it is also substantially at odds with current practice. In elementary school mathematics, for example, 70-75 percent of instruction time is spent on computational skills, with the remaining 25-30 percent divided between conceptual understanding and problem solving. And even the small amount of time devoted to problem solving contains drill and practice on highly structured word problems (Porter, 1989).

In pursuit of the new goal of achieving both basic academic knowledge and conceptual understanding and problem-solving skills for all students, many people have concluded that schools do not merely need to be improved; rather, a fundamental restructuring in the nature of schooling is necessary. Among the solutions proposed by advocates of school restructuring are national goals and national achievement tests; school-site management; schools of choice; career ladders for teachers, with new roles and responsibilities; abolition of tracking and homogeneous ability groupings for students; outcome-based curriculum; reduced school size; smaller, stable, family-like instructional units of students and teachers; portfolios of student work replacing standardized tests; parental control of schools; team teaching; teacher participation in school management; ongoing staff development; deep coverage instead of broad coverage as a curriculum principle; interdisciplinary curriculum; community-based learning; and integration of community resources to serve students (Newmann, 1990; Smith and O'Day, 1990). Although the reform sentiment is strong, most of these proposed alternatives are not fully articulated and are of unknown merit.

The ambitions of today's proposed reforms are equal to the size of the problems confronting the nation's schools. But what is much less clear is whether these ambitions can be realized. As a society, the United States has been good at launching reforms; it has been less good at continuing them to completion (Cuban, 1990; Elmore and McLaughlin, 1988). And despite the growing national consensus that the nation faces a major problem in education from kindergarten through high school (K-12), fixing the problem—or even defining it adequately—remains a daunting challenge.

Education in the United States exists on a vast scale. Just the K-12 component involves 45 million students, almost 3 million teachers, about 100,000 schools, and annual budgets of more than $240 billion (National Center for Education Statistics, 1991b). The total education enterprise—

encompassing higher education, industrial education, and supporting organizations (from textbook publishers to state education agencies)—involves an estimated annual budget of more than $375 billion. How can an enterprise of this size be nudged, let alone turned around?

Both the scale and the decentralized character of education in the United States make the imposition of central solutions impossible. If schools in the United States are going to get better, it will require the combined efforts and commitment of all concerned—parents, teachers, administrators, and government officials. The challenge for federal and state policy makers is to create conditions that will make education reform more likely—to help schools and communities equip themselves with the tools of reform. When schools have an internal capacity for improvement, they can respond not only to today's reform imperatives, but also to future challenges. To achieve lasting and self-renewing education reform, the nation needs to enable schools and other educational institutions to continually learn from their own experience and from other resources. Research can make important contributions to this transformation.

At the present time, the formulation of education policy is running far ahead of education research. Whether the initiative is school choice or national testing, new ideas are being advanced and implemented with little knowledge about how they might work. This is not all bad: trying new approaches opens the possibility of learning from failures as well as from successes. But if new policies often fail, interest in education reform may be closed off prematurely—until the next wave of societal change sweeps across an unprepared education system. Research is essential in order to know which new ideas are worth exploring and which are ready for widespread implementation. It is essential for developing new ideas to their full potential, and it is essential for building capacity in the education system for continuous learning and renewal.

THE ROLE OF RESEARCH

The imagery that often dominates the discussion of education research assumes that researchers do studies, developers translate study findings into products and packages (such as new curricula), the products are delivered to schools, the schools adopt the products, and education is improved. This linear model represents only one subset of real-world experiences, and it creates unrealistic and unrealizable expectations for what research can contribute to education.

There are three major flaws in this image of the research-to-practice process. First, it assumes that all research is, or should be, suitable for development into prescriptions for practice. Although a large subset of education research is directed toward such ends, another part of the enterprise serves other functions that are equally important for the improvement of education (Weiss, 1989). Research *provides warnings* of problems in education, as in the international comparative studies that have repeatedly shown U.S. students' doing relatively poorly in science and mathematics. Research *informs policy debates* by testing the assumptions that underlie arguments on all sides of an issue, such as the determinants of parents' choices of schools for their children. Research *evaluates* the consequences of programs and policies, such as open-enrollment options. Research *provides new insights* into basic processes of individual and organizational functioning, such as the neurological networks activated in the human brain during learning or the situational stimuli for group leadership. Research *provides enlightenment*—new perspectives, new ideas, new conceptualization of problems, and new priorities. In other words, education research contributes considerably more than just the production of curricula and methods that can be adopted by schools.

Second, the linear image of research-to-development-to-dissemination-to-practice misconstrues the ways in which people learn. It is another version of the "empty vessel" image of students—students enter school empty and the teachers fill them with knowledge—that has been discredited by more than two decades of research in cognitive science. The work of teachers and principals over the course of their careers is a search for understanding and improved practice. Teachers and principals need a continuing dialogue with researchers, policy makers, and administrators about the interpretation and implications of research findings. There must be time to try new methods and approaches for the specific situations of their schools and students. Opportunities should allow collaborative inquiry to identify problems, develop solutions, and refine practices for immediate application.

A third flaw in the popular image is that it implies that school reform can be effected by research and researchers. If education does not improve, the onus can be laid at the feet of the research community: they did not choose the right topics; they did not do quality research; above all, they did not adequately disseminate their findings to teachers and administrators. There is some truth in these statements, but they are only a small part of a much larger reality. The reform of education requires the effort, will, and knowledge of millions of teachers, administrators, and policy makers, as well as students, parents, and the public. Research can help them, but they have to want research, value the insights and ideas from research, and take research ideas into account; otherwise, no "dissemination" strategy will make a difference. To date, the *demand* for research from the real world of education practice has been weak (see Chapter 4). Even if the relevance and accessibility of research are improved, the situation would not change markedly. There has to be a mutual recognition that the challenges that education currently faces require not only the best research, but also a demand for and use of that research.

A central premise of this report is that reform is an organic, developmental process. In place of the linear model discussed above, we visualize the reform of education as an evolutionary process that involves new research findings, the experiences of practitioners, the course of public policy, and other forces. This dynamic image of reform calls on the active participation of researchers, school administrators, teachers, federal and state agencies, and policy makers—a community who are at once learners and contributors to the process.

A number of scholars have given thought to what such a learning community would look like at the school and district level (Fullan, 1991; Little, 1982; Rosenholz, 1989; Skrtic, 1991; Tikunoff and Ward, 1983). They argue that to develop a productive vision of education reform, it is important to see teachers and other school professionals as the instruments of new knowledge and change. Teachers' opportunities to learn have a profound effect on the course of change; when learning opportunities are shortchanged, the outcome will be disappointing. The image of the way teachers learn must cast them in an active role: they are not empty vessels to be filled with facts and skills, but active agents in the construction of knowledge (Anderson, 1980; Simon, 1974).

The idea of schools as parts of learning communities changes the conventional view of how research can contribute to improvements in education. In that view, researchers dispense their wisdom—ideally in a well-packaged, easy-to-use format—to a relatively passive audience of teachers and administrators, and the reason for building a strong infrastructure of research, development, and dissemination is to transmit knowledge about education from a central vantage point (the government or a university) to schools, classrooms, and homes. Unfortunately, this view of knowledge development and transmission does not fit the realities of school improvement. It is far too mechanical, and it places practitioners' learning at the margins of the system rather than at its center.

The research literature on school change that has developed over the past three decades makes clear that successful reform in schools takes place through a complex and lengthy process (Elmore and McLaughlin, 1988; Fullan, 1991; Gross et al., 1971; Sarason, 1971). The process has to overcome many barriers to reform, including inadequate programs of teacher education and professional development (Goodlad, 1990), severe time pressures on teachers and administrators (Goodlad, 1984), a culture of schools that does not value change (Sarason, 1971), a lack of community demand for substantial improvements (Elam, 1990; Elam et al., 1991), inadequately developed models for change, and tight school budgets. Most past efforts at school reform have failed because they did not take into account the many complexities of the process. However, there have also been initial success stories that have helped to define some effective steps for the initial stages of reform (Crandall and Loucks, 1982; Louis and Miles, 1990; Turnbull, 1991).

The main task of reform is not to install new practices in schools the way one would install appliances; nor is it to overcome resistance to new knowledge. Instead, it is to foster learning, which is a very different and more complex endeavor. In our vision, successful change in schools requires participants at all levels of the learning community—policy makers, agency representatives, researchers, practitioners, and parents—to work together, to initiate and examine new ideas, to share new knowledge, and to test, refine, and rebuild programs. Each level of the community brings it own unique contribution to the reform effort: by working and learning together the participants can create the conditions and opportunities for increasingly effective reform.

This committee was asked to determine how federally sponsored education research could better contribute to improved education, with particular focus on the mission, organization, and operations of Office of Educational Research and Improvement (OERI). The committee does not believe that research provides simple solutions to the problems of education practice. However, a sustained investment in research is an essential ingredient in an overall effort to improve education. Research has served and continues to serve several key roles:

• Research expands understanding of the fundamental aspects of human development, learning, teaching, schools, and their environmental contexts.

• Research points the way to the discovery of effective elements of curriculum, instruction, and school organization.

• Research provides the best basis for distinguishing worthwhile innovations and policies from fads.

• Research assesses the status of education systems and their progress towards various goals.

In addition, research can contribute many ideas about how the process of reform works and how it can be helped along. This line of inquiry includes investigations that provide valuable lessons about reform efforts that have failed, as well as those that have had some success.

In considering how OERI can fulfill its mission for education research, one can learn from many different approaches to the conduct of research, development, and dissemination in federal agencies, as well as in the private sector. From the National Science Foundation, one can see how allowing scientists throughout the country to propose their own research directions and pursue new ideas has produced major breakthroughs in knowledge and understanding. From the National Institutes of Health, one can see how broad-based and coordinated research and development, focused on long-term problems, can yield dramatic solutions. From the commercial development of electrical power systems and worldwide air transportation, one can see that repeated iterations of research, development, testing, and re-finement—increasingly complex and expensive—are necessary to overcome failures, maximize effectiveness in diverse settings, and reduce costs sufficiently to allow widespread application. From the Agricultural Extension Service, one can see that long-standing, face-to-face relationships are often essential for fostering the use of even relatively easily implemented innovations.

Learning communities would be another approach to research, development, and dissemination. They would not exclude traditional approaches, and they would not be the exclusive approach for education research; instead, they would be a new arrangement within which some, and perhaps eventually, many research and related activities would be conducted. The communities would be partnerships among researchers, practitioners, and policy makers, in which each becomes involved in disciplined inquiry and each contributes to the learning of the others.

One form of partnership would focus on sharing the needs of each group with the other groups. In this form, research would be closely informed by the needs of practitioners and policy makers, and the latter would be informed of researchers' needs. A second form of the partnership would focus on sharing the expertise of each group. In this form, research would make more use of the expertise of practitioners and policy makers, and each of those groups would in turn make more use of the expertise of researchers. In a third form the partnership could include collaborative efforts. For instance, some practitioners and policy makers could work with researchers in the design of their studies, in review of the initial results, in the formation of follow-up questions for analysis, and in the interpretation and dissemination of the results.

Our view of the structure and functioning of learning communities is very preliminary: there needs to be further conceptualization, development, experimentation, assessment, and refinement of them. OERI can help encourage and foster learning communities, but their establishment and functioning will depend on the support of all the groups involved in education—federal policy makers, state legislatures and education agencies, professional associations of teachers and administrators, local school districts, parents, students, employers, and community organizations.

This report assesses the current structure and operations of OERI and examines the ways in which it can contribute more to the understanding and improvement of education. First, however, in Chapter 2 we discuss several examples of the contributions of research and development activities to the improvement of education. In Chapter 3 we turn to the organization, programs, and key operations of OERI. Chapter 4 presents an appraisal of the agency and the challenges that it has faced. The final chapter provides a series of governance, organizational, operational staffing, and funding recommendations designed to strengthen OERI for the traditional roles of research and for developing learning communities to conduct and use research.

2

Research and the
Improvement of Education

Few Americans would question the proposition that research has been a potent force for improved medical care in the twentieth century. Few would deny that research has played an equally powerful role in the emergence of modern agriculture. When it comes to education, however, research enjoys no such flattering reputation. Whether or not the judgment is justified, research in education is more likely to be dismissed as trivial or irrelevant than it is to be considered a fundamental ingredient in understanding how children learn and in improving how they are taught.

One example of this low regard is the very small portion of federal research and development funding that goes to education: slightly more than $350 million of $64.1 billion in fiscal 1991—one half of 1 percent. In comparison, the federal government spends 3 times as much on research and development activities for agriculture, 21 times as much for space research and development, and 30 times as much for research related to health. If relative funding levels are any indication, Congress is clearly not convinced that federal support of research can benefit public education in the way it has benefited the nation's health and agriculture. Members of Congress are not alone in their general low regard for research as an integral part of a robust system of education: teachers commonly indicate that they do not use research and do not see its connection to what they do on a daily basis in the classroom (Louis et al., 1984).

There are many reasons for the undistinguished reputation of research in education, only some of which are well founded. Part of the cause can be found in the practical orientation of teacher education. Schools of education generally do not prepare the nation's future teachers to value disciplined inquiry or even, at a more mundane level, to keep track of relevant research. Once on the job, the conditions of work do not encourage school teachers to study the research literature. No matter how enlightening research may be, it cannot contribute to improvements in education if it is not understood, used intelligently, and refined in the context of local experience.

This situation is aggravated by the national tendency to want quick solutions to problems—even if they have been generations in the making. Much of the public discussion of education research has a distinctly utilitarian cast: it assumes that researchers conduct studies, their findings are translated into products or programs for use in the schools, and education is improved. This view is at once too narrow and too grandiose. It implies that the only valuable research is research that can be directly translated into classroom practice, a view that gives short shrift to much research. And it encourages unrealistic expectations about what research can—or should be able to—accomplish.

The effects of research on educational practice are seldom straightforward and quick. As in other fields, there are few definitive studies, but rather a gradual accretion of knowledge drawn from overlapping studies in many fields of study, conducted over a long period of time, punctuated by an occasional breakthrough. In physics and chemistry, as well as social and behavioral science, decades of basic research provide the seed bed for new approaches and methods. Improvement in education will occur only if all participants—parents, students, teachers, the public, and policy makers—are willing to make strong intellectual commitments to work together using new insights, approaches, and techniques to improve education.

The undistinguished reputation of education research is also partly attributable to some of the work. There has been some methodologically weak research, trivial studies, an infatuation with jargon, and a tendency toward fads with a consequent fragmentation of effort. The committee, however, does not share the widespread negative judgments about the contributions of research to the reform of education. Our review of research-based programs to improve teaching, strengthen curricula, restructure institutions of learning, and assess and monitor the progress in U.S. schools has convinced us not only that research can improve education, but also that it has been demonstrably useful.

This chapter provides a brief introduction to a few of the contributions from research and development for education. Some of the work has been funded by the Office of Educational Research and Improvement, some has been funded by the National Institute of Child Health and Human Development and the National Science Foundation, and some by other federal agencies. We first discuss just one stream of basic research, cognitive science, and how it has informed understanding of the teaching and learning of mathematics and reading. We next introduce seven innovative curricula and teaching approaches, several of which are based partly on the findings from cognitive science, and then two school restructuring processes, based on other research from the social sciences. The third section describes some of the major efforts to monitor the status of American schools and teachers and the achievement of students. Finally, we discuss some of the ways in which Congress and congressional agencies have used education research.

There is much research and development that we have not covered, such as work on the social and cultural contexts of school and learning, school finance, the economics of education, administrative and organizational studies, classroom observational studies, curriculum analysis, and studies of postsecondary education. Our exclusion of these lines of work is no reflection on their importance but rather a result of the committee's limited time and our decision to cover fewer topics in greater depth. For a broader introduction to the field, see the *Encyclopedia of Educational Research* (Alkin, 1992).

BASIC RESEARCH IN COGNITIVE SCIENCE

Research has enriched knowledge of learning and teaching in many ways. One of these is knowledge about early development of thinking, reading, and mathematics skills. A number of the basic theories of the development of cognitive processes presented in this section informed the design of programs discussed below. In some cases, the findings of cognitive researchers have reinforced traditional practices used to assist children in acquiring reading and mathematics skills. For instance, the practice of reading with a child and discussing the story has been shown to build cognitive skills of summarizing, clarifying, predicting, and questioning. But just as often, cognitive researchers working in areas such as artificial intelligence and expert systems have suggested new approaches to teaching.

For many years the principles espoused by B.F. Skinner dominated human experimental psychology. His approach was based on determining the relationships between observable stimuli and observable responses, with little consideration for what went on in between. Since the late 1960s, however, the emphasis has shifted to the study of cognitive processes, modeling what the mind knows and how it knows—an approach that is more compatible with providing guidance for teaching and learning. According to Resnick (1987a:7):

> The process of making explicit the abilities formerly left to the intuitions of gifted learners and teachers is precisely what we need to establish a scientific foundation for the new agenda of extending thinking and reasoning abilities to all segments of the population.

Cognitive scientists—including researchers in psychology, computer science, linguistics, neuroscience, and anthropology—have differentiated and expanded understanding of how thought and knowledge develop and interact. The notion of schemata, first discussed by Bartlett in 1932, has reemerged as a principal concept. A schema is a mental framework for acquiring and organizing new knowledge and skill and interpreting new experience; it also contains both the elements of knowledge and the rules for relating the elements. The development of expertise involves more than the acquisition of new knowledge, it involves the remodeling of one's prior perspective. According to cognitive theorists, individuals have several schemata, each of which may result in a different interpretation of an event.

Thinking skills are sets of strategies for analysis and self-regulation that build on prior knowledge and experience and generate increasingly complex frameworks for understanding (Chipman et al., 1985; Glaser, 1984; Resnick, 1989). Some aspects of thinking are common across domains; others are quite specialized and domain specific (Benton and Kiewra, 1987). And thinking is influenced by social support, shared experience, and role models (Brown and Palincsar, 1989; Rogoff and Lave, 1984).

In the past it was believed that young children were essentially empty vessels to be filled with knowledge, and when faced with unfamiliar problems, their errors were the result of random guessing. Work in cognitive science has since shown that many errors made by children in the first grade of school are based on the consistent application of incorrect rules (Brown and VanLehn, 1982; Fisher and Bullock, 1984). With this new understanding of learning processes, cognitive scientists began to explore and categorize faulty rules, looking for the principles underlying the errors made in different learning tasks. The results of this work have provided the ability to identify the cause of children's errors and to design instructional strategies to eliminate them.

One approach to supporting cognitive development in young children is guided intervention, a collaborative process based on shared experiences and understanding (Vygotsky, 1978). In this approach, children develop thinking and subject-related skills through guided, social contact with adults. The adult models a behavior that is slightly beyond the child's current capabilities, coaches the child in the behavior, and guides him or her in reflecting on the new experience for purposes of mastering the behavior. In this way, the child acquires not only the new skill but also the adult's understanding of the skill.

Another important line of research in cognitive science is modeling the knowledge structures and judgments of experts and novices and then comparing the two as a way to understand the nature of expertise and the training needed to turn novices into experts. For example, Chi et al. (1981) have examined the differences in the knowledge structures and problem approaches of expert and novice physicists to better understand how the acquisition of knowledge and rules affects problem-solving strategies. The schemata and algorithms used by experts can be studied by using such methods as cognitive task analysis or think-aloud protocols (Newell and Simon, 1972). According to Glaser et al. (1991), models representing stages in the progression from novice to expert skill would be useful in guiding the learning process.

The principles of cognitive science have provided important guidance to the developers of many promising programs on curriculum design and teaching approaches. Two examples are Cognitively Guided Instruction and Reciprocal Teaching (described below).

Mathematics Education

Recent research on mathematics learning shows that preschool children develop mathematical concepts that they apply to a variety of practical situations. Not surprisingly, many of their concepts and algorithms are incorrect. In a careful study of the processes used by children in multidigit subtraction, Brown and VanLehn (1983) found that many errors were systematic and consistent and could be traced to erroneous variations in procedures known as "bugs". For example, when the top digit is smaller than the bottom digit, children often subtract the top digit from the bottom digit instead of borrowing. At the time of their article, Brown and VanLehn had found 88 primitive bugs and 300 combined bugs based on children's flawed hypotheses.

Many children experience difficulty in learning mathematics in school because they and their teachers do not understand the relationship between the rules and algorithms taught in school and the children's own, independently developed mathematical intuitions. Understanding the rules followed by children as they make errors can be useful in diagnosing specific learning problems and in developing effective instructional strategies. For instance, researchers at the Learning Research and Development Center are currently working on a reasoning-based mathematics program designed to help children build on their intuitions, showing them how to correct and extend them. At the Wisconsin Center for Educational Research, Fennema et al. (1989) developed a taxonomy of word problems in addition and subtraction. The taxonomy helps teachers identify the mathematical concepts a student understands and those that must be mastered to solve given problems correctly.

Reading

Several lines of research have contributed to understanding how to teach beginning reading. One central stream is the decades of work on alphabetic

coding, phoneme awareness, and word recognition. Adams (1990), a researcher at the OERI's Center for the Study of Reading, provides a detailed
analysis of this work. She describes the reading system, based on four
processors: the orthographic processor perceives the sequence of letters in
the text; the phonological processor maps the letters onto their spoken equivalents;
the meaning processor generates meaning from words; and the context processor constructs an on going understanding of the text. Experimental research on eye movements and fixations of skilled readers provides important insights into how each of these processors is used and how they interact
as a reader moves from print to meaning.

Phoneme awareness has been shown to be a prerequisite for mapping
alphabetic symbols to sound, and alphabetic mapping is believed to be necessary for learning to identify words. Chall (1983) found that the two best
predictors of early reading achievement are letter knowledge and the ability
to discriminate phonemes. Findings reported by Adams (1990) and Vellutino (1991) suggest that strategies based on the direct teaching of letter-sound
combinations to facilitate the generative use of sounds for word decoding
are necessary but not sufficient conditions for learning to read: meaning-
based strategies are also important for comprehension.

Skilled reading requires mastering the basic processes of letter and
word recognition to the point that they are automatic. When reading is not
fluent, comprehension has been found to be deficient perhaps because "less
than optimum facility in word identification drains off cognitive resources
that would normally be diverted to comprehension processes, thereby im-
peding these processes" (Vellutino, 1991:438).

In 1972 a small group of distinguished social scientists was assembled
by OERI's predecessor, the National Institute of Education (NIE), to examine written and oral communication from the standpoint of information processing theory. The group concluded (Miller, 1973): "NIE should actively
support efforts to understand the cognitive processes involved in acquiring
basic reading skills and the cognitive processes involved in comprehending
linguistic messages." More than 100 researchers were subsequently involved in a consensus building process to plan an appropriate research program. In response to the ensuing request for field-initiated proposals, 100
were received and approximately 25 were funded. Funding was also provided to the Center for the Study of Reading and the Center for The Study
of Writing.

This work and that supported by other federal agencies substantially
expanded understanding of cognitive aspects of learning to read. In a major
summary of the work 10 years later, Anderson et al. (1985) indicate that
constructing meaning from written text is central to the reading process and
that this involves selecting and using knowledge about people, places, and
things, as well as developing the skills of summarizing, clarifying, and

predicting. Skilled readers use prior knowledge about the topic and about the syntax of language to fill in gaps, integrate different pieces of information, and infer meaning. Consequently, skilled readers are strategic: They assess their prior knowledge on a topic; adjust their approach on the basis of the complexity of the text, their familiarity with the topic, and their purpose for reading; and monitor their comprehension.

It has long been known that parents reading to young children is useful for intellectual, social, and emotional development. In addition, however, research has shown that the intellectual stimulation is enhanced if the parent engages the child in discussions of the stories. Asking children to recall facts, provide descriptions, and reflect on the experiences in the stories introduces them to reading as a constructive and strategic process (Anderson et al., 1985; Dole et al., 1991). Another new research finding involves writing. It used to be thought that young children could not learn to write meaningful text until they mastered basic reading skills. However, when researchers tried to teach writing and reading simultaneously to first and second graders, they were not only successful, but they also serendipitously found that writing instruction accelerated the acquisition of reading skills (Graves, 1983).

Research on reading and writing has contributed to the development of innovative programs, such as Reciprocal Teaching, Reading Recovery and Success For All, and has informed parents, teachers, and policy makers through a series of widely distributed publications. A popular summary of the research work, *Becoming a Nation of Readers* (Anderson et al., 1985) was published by the Center for the Study of Reading and sold 250,000 copies. In addition, OERI published nearly a million copies of three companion booklets—for parents, for teachers, and for principals.

CURRICULUM DEVELOPMENT AND IMPROVED TEACHING APPROACHES

The committee's informal search for examples of programs designed to improve curriculum was not comprehensive—programs suggested by committee members and a review of *Educational Programs That Work* (National Dissemination Study Group, 1990) produced a list of 30 candidates. From those we selected seven that appeared to have at least moderately credible evaluation data, that had evidence of at least moderate impact, and that illuminated a variety of approaches. We did not assess whether the examples are the most effective or efficient programs available for a given purpose.

The programs selected for discussion are striking in their variety, but all provide evidence that the translation of research to improved teaching and learning is a lengthy and expensive process that often requires numerous iterations of research, development, and refinement. Two of the programs are still in the early stages of research, but all are the product of 4 or more years of work, and several have been in various stages of development or dissemination for more than 10 years.

In-service teacher education and development is part of each program. For most of the programs, initial training is for less than 1 week, but Cognitively Guided Instruction requires a 4-week seminar, and Reading Recovery requires a full year of training.

Federal funding for research and development portions of the programs ranged from $330,000 to $8 million. Many of the innovative programs were also supported by state and private funds and by the in-kind contributions of school districts that participated in their development and demonstration.

The seven programs reviewed in this section present examples of promising programs in four areas: higher order thinking skills, reading, mathematics, and generic instructional approaches for use in any subject area. The first program, Project IMPACT, integrates instruction in thinking skills into the curriculum as part of each subject-matter course. The next two programs are designed to enhance reading instruction, and they draw on research in both reading theory and cognitive science. One of the programs, Reading Recovery, is described in detail because it offers an example of a fully developed program for the poorest readers in the first grade that has been demonstrated to have a continuing positive effect over at least the next two grades. The other reading program, Reciprocal Teaching, demonstrates Vygotsky's model of guided intervention and provides a direct test of the theory of the centrality of comprehension monitoring in strategic reading. Reciprocal Teaching also offers an example of an extensive basic research program designed to study metacognition that has also begun to benefit educational practice.

The two mathematics programs are the Comprehensive School Mathematics Program (CSMP) and Cognitively Guided Instruction. CSMP offers an interesting example of a field-initiated effort based on new concepts of instruction that was subsequently developed by a laboratory of NIE. The idea of including thinking skills in the instruction of mathematics is now becoming more widespread. Cognitively Guided Instruction provides an example of how teachers can learn to diagnose a child's level of comprehension and create instruction that builds directly on that level. The program draws on research examining the mathematical concepts of preschool children conducted at the University of Wisconsin and the Learning Research and Development Center.

The final two examples, computer-assisted instruction (CAI) and cooperative learning, are illustrative of successful, widely disseminated approaches that are used for instruction in all subject areas. Both approaches have a history of at least 25 years of research, development, refinement, and application, and both have been studied extensively by several researchers. These long-term efforts illustrate the usefulness of research in identifying and confirming innovations that can make a positive difference in education. Student Team Learning, a cooperative learning program created by researchers at the Johns Hopkins Center for Social Organization of the Schools, is an example of a program based on prior research in social and organizational psychology and modified by the developers' own subsequent research and evaluations.

All of the programs described in the section used research designs in which the performance of students in an experimental group was compared with national norms or with the performance of students in a control group. However, the committee, was generally disappointed in the quality of the evaluations available from these programs, which exhibited several problems. Part of the gains reported for some of the evaluations may be due to a statistical artifact known as regression toward the mean, a problem that occurs when subjects for a remedial treatment become candidates for selection by exhibiting lower than average achievement scores. The most commonly used criterion for program success was a statistically significant increase in performance on a standardized achievement test. Although these tests are useful, they often provide a relatively narrow indication of student achievement. In addition, few of the programs have collected follow-up data to determine whether initial effects were maintained after students left the program. In many cases, the evaluation data are only from carefully managed demonstrations and not from subsequent dissemination sites except for computer-assisted instruction and cooperative learning, where full adoption of the program is not assured. Moreover, except for computer assisted instruction and cooperative learning, all of the evidence for effectiveness has been provided by program developers. Lastly, the reports of evaluations were often less thorough than we would have liked.

Despite these limitations, the programs have been subject to two or more evaluations, often using different approaches, and the results were similar. This increased our confidence in the findings. Nevertheless, because of the important limitations in the evaluations, most of the programs and approaches described should be considered promising, rather than of proven effectiveness.

Project IMPACT

Program Description

Project IMPACT was designed to improve the critical thinking of students by incorporating instruction in thinking skills into the regular course work of reading, mathematics, and science. Development of this field-initiated program began in 1979 with remedial students in grades 6-9; it has since been expanded to include all grades from kindergarten through high school. The premise of the program is that all students with intellectual potential at or near the normal range will benefit from instruction in higher level thinking skills.

The IMPACT program provides curriculum materials and training. The first section of the materials is designed to assist curriculum planners in analyzing existing courses for embedded instruction on thinking skills: classifying, seeing cause-and-effect relationships, making generalizations, forming predictions, and making assumptions. The second section of the program materials is designed to help teachers fill in identified gaps in thinking skills instruction. These materials contain lesson plans for classifying and categorizing information, ordering and setting priorities for information, formulating effective questions, and various reasoning exercises (Winocur, 1987).

Training is available at two levels. At the first level, teachers participate in a 3-day in-service workshop in which they are provided with strategies for introducing and guiding the process of critical thinking within the context of various subject areas. Special instruction is provided in effective use of Project IMPACT curriculum materials. The second level of training is designed to prepare graduates of the first level of training to act as trainers and disseminators in their local school districts.

Testing and Evaluation

The original evaluation study was conducted in 1983 and involved four school districts. All student subjects were in the seventh, eighth, or ninth grades and were enrolled in remedial reading or mathematics classes. The students selected to participate in both the experimental and control groups were those who failed to pass their district proficiency test and scored at or below the 37th percentile in reading comprehension on the Comprehensive Test of Basic Skills. The 426 students in a remedial IMPACT classes were taught by IMPACT-trained teachers; the 352 students in remedial control classes were taught by regular teachers. Standardized tests of basic skills and the Cornell Critical Thinking Test were used as measures of students' gains. Pretests were administered in September and posttests in February; all testing was conducted by classroom teachers. The results show that students in the Project IMPACT classes significantly outperformed students in control classes in thinking skills, mathematics, and reading at all three grade levels. According to the analysis, the magnitude of the gains for IMPACT students was 1 standard deviation on both the Comprehensive Test of Basic Skills and the Cornell Critical Thinking Test, compared with an average gain of 0.1 standard deviations for students in control classes (Winocur, 1983).

Results obtained in a later study by the same investigator showed that 83 students in seventh grade classes taught with IMPACT significantly improved their reading comprehension between the pretest and the posttest (as measured by the Comprehensive Test of Basic Skills): the mean performance of these students increased from the 40th percentile to the 51st percentile of the norm group, which included a nationally representative student (Winocur, 1987).

Project IMPACT offers an approach that can be embedded into most curricula and used as part of most teaching methods. As a result, the program appears to have widespread utility. Since 1983 the National Diffusion Network has helped disseminate this program. According to IMPACT staff, there have been approximately 6,500 adoptions across all grades.

Reading Recovery

Program Description

Reading Recovery is an early intervention program designed to assist the lowest 20 percent of readers in the first grade, as determined by a special battery of diagnostic tests developed by Marie Clay (1985). The goal of this field-initiated program is to teach these children reading skills that are comparable to those of the average students in their class. Current data show that 86 percent of the children in Reading Recovery have successfully met that goal within 12 to 20 weeks.

The Reading Recovery program is designed to be supplementary to regular reading instruction in the classroom. A child in the program leaves the classroom to work one-to-one with a specially trained teacher for 30 minutes every day. Within a lesson, reading and writing activities are integrated, based on the idea that development in one skill area supports advancement in the other. Program materials include several hundred small books graded at 20 levels of difficulty. The easier levels of these books contain illustrations on every page and are written in predictable language patterns compatible with children's ability to understand.

The approach is to encourage children to read by building on the knowledge and skills they already have. In the early stages of the program, a teacher works very closely with a child, examining each word and each sentence in a small story for recognition, pronunciation, and meaning. Throughout the story reading, the child and the teacher discuss what the characters might do next. As the child progresses through the lessons, he or she is supported by the teacher in the development of strategies that good readers appear to acquire naturally, such as summarizing, clarifying, and predicting. Teachers stress meaning cues and comprehension in both reading and writing activities. Children are considered ready to leave the program when they have demonstrated the ability to use these strategies on their own and when they have reached the average reading level of their class.

A critical component of the Reading Recovery program is teacher preparation. Teacher leaders go through a year-long program at a university training site and then return to their local regions to provide a full year of training for other teachers. During training the teachers learn how to prepare lesson plans and administer the program, how to create diagnostic summary reports, and how to assess student progress. They also practice working with a child behind a one-way glass while being observed by the other teachers in the program. As a teacher works with a child, the observers comment and discuss the process. Teachers also keep records on every aspect of the process. Throughout the training year, teachers work with students in their schools using the Reading Recovery methods.

Research and Development

Maria Clay, who developed Reading Recovery in New Zealand in the 1970s, spent several years reviewing theories of reading and studying the reading behaviors of young children. As a result of her field-initiated work, she found that children use phonological awareness, syntax cues, and their knowledge of subject matter when extracting meaning from text. Her approach to teaching reading immerses learners in high-interest, authentic literary tasks instead of drills and exercises; and teachers coach students in using all three strategies for extracting meaning.

Reading Recovery also incorporates a number of principles from Vygotsky's work on learning through social interaction and from Piaget's work in the genetic or historical reconstructive method. Essentially, these developmental theories suggest that instruction be provided as guided reinvention—a process that offers a structure for a teacher to share activity with a child in a way that the growth of the child is maximized. As the child gains competence, new levels of knowledge are jointly explored. Reading Recovery adopts these principles in its interactive lessons and in the adjustments made from lesson to lesson on the basis of the progress of the child. When a child successfully completes the program, he or she has internalized the skills necessary to continue to learn to read alone. According to Clay and Cazden (1990:207):

> The end point of early instruction has been reached when children have a self improving system: they learn more about reading every time they read, independent of instruction. When they read texts of appropriate difficulty for their present skills, they use a set of mental operations, strategies in their heads, that are just adequate for more difficult bits of the text. In this process they engage in reading work, deliberate efforts to solve new problems with familiar information and procedures. They are

working with theories of the world and theories about written language, testing them and changing them as they engage in reading and writing activities.

The first field studies of the Reading Recovery program were initiated in 1978; they were designed to answer questions about the program's impact on students as well as the influence of various school characteristics on the effectiveness of the program. Early successes in New Zealand led to interest from researchers in the United States. In 1983 Pinnell and Huck transferred the program to Ohio State, where several additional field tests were conducted. Between 1984 and 1986, $1.5 million was invested in the program's development by state and local funding sources in Ohio.

Testing and Evaluation

In the first full year of implementation in Ohio (1985-1986), urban school students in the lowest 20 percent of their first grade classes, as determined by Clay's diagnostic test battery, were randomly assigned either to Reading Recovery (133 students) or to a control group that received a commonly used remedial reading curriculum (51 students). After 15.7 weeks the results appeared impressive: Reading Recovery students performed significantly better than control students, and 73 percent of the children reached average levels of achievement in reading for their respective first grade classes. In addition, the developers found that Reading Recovery students made an average normal curve equivalent gain on the Comprehensive Test of Basic Skills of 8.6 for the school year, compared with –0.2 for students in the control group. At the end of the first grade, Reading Recovery students (the 73 percent who had successfully completed the program) were reading and writing at or above the average level of their classmates; when entering the third grade, they were reading at a 3.1 grade level.

Because Reading Recovery is labor intensive and thus very expensive, developers have been exploring ways to reduce the amount of time a teacher spends with each child. In a recent study supported by the MacArthur Foundation, Pinnell et al. (1991) compared four reading instruction methods with one another and with a control group. The four methods included (1) regular Reading Recovery, (2) Reading Recovery with teachers who received a shortened training course, (3) a one-to-one practice model (Direct Instruction Skills Plan), and (4) group lessons by a Reading Recovery Teacher. The sample included 324 students in 10 school districts. According to Pinnell et al. (1991:1):

> Regular Reading Recovery was the only group for which the mean treatment effect was significant on all four measures [of reading ability] at the conclusion of the field experiment and was also the only treatment indicat-

ing lasting effects. Results of this study indicate that one-to-one instruction is a necessary but not sufficient factor in Reading Recovery's success. Quantitative results and the qualitative analysis of videotapes indicate that Reading Recovery training is a powerful influence on teachers and makes a difference in student success.

Over the past decade Reading Recovery has spread to 33 states and two sites in Canada. In 1991 there were 84 teacher leaders, 1,906 teachers, and 12,902 children involved in the program. According to the developers, approximately 86 percent of those students completed the program successfully in 12-20 weeks, demonstrating reading skills at the average level for their class.

A critical element in the success of this program is the central quality control over the program provided by the staff at Ohio State University. Not only is the staff responsible for ensuring effective training, they also analyze the results for every student enrolled in Reading Recovery. Based on the results to date, the program continues to be effective from entry to the third grade. OERI's National Diffusion Network certified Reading Recovery as an effective program in 1987 (see Chapter 3) and has helped disseminate it since that time. A key goal for the future is to develop Reading Recovery as a group instructional program to reduce operating costs.

Reciprocal Teaching

Program Description

Reciprocal Teaching is a 10-year, field-initiated program of basic research funded by the National Institute of Child Health and Human Development to test the theory that the skills that define "comprehension monitoring" are central in strategic reading. The comprehension monitoring activities selected for study include summarizing (self-review), questioning, clarifying, and predicting. The approach is to instruct students in the use of these skills by encouraging them to participate in guided activity before they are asked to perform independently (see Brown and Palincsar, 1989; Palincsar and Brown, 1984). "In these teaching situations the novice carries out simple aspects of the task while observing and learning from an expert, who serves as a model for higher level involvement" (Palincsar and Brown, 1984:123). Initially, research on Reciprocal Teaching focused on reading and listening; more recently, it has been extended to include mathematics (Campione, et al., 1988).

In Reciprocal Teaching of comprehension, a teacher and a student take turns leading a discussion concerning sections of the text: the task includes clarifying complex sections, asking questions, making predictions, and generating summaries. Initially the teacher models the activities, and the students are encouraged to work at whatever level they can; the teacher then provides guidance at the appropriate level for each student. In the beginning, students have a great deal of difficulty with the process of becoming a leader. However, as the Reciprocal Teaching progresses, with the teacher providing directed feedback and guidance, the students become much more competent and comfortable.

Testing and Evaluation

The first two experiments of reciprocal reading were conducted with seventh grade students who could read but were at least 2 years behind on standardized scores of reading comprehension (Palincsar and Brown, 1984). In the first study, some students received the Reciprocal Teaching approach from the program developers, and other students were assigned to one of three comparison groups. Program developers worked with students in pairs in the Reciprocal Teaching group, giving them an overview of the lesson, having them read a passage silently, asking one to take the role of teacher, and as the lesson progressed, providing corrective and supportive feedback. Students were told that the strategies they were learning were general and would help them understand as they read. Each day students took three unassisted assessments (before, during, and after training) in which they read a passage and answered ten questions.

The results provide impressive support for the efficacy of Reciprocal Teaching. Average performance in the comparison groups did not improve and remained at around 40 percent comprehension. In the Reciprocal Teaching treatment, students became more like the adult model: they began to use their own words, and main idea summaries became more and more frequent. All six students in the program reached a stable level within 12 days of instruction, and five of the six were operating at a level of 70-80 percent comprehension. Moreover, five of the six students improved their classroom comprehension on other tasks. These improvements were still in place 8 weeks after the Reciprocal Teaching program.

In the second study, regular classroom teachers provided Reciprocal Teaching to three seventh grade and one eighth grade reading class (ranging in size from four to seven students). The student selection criteria and the materials and procedures for Reciprocal Teaching were the same as those used in the first experiment. After 15 days of Reciprocal Teaching, students were demonstrating comprehension of 75-80 percent on daily assessments— up from 40-50 percent at the beginning of the intervention. By the 25th day, many were at 100 percent of comprehension and these levels were maintained on the 8-week posttest. As with the first experiment, there was also evidence that the comprehension skills transferred to other subjects such as mathematics. Moreover, combined results from the two studies show that students receiving Reciprocal Teaching gained an average of 20 months in comprehension in comparison with a 1-month average gain by control students; Reciprocal Teaching students also improved their percentile rankings by more than 40 points in social studies and science in comparison with a randomly selected sample of all seventh graders in the schools where the experiments were conducted.

In 1987 Palincsar et al. reported on the results of a study using peer tutors as Reciprocal Teaching instructors. In addition to providing another demonstration of the effectiveness of Reciprocal Teaching, this study examined the effectiveness of instructional chains—one group of individuals is taught an activity and then becomes responsible for teaching the activity to others. The nine peer tutors, selected from developmental reading classroom students, were taught by teachers for 10 days; they then taught one or two other students in their class for 12 days. During the study the peer tutors' comprehension rose from an average of 72 percent correct to an average of 87 percent correct during their training and tutoring, and the tutorees comprehension rose from an average 53 percent to an average of 77 percent correct.

In another study using Reciprocal Teaching to develop listening skills, Brown and Palincsar (1989) collected data on 17 first grade teachers, 132 experimental children whose comprehension abilities were severely impaired, and 66 children of comparable ability in a control group. After 20 days of Reciprocal Teaching, 78 percent of the students showed consistent gains in comprehension (either reaching a criterion of 70 percent correct or improving comprehension by at least 20 percentage points); in comparison, only 28 percent of students in the control group showed such gains.

According to program researchers, Reciprocal Teaching instruction has been conducted with approximately 50 teachers and 1,000 students under highly controlled experimental conditions. The method has begun to spread as a teaching strategy, but it has never been formally disseminated or evaluated in the nonexperimental dissemination sites.

The Comprehensive School Mathematics Program

Program Description

The Comprehensive School Mathematics Program (CSMP) was initially designed to develop thinking skills as part of mathematics instruction for children of all ability levels in grades K-6. Specifically, the program addresses: (1) the need to expand the definition of basic skills beyond computation; (2) the need for problem solving to be the focus of mathematics; (3) the need for developing such skills as reasoning, analyzing, estimating, and inferring; and (4) the need to increase emphasis on numeration and number sense, patterns, probability, logic, geometry, algorithmic thinking, and mathematical connections. Two important features of CSMP are that students are taught through interrelated experiences and problems that are appropriate to their natural instincts and level of understanding. When CSMP was developed, however, the notion of integrating thinking skills with content differed dramatically from the prevailing emphasis on drill and practice. CSMP is one of the few mathematics programs that conforms to many of the elements of the recently developed *Curriculum and Evaluation Standards for Schools Mathematics* (National Council of Teachers of Mathematics, 1989).

The program uses a "pedagogy of situations"—gamelike problem situations and story settings to teach both content and processes. Specifically, content is presented as an extension of a child's everyday and fantasy experiences. Three special languages are used: the language of strings (notion of sets), the language of arrows (notion of relations and functions), and the language of Papy Minicomputer, which models the positional structure of the Western system of numeration. A key feature of CSMP is the sequencing of the curriculum in a spiraling form: "each student spirals through repeated exposures to the content, building interlocking experiences of increasing sophistication" (Heidema, 1991).

Research and Development

According to Claire Heidema, the initial planning for CSMP began with mathematician Bert Kaufman in 1966; he brought the program to the Central Midwestern Regional Educational Laboratory (CEMREL)—a laboratory supported by NIE—in 1970. Kaufman, an active researcher in mathematics education, was joined by Belgium mathematician Frederique Papy in 1972. Papy provided the fundamental concept of using situations as a basis for instruction.

CSMP was field tested and revised over a 5-year period. In the first year, instructional materials were used by CSMP staff in both public and parochial school classes. The second year was devoted to a local pilot test in which revised materials were used in about ten regular classrooms in St Louis. During the third and fourth years, an extended pilot trial version (based on revisions from the local pilot test) was evaluated in a national network of cooperating schools. In this test, CSMP classes were compared with non-CSMP classes, and the materials were revised again. In the fifth year, the material revisions from the extended pilot trials were prepared for publication. Throughout the 5-year process, an independent unit of CEMREL conducted evaluations of the program. Altogether, the Department of Education provided $8 million dollars for development of the program.

Testing and Evaluation

CSMP developers claim that students using the curriculum are better able to apply the mathematics they have learned to new problem situations and perform as well in traditional basic computational skills. Two types of studies have been used to compare CSMP students with non-CSMP students. In the first type, the same teachers taught two courses—the first year they taught the regular mathematics course and the second year they taught the CSMP curriculum—and the students' scores were compared. In the second type, matched groups of students were taught CSMP or the regular mathematics curriculum by different teachers in the same year. In the spring of each year the students were tested using a standardized mathematics test and a specially designed test to measure thinking skills—MANS, Mathematics Applied to Novel Situations. MANS was developed by researchers at CEMREL; it tests skills in estimation, mental arithmetic, representations of numbers, number patterns and relationships, word problems, and production of multiple answers.

The research sample included grades 2-6 in nine school districts (more than 300 students): six of the districts used the different teacher model, and three used the same teacher model for data collection. Prior to the experiment, each class (both experimental and control) was given the Gates MacGinitie Vocabulary Test; CSMP students scored slightly higher on average than non-CSMP students (between 1 and 2 items correct out of 45).

When the two groups were compared on the MANS test, CSMP students performed consistently and significantly better than students in the regular curriculum on all scales except "producing multiple answers," for which there were no difference. These data support the claim that CSMP students are better able than comparable non-CSMP students to apply the mathematics they have learned to new problem situations. When the two groups were compared on a standardized test of basic mathematics, there were no differences, except for the second grade, in which CSMP students performed better than the control group. More recently, the sample has been expanded to over 30 school districts, and the findings confirm those obtained in the earlier studies.

CSMP is currently being disseminated by the OERI-supported Mid-continent Educational Laboratory (McREL) and the National Diffusion Network. The program has been adopted in more than 125 school districts in 34 states, Washington, D.C., Puerto Rico, and Canada.

Cognitively Guided Instruction

Research Description

Cognitively Guided Instruction (CGI) is a program developed at the University of Wisconsin to help teachers understand how students think about mathematics and then to use this knowledge in making instructional decisions in classroom activities. Current project research activities are focused on students in kindergarten and the first grade. Teachers in the program are given training in problem types (a taxonomy of addition and subtraction problems graded in difficulty), in children's early cognitions of mathematics, and in how to build on what children do naturally to reach an understanding of symbols and principles.

The teachers use this knowledge and skills with their existing curriculum materials to assist their students in gaining correct mathematical concepts. In a CGI classroom, teachers work interactively with the whole class, asking all children to participate by giving their solutions to interesting, everyday problems that represent problem types in the addition-subtraction word problem taxonomy developed by program researchers. Teachers begin with the easiest problem types and work towards the more difficult ones. Teachers encourage students to find alternative ways of solving a given problem as a basis for building understanding.

CGI grew out of two principal lines of research. One focused on creating a taxonomy of addition and subtraction word problems and developing a detailed understanding of the development of preschool children's conceptions of addition and subtraction (Carpenter et al., 1989). The second line of research focused on teachers' beliefs about students abilities, on teaching behaviors, and on how various types of teacher behavior relate to student achievement. One of the basic strategies of CGI was to modify both teachers' attitudes and instructional behavior.

Testing and Evaluation

An evaluation of CGI was conducted with 40 first grade teachers assigned randomly either to an experimental or a control group (Carpenter et al., 1989). The 20 experimental teachers participated in a 4-week summer workshop in which they were provided with information about the CGI approach to teaching and learning. During the workshop, teachers worked on designing their own programs of instruction on the basis of the principles discussed. In addition, all teachers participating in the workshop were given readings on the problem taxonomy and on research studies describing children's solutions to addition and subtraction word problems.

The evaluation was conducted over 1 year. Throughout that school year, project researchers systematically observed and measured classroom teachers' knowledge and beliefs and their students' learning. The results suggest that CGI teachers taught problem solving significantly more, and number facts significantly less, than teachers in non-CGI classes. In addition, CGI teachers encouraged students to use a variety of problem solving strategies, and they listened to the students explain their processes significantly more than did control teachers (Carpenter and Fennema, 1992). Even though CGI teachers spent about half as much time teaching number facts as other teachers, CGI students exceeded non-CGI students in number fact knowledge, problem solving, and reported confidence in their problem-solving abilities.

During the experiment, six detailed case studies were conducted to learn how teachers gained an understanding of their students and how they used this knowledge to build on their students' informal knowledge. In most cases, assessments were an ongoing part of the instruction—the teachers continually asked students to describe their solutions to a given problem and to discuss the process they used to arrive at the solution. The problem taxonomy was particularly useful for organizing the problems and processes used by children in solving each problem type. The taxonomy gave the teachers some direction on what questions to ask and what to listen for in the students' solutions. The children learned through interaction with the teacher and through listening to the solutions presented by other children: this is a common thread with Reciprocal Teaching (Palincsar and Brown, 1984).

Computer-Assisted Instruction

Program Description

According to Becker (1990), by the end of the 1980s there were more than 2.5 million microcomputers in the schools (approximately 1 per classroom), and many new applications, such as hypertext and advanced graphics, are being developed. Computers have been used in education for several purposes. Niemiec et al. (1987) present the following taxonomy:

• Computer-managed instruction (CMI): the computer serves a clerical function; it assesses student progress toward curriculum goals, indicates needed instruction, and tracks progress.
• Computer-aided drill and practice: the student interacts directly with the computer in learning and recalling factual information. Drill and practice supplement the curriculum by providing students with additional practice on lower order learning skills.
• Computer-aided tutorials: the computer works in an interactive mode with students by presenting concepts and providing feedback and direction; the software reinforces correct responses and assists in correcting errors.
• Computer-aided problem solving: the computer is used by students as a tool for deriving information and conducting analyses needed to solve a problem.

Testing and Evaluation

Over the years, thousands of articles evaluating or discussing CAI and its implications for educational practice have been published. Some of these articles—Colorado (1988); Kulik et al. (1985); Kulik and Kulik (1986, 1987); and Niemiec et al. (1987)—provide reviews of many studies. In their 1987 article, Kulik and Kulik summarize findings from 199 studies of CAI used primarily as a supplement to regular classroom instruction at all levels from elementary school through college. Although these studies include a wide variety of computer-assisted approaches and instructional settings, the overall results indicate that CAI generally increased student performance and decreased learning time. More specifically:

• For all levels of schooling taken together, CAI students' performance was 11 percentile points higher than that of students not using CAI, and their instructional time was 32 percent less.

• The average performance of students in elementary school using CAI was 18 percentile points higher than the average performance of students in control groups (the average effect size was 0.47 standard deviations).

• Low-aptitude students were more favorably affected by computer-delivered instruction than high-aptitude students.

• There was no significant difference between tutorial programs and drill and practice programs in terms of their effect on student performance.

• Students were more positive towards computers after they had used them as part of the instructional process (effect size of 0.33).

Another study (Levin et al., 1987) compared the cost-effectiveness of CAI with cross-age tutoring (peer tutors from the upper grades), reduced class size, and increased instructional time. The results show that peer tutoring and CAI were equally cost-effective, and both were superior to the other two approaches.

Cooperative Learning

Program Description

Cooperative learning is an approach that encourages learning as a social process and facilitates the building of learning communities in the schools (E. Cohen, 1986; Johnson and Johnson, 1990; Slavin, 1990). One example of a successful cooperative learning program is Student Team Learning, developed by Slavin and his associates at Johns Hopkins' Center for Social Organization of the Schools, which was supported by OERI and NIE from 1967 to 1985. Student Team Learning, designed primarily for elementary education, includes three programs—Student Teams Achievement Division, Teams-Games-Tournament, and Cooperative Integrated Reading and Composition. All of these programs involve students' working together on common topics. Students are scored individually on the basis of the amount of improvement they make from one test or graded exercise to the next. Individual scores are combined to obtain group scores, which are used to determine group rewards.

In Student Teams Achievement Division, students are assigned to four- or five-member teams made up of high-, average-, and low-performing students, males and females, with different ethnic backgrounds. After a weekly topic has been presented by the teacher, students work in their teams, studying worksheets as individuals or in pairs, quizzing one another, and holding group discussions to learn the material. Students understand that they are not finished studying until they are sure that all the team members have mastered the topic. When the teams have completed their preparation, each individual is tested and scored—and teams earn recognition based on the improvement made by all students. Teams-Games-Tournament is the same except that instead of taking quizzes, students are drawn from their Student Teams Achievement Division teams to play games and show their academic mastery of a particular subject matter in tournaments held each week. Students from different teams who have demonstrated comparable performance in the past are pitted against each other in groups of three. In Cooperative Integrated Reading and Composition, students work on basic reading activities, comprehension, and writing in cooperative groups similar to Student Teams Achievement Division teams.

Research and Development

Student Team Learning was designed to evaluate the effects of heterogeneous groupings, cooperative tasks, and group rewards on student learning. Slavin and his associates have conducted at least 35 studies on activities that are currently incorporated into Student Team Learning (Slavin, 1986). Research began in 1972 and is still continuing. In 1975 Teams-Games-Tournament was certified as effective by OERI's National Diffusion Network for dissemination (see Chapter 3); in 1978 Student Teams Achievement Division was added; and in 1988 Cooperative Integrated Reading and Composition was accepted.

Testing and Evaluation

In 1983 Slavin conducted a "best evidence synthesis" of 42 relatively high-quality field experiments of cooperative learning. For purposes of analysis, the studies were grouped into four categories: group study and group reward for learning (25 studies); group study but no group reward (9 studies); task specialization and group reward for learning (1 study); and task specialization but no group reward (6 studies). All three programs in Student Team Learning fall into the first category.

The results showed that the experimental treatment with the most positive effects was the combination of group study and group reward: 22 of the 25 studies showed students' performing significantly better under this condition than under control group conditions. In the other three categories of treatment, only 4 of 15 studies showed statistically significant results for the experimental treatment. Slavin's (1990) conclusion is that "cooperative learning methods that use specific group rewards based on group members' individual learning consistently increase achievement more than control methods."

The work of the Johns Hopkins Center is a excellent example of mixing research, development, evaluation, refinement, and persistence in the pursuit of better education. Its two-decade program of work along a specific line of inquiry and development is not uncommon in the natural sciences, but it is rare in education research and development.

SCHOOL RESTRUCTURING

Research provides important insights into the processes involved in school change. School restructuring goes beyond the adoption of innovative curricula or teaching methods: it calls for a fundamental rethinking of the process of schooling. According to Smith and O'Day (1990:2):

> In this "new" conception, the school building becomes the basic unit of change and school educators (teachers and principals) are not only the agents but also the initiators, designers, and directors of change efforts. In addition to an emphasis on process, student *outcomes* are also key in this new approach. The principle underlying many of the second wave themes— from school-site management to teacher professionalism to parental choice— is the notion that if school personnel are held accountable for producing change and meeting outcome objectives, they will expend both their professional knowledge and their creative energies to finding the most effective ways possible to do so.

Two examples of promising field-initiated, school restructuring projects are James Comer's School Development Program and the Outcomes Driven Development Model (ODDM) created by the Johnson City Central School District in New York. Both are aimed at coordinated change in the organization and operation of schools, in the beliefs and behaviors of staff and parents, and in the design and delivery of instruction. Like the projects discussed in the previous section, the evaluations of these programs are limited, and thus we consider them promising but not proven. Neither program is an all-encompassing prescription for a school, but, rather, a restructuring process that establishes administrative mechanisms and a climate for cooperation and change. Specific changes can vary moderately from one school to another under the School Development Program, and they will vary substantially when using ODDM.

School Development Program

Program Description

The School Development Program was initiated in 1968 in two New Haven elementary schools as a joint effort between the Yale Child Study Center and the New Haven School System. According to Comer (1980), the program's hypothesis is that:

> the application of social and behavioral science principles to every aspect of a school program will improve the climate of relationships among all involved and will facilitate significant academic and social growth of students.

Psychiatrists, psychologists, and social workers at the Yale center drew on their knowledge of child development and organizational change to develop and implement the program. By 1988 Comer reported that the program had been adopted throughout the New Haven School System and in 150 schools in 16 other school districts. The program is currently being extended to dozens of urban schools in New Jersey (Schmidt, 1991).

The School Development Program was initially supported by the Ford Foundation as one of several cooperative projects between universities and public school systems. The first two schools were located in low socioeconomic neighborhoods and served a student population that was 98 percent African American. Records indicated that at the beginning of the project these students were lowest in academic achievement in the city, and there were reports of serious attendance and behavior problems.

The basis of the program is to actively involve school administrators, teachers, parents, and mental health specialists in creating a secure and accepting environment for student learning. Most of the underlying concepts for the program are drawn from developmental and social psychology and are used to educate administrators, teachers and parents in how to assist children in emotional, social, and academic growth.

As described by Comer (1980), the School Development Program was designed to include: (1) a steering committee composed of school administrators, teachers, parents, and representatives from the Yale Child Study Center; (2) a pupil personnel team composed of mental health workers and speech and hearing therapists; and (3) three school committees—curriculum, personnel, and evaluation—each of which included the principal, the social worker from the mental health team, teachers, and elected representatives from the parents' group. The work of these groups was supported in part by workshops, an extended-day program in which teachers learned more about child development and behavior, and a program for parents to participate as teacher aides in the classroom. Small stipends were provided for parents and for teachers in the extended-day program.

Throughout the program's development and implementation, the focus was on involving the parents, encouraging participation among all interested parties, and working to create an understanding of children's emotional, social, and academic needs. The mental health team worked with children and taught their teachers how to respond appropriately to disruptive or antisocial behavior. A special program, the discovery room, included a variety of tools, toys, and material for students to use individually, in pairs, or in groups, and was staffed by an understanding and accepting teacher who helped the children work through their fears, anxieties, and anger. Many of the children in these schools were not emotionally or socially prepared for school: they came from insecure family environments that did not encourage cognitive or emotional growth. As a result, it was necessary for the school to provide an environment for this growth. In addition, to create more stability for the children, they were assigned to the same teacher for 2 years.

Administrators, parents, and teachers worked together on all aspects of the schools' programs. Curriculum changes and the introduction of special innovations, such as the discovery room, were contingent on the approval of parents. According to Comer (1980, 1988), parental participation was critical to program success. The first year of the project was marked by dissension and lack of parental support, but by the second and third years there was growing cooperation and participation. In the second year, teachers developed a set of guidelines for parents to use when observing a class: what to look for, what sorts of questions to ask, etc.

Testing and Evaluation

Data reported by Comer (1988) show marked improvement for mathematics and reading scores of fourth graders attending the first two New Haven Schools; no performance data have been provided on students in other grades. In 1969 the fourth grade students in these schools were functioning slightly below a third grade level; 10 years later they were performing at grade level; and by 1984 they were scoring 2 years above grade level. Moreover, school attendance, at all grade levels, improved to second highest in the city, and student conflict was reported as minimal.

The program was further evaluated by developers in a 1987 study using a randomly selected sample of 306 African American students in grades 3-5. Of the total sample, 176 students were attending seven School Development Program schools around the country, 91 were attending four control schools (comparable schools not using the program), and 39 were in three special schools. The results show significant gains in reading scores, as measured by classroom grades, for students in program schools but not for students in control schools; there were no significant gains in mathematics for either group. Children in program schools were significantly more positive toward their classroom environment after the program was introduced, and absenteeism declined significantly (Comer et al., 1989).

In another study, students in ten predominantly African American schools in Prince Georges County (Maryland) using Comer's program showed significantly higher percentile gains on the California Achievement Test than those reported for the district as a whole (Comer, 1988). Between 1985 and 1987 third grade students in Comer's program schools gained 18 percentile points in mathematics, 17 in language and 9 in reading; throughout the district, students gained 10 percentile points in mathematics, 8 in language, and 5 in reading. At the fourth grade level, students in the program schools gained more than 20 percentile points in mathematics, 12 in language, and 7 in reading, compared with district-wide gains of 11, 7 and 4 percentile points respectively. Prince Georges County is the fifteenth largest in the country and has 105,000 students, 62 percent of whom are African American.

Outcomes Driven Development Model

Program Description

Development of the Outcomes Driven Development Model (ODDM) began in 1971 in response to dissatisfaction with student performance of administrators and teachers in New York's Johnson City Central School District. ODDM is a procedural model involving the direct participation of teachers, administrators, and boards of education in restructuring all aspects of a school to achieve a specified set of outcomes.

ODDM provides a set of procedures for aligning all facets of a school or district with a goal of excellence in student achievement and for guiding teachers and administrators in using the best research available for these purposes—research on instructional practices, curriculum design, school climate, change theory, and school management. One of the first steps involves changing the belief systems of teachers and administrators concerning student capabilities. ODDM creates conditions in which all teachers and administrators can participate in decisions that influence the direction of the organization. Restructuring also involves changes in the administrative supports, the classroom supports, and the community supports: ODDM provides a blueprint for making these changes.

All adopters are required to follow an eight-phase training plan over a 2-year period, starting with the development of a leadership team and ending with diffusion; the training is provided by Johnson City Central School District staff and other certified trainers. All adopters are also required to carry out the full ODDM process. Since the first work at Johnson City, the program has been expanded to serve high schools.

Testing and Evaluation

For the developers, the original goal was to have at least 75 percent of the students achieve scores of 6 months above grade level in reading and mathematics by the end of the eighth grade. In 1976 the percentage of eighth grade students at or above this level was 44 percent for reading and 53 percent for mathematics; 7 years later the percentages were 75 percent for reading and 80 percent for mathematics. In Utah, five districts have used ODDM for 3 or more years; four of them have data showing dramatic improvements, using pretest and posttest performance on the Comprehensive Test of Basic Skills. One district showed average increases of two and three grade levels by fifth and sixth grade students; a second showed math score increases of 1.5, 2.0, and 3.0 grade levels by students in the third, fourth, and fifth grades, respectively; a third raised the average reading percentile approximately 5 points and the average math percentile by 10-20 points; and the fourth raised reading and language arts percentiles by approximately 10 points and mathematics percentiles by 15-20 points. A particularly encouraging aspect of these findings is that the effects appear to be cumulative—probably because of the systematic redirection of instruction throughout all the grade levels in a school or district.

ODDM has been actively disseminated through the National Diffusion Network since 1985. Future plans for the project involve additional evaluation and continuing dissemination.

MONITORING THE STATE OF PUBLIC EDUCATION

One important function of education research is to inform policy makers about the course of education. In this regard, the federal government, principally through the National Center on Educational Statistics (NCES), has long played a major role by large-scale collection of data on the condition of education in this country. NCES produces data on the demographic, financial, physical, and performance characteristics of U.S. school systems. In this section we discuss some of the most widely used databases and reports prepared by NCES, including statistical compilations describing current conditions, longitudinal studies, national assessments of student performance, and international comparisons.

National Statistics

The principal descriptive databases currently prepared by NCES include the Common Core of Data, the Schools and Staffing Survey, the Integrated Postsecondary Education Data System, the National Postsecondary Student Aid Survey, and the Survey of earned Doctorates Awarded in the United States.

The Common Core of Data (CCD) on state education agencies, local education agencies, and public schools is collected annually. It includes enrollments by grade, the racial and ethnic composition of the enrollments, the percentage of students eligible for the free lunch program, number of handicapped students, number of graduates, number of teachers and other staff, teacher salaries, and an array of other financial data. The Schools and Staffing Survey (SASS) collects more detailed information on school staff and workplace conditions from a sample of public and private schools.

The Integrated Postsecondary Education Data System (IPEDS), which superseded the Higher Education General Information Survey (HEGIS), collects data on types of programs offered; tuition; full- and part-time enrollment; racial and ethnic characteristics of students; age distributions of students; degrees completed by race, ethnicity and gender; full-time equivalent staffing; rank, tenure, and salaries of staff; and various other financial data. The National Postsecondary Student Aid Study (NPSAS) provides the most comprehensive nationwide data on how students and their families pay for postsecondary education. The Survey of Earned Doctorates Awarded in the United States has been conducted each year since the 1920s.

Drawing on these databases, NCES regularly publishes three major compendia of statistics: *Condition of Education, Digest of Educational Statistics,* and *Projections of Education Statistics.* NCES also publishes numerous annual and biennial reports from the individual databases, and special reports on specific topics. The reported statistics are used by Congress, federal agencies, state and local education agencies, professional associations of educators, researchers, businesses that sell goods and services to schools, the media, and officials in other nations. They are used to project future enrollments at each grade, assess the supply and demand of teachers, profile the teacher work force, portray school climate and working conditions, describe various characteristics of the educational programs, compare public and private schools, examine educational attainments, and monitor expenditures.

Longitudinal Studies

Longitudinal studies provide important information about the changes in the behavior and performance of a cohort of students over time. NCES has supported three particularly notable large-scale longitudinal studies of students: the 1972 National Longitudinal Study, the 1980 High School and Beyond Study, and the 1988 National Educational Longitudinal Study. These studies have been "valuable in basic scientific and policy research, and they have occasionally been useful in monitoring trends in educational transitions" (Hauser, 1991:3).

The 1972 National Longitudinal Study (NLS-72) was designed to describe the transition of students from high school to college and then into the work force. The sample was composed of 16,683 high school seniors around the country. The data that were collected included demographic and school characteristics, courses taken, academic achievement, and current status of and future plans for both education and work. Follow-up data were collected in 1973, 1974, 1976, 1979, and 1986 to determine changes in education, work, and marital status. NLS-72 has provided the basis for hundreds of studies. One example is *Student Progress in College: NLS-72 Postsecondary Education Transcript Study* (Knepper, 1989), which examined patterns of student progress through the postsecondary education system. Although the majority of 1972 high school seniors went on to postsecondary education, most did not follow the traditional pattern of completing college within 4 years. Students who attended 4-year schools entered sooner after high school graduation than those who began other forms of postsecondary education. Generally, men took longer than women to complete each level of education. Transfer students generally took an average of 8 months more to complete a B.A. degree than nontransfer students.

High School and Beyond was designed to provide additional data on the school-to-work transition, particularly in light of concerns raised by increases in school dropout rates and decreases in academic achievement. In 1980 a sample of 28,000 sophomores and 30,000 seniors was drawn from a highly stratified national probability sample of 1,100 secondary schools. The longitudinal design included follow-up surveys of large subsets of the two cohorts in 1982, 1984, and 1986, with another follow-up of the sophomore cohort scheduled for 1992. The High School and Beyond study expanded the data collection categories used in NLS-72 to include parents' attitudes and financial planning, teachers' observations, and students' scores on a variety of achievement tests. The findings from the first follow-up study of sophomores provided important information concerning school dropout problems and the factors that influence student aspirations during the last 2 years of high school (National Center for Education Statistics, 1991c). Comparisons between the results of NLS-72 and High School and Beyond provide insight into the effects of social and cultural changes on the attitudes and performance of high school students. The 1988 National Educational Longitudinal Study (NELS-88) was designed to examine the major factors contributing to student achievement, persistence in school, and participation in postsecondary education. The study will follow a cohort of 25,000 eighth graders for a decade, and it will collect more data on family, school, and classroom characteristics than NLS-72 and High School and Beyond. Tests of reading, mathematics, science, and social science skills were administered in 1988 and 1990 and will be administered again in 1992. Although most of the questions being addressed by NELS-88 cannot be answered for several years, the first round of data provides some important baseline information concerning the eighth grade students in the sample: 44 percent of African Americans, 39 percent of Hispanics, and 36 percent of Native Americans have two or more background characteristics that put them at risk for school failure. The risk factors are single-parent family, family income less than $15,000 annually, child home alone more than 3 hours per day, parents without a high school diploma, a sibling who has dropped out of school, and limited English proficiency. These data also reveal that eighth graders spend an average of 21.4 hours per week watching television, 5.6 hours doing homework, and 2 hours doing outside reading.

National Assessment of Educational Progress

Development of the National Assessment of Educational Progress (NAEP) was initiated with federal funds in the late 1960s to measure the achievement of elementary and secondary school students in science, mathematics, reading, writing, citizenship, history, geography, social studies, art, music, and literature. NAEP is now conducted in even-numbered years using samples of students in the fourth, eighth, and twelfth grades. Currently, reading and mathematics are assessed every 2 years, writing and science every 4 years, and the other subjects on an irregular basis.

NAEP is both a product and a source of education research and development. The matrix sampling of test items, the analysis of potential items for bias, and the scale scores used in reporting findings are the result of complex psychometric work accomplished over the past three decades by psychologists, statisticians, and education researchers. Without this work, NAEP would have been more time-consuming for students to take, more expensive to administer, and less accurate as a measure of achievement.

NAEP has revealed much about students' knowledge and how their knowledge has changed over time. In 1990, only 74 percent of twelfth graders knew how many hours equal 150 minutes; only 49 percent knew what percent 7 is of 175; and only 15 percent knew how much a $1,000 deposit would be worth after 6 months if it earned interest of 1 percent per month on the initial amount (National Assessment Governing Board, 1991). Trend data indicate that reading and mathematics skills have increased only slightly over the past two decades while science achievement declined and then rose to about the 1970 levels (National Center for Education Statistics, 1991d). One of the lesser known trends is that the reading and mathematics scores of African American and Hispanic students have been rising faster than the national average. The first decade of NAEP data partly provoked the 1980s school reform efforts (National Research Council, 1986); the second decade of data has prompted policy makers to rethink their reform strategies because the effects of those reforms on NAEP scores have been less than they had hoped.

Despite its prominence and use, NAEP is the target of controversy and misunderstanding. There is debate over which knowledge and skills should be assessed and how they should be measured. Some observers are concerned that students do not try to do their best because the scores have no personal consequences. And many people do not realize that changes in scores, or lack thereof, reflect changes in the student populations and social conditions as well as changes in school instruction. If the quality of instruction in schools improved, there would be no change in the scores if, for instance, the level of student motivation and family support declined. Conversely, increases in scores are not necessarily evidence that school instruction has improved.

International Studies

International studies are helpful in interpreting the educational achievement of U.S. students. NCES has been a major contributor of resources and data in coordinating comparisons among countries. For example, NCES has contributed to the 1982 Second International Mathematics Study, the 1984 International Education Association (IEA) Writing Study, the 1985 Second International Science Study, the 1988 International Assessment of Education Progress, and the 1991 IEA Reading Literacy Study, and it is currently funding the planning of performance assessments for the upcoming Third International Science Study (TIMSS).

Although each of the studies has some limitations, they have repeatedly found that American students' academic skills lag behind those of many other nations. For instance, the Second International Math Study found that U.S. eighth graders were slightly above average in arithmetic calculation, but well below average in problem solving. The results of international studies of mathematics and science achievement were cited prominently in *A Nation At Risk* (National Commission on Excellence in Education, 1983), a publication that helped precipitate the school reform efforts of the 1980s. These results also inspired one of the National Goals for Education: "By the year 2000 U.S. students will be first in the world in science and mathematics achievement."

Several of the above studies, particularly the more recent ones, have collected some data on characteristics of the schooling provided in each country. These data permit analysis of the relationships between school achievement and such factors as curricula, amount of time spent on school work, teacher development, classroom size, parental involvement, and other factors. Other international studies focus intensively on comparisons of curriculum and teaching practices in different countries. For example, it has been found that American mathematics textbooks often develop ideas by progressing slowly through a hierarchy of learning tasks, while textbooks used in several Asian countries immerse students in more demanding problems from the beginning (Fuson et al., 1988). The recently developed and widely hailed standards for mathematics teaching in this country endorse the latter practice (National Council of Teachers of Mathematics, 1989).

CONGRESSIONAL USE OF
EDUCATION RESEARCH

There are four agencies that serve as conduits for education research and development information to Congress. They are the Congressional Research Service (CRS), the General Accounting Office (GAO), the Congressional Budget Office (CBO), and the Office of Technology Assessment (OTA). The committee interviewed 17 of the education specialists in the first three agencies and reviewed the OTA publications that deal with educational matters. Of the specialists, 14 indicated that they often use data or reports from NCES; 13 often use the bibliographic and document retrieval system of OERI's Educational Resources Information Center (ERIC). Only 3 of the specialists said they often use the studies of the OERI laboratories and centers (see Chapter 3) or consult with their staff, but another 9 do so occasionally. Several of the education specialists also mentioned using the results of education research and development from the National Science Foundation (NSF), the Department of Health and Human Services, and the National Institute of Mental Health.

All four congressional agencies have used reports from NCES's High School and Beyond study, and one staffer described it as a "treasure trove." Several staff members mentioned that the federal government is usually the only source of longitudinal studies, and several reported using NAEP data and reports. Staff at one congressional agency found that the work they were planning was already under way at OERI centers and laboratories. And when staff at a congressional agency were working on testing issues they used data from OERI's Center on Assessment and Evaluation and "consulted regularly" with its director. Another agency staffer, with a Ph.D. in economics, described the work of the former Center on Education and Employment as "impressive high quality research."

An examination of OTA's reports covering education reveal use of a broad range of OERI work, including NAEP, High School and Beyond, the National Longitudinal Survey, the *Digest of Education Statistics*, the *Condition of Education*, NCES bulletins, and reports from the laboratories and centers. NSF's work is also frequently cited.

Several staff in the congressional agencies noted a marked improvement in NCES's services since 1987. Suggestions for additional change included more timely collection and delivery of data, release of confidential data with appropriate safeguards, more longitudinal studies with broad scope, consultation between NCES and congressional agencies when planning data collection efforts, and easy access to the ongoing work of the centers and laboratories.

One example of an education research study that directly influenced policy is the National Assessment of Vocational Education, completed in 1989 (Wirt et al., 1989). According to the counsel for the House Education and Labor Committee, Congress was much influenced by the study when drafting the Perkins Vocational and Applied Technology Act. This legislation focused federal support for vocational education on districts that have the highest proportion of poor families, that integrate academic and vocational instruction, and that operate effective programs and produce the desired results. The legislation also encouraged an easing of state regulatory burdens and the transfer of more authority over these programs to the local level (Jennings, 1991).

Why did this study have a major impact on Congress? At least four factors seem to have contributed: the study was mandated by Congress to help inform its reauthorization of the Perkins Act; the researchers consulted with Congress on the design of the study; interim findings were released as they became available; and the researchers responded with additional analyses that were requested by Congress. In short, the researchers worked closely with Congress to make the study meet its needs.

CONCLUSIONS

The programs discussed in this chapter are examples of how research has (1) expanded fundamental understanding of child development, learning, and teaching; (2) pointed the way to the discovery of effective elements of curriculum, instruction, and school organization; (3) provided a basis for evaluating worthwhile innovations; and (4) monitored the progress of reform efforts, assessing whether the reforms have been implemented as planned and are having the intended effects.

Findings from basic research have significantly broadened knowledge concerning the underlying processes of acquiring, organizing, storing, and retrieving information. Moreover, researchers studying early cognitive development have provided important insights into preschool children's understanding of mathematical and language concepts, thus giving developers of educational programs important guidelines for enhancing instruction. Two of the programs—Reciprocal Teaching and Cognitively Guided Instruction—were designed as basic research on theories developed by cognitive scientists, but they have also led to some practical guides for classroom instruction. Several of the other programs also drew heavily on one or more of the concepts developed by cognitive scientists. The focus in this chapter has been on the contributions of cognitive science to learning and teaching, but many other disciplines have made important contributions to the process of education: some of this research is at a detailed physiological level; other research concerns the functioning of groups and organizations.

Our review shows that the effects of research on educational practice are for the most part indirect and slow. The programs examined in this chapter range in development time from 4 to more than 20 years and are based on decades of research work. Some of the programs are heavily grounded in basic research; all of them have made use of principles drawn from basic research. The three most highly developed programs—Reading Recovery, Comprehensive School Mathematics Program, and Student Team Learning—have had the advantages of continuous support and the work of dedicated researchers since the initial stages of research, and all have been under development for longer than 20 years.

One important shortcoming of most of these innovative programs is the lack of follow-up assessment to determine if the gains measured at the end of the treatment are maintained over time. Another shortcoming is the lack of evaluations at dissemination sites where the programs are no longer under the direct control of the developers. Once a program is disseminated, evaluation activities are usually reduced or discontinued because of logistical difficulties and the lack of funding. A third shortcoming of most of the programs is the limited number of adoptions—without adoptions, programs cannot have impact.

Both the laboratories and centers that are supported by OERI and individual scholars have been responsible for producing promising research and innovative programs. The Learning Research and Development Center and the Wisconsin Center for Educational Research have been leaders in research on cognitive science and its contributions to education; the Center for the Study of Reading has been a leader in reading research (and produced A Nation of Readers); the Central Midwestern Regional Laboratory designed the Comprehensive School Mathematics Program, and the Midcontinent Regional Educational Laboratory disseminated it; and the Johns Hopkins' centers have developed and expanded Student Team Learning.

Field-initiated research and development has also been a rich source of ideas and has provided a wide range of promising programs for schools. Most of the innovative programs we reviewed were built on a research base accumulated largely from the field-initiated work of individual social and behavioral scientists. In addition, many of the innovative programs were developed by individuals working on their own initiative. For example, the use of computers in the schools was introduced and tested through numerous field-initiated efforts; Reading Recovery is based on the research of Marie Clay, who then proceeded to develop this powerful intervention; IMPACT was a field-initiated effort aimed at integrating instruction in thinking and reasoning into content courses; and the developers of both the School Development Program and the Outcomes Driven Development Model combined prior basic research and their own practical experience to create comprehensive approaches to school restructuring.

Research has also informed policy makers and the public about the status of the U.S. education system, it problems, and the progress towards reaching the nation's goals in education. The major activities of the National Center for Educational Statistics and the data it collects and reports are invaluable to congressional agency staff and to social science researchers in general.

Our review demonstrates that successful education research and development requires a sustained investment of time and money for research, development, and dissemination. We conclude that no one mechanism for the support of research should dominate federal grant-making policy. A vigorous program for support of field-initiated research is as important as the support of laboratories, centers, and other such institutions. Furthermore, no one discipline should be given priority. Advances in education have been built on research in the cognitive sciences, psychology, sociology, anthropology, organizational behavior, and clinical work in and outside of classrooms.

3

The Office of Educational Research and Improvement

The Office of Educational Research and Improvement (OERI) in the U.S. Department of Education is the federal government's lead agency for educational research and development. Its goals are to promote quality and equity in education. OERI collects statistics on the status and progress of schools and education throughout the nation; funds basic research aimed at enriching fundamental understanding of learning, teaching, and schools; supports applied research to improve curriculum, teaching, schools, and assessment; develops new learning aids, teaching techniques, and means of organizing and administering schools; demonstrates and evaluates promising educational approaches; disseminates information; and provides technical assistance to those who seek to improve education.

OERI's immediate predecessor was the National Institute of Education (NIE). Because NIE had essentially the same mission as OERI, and shared similar problems, it is included in the discussion in this and the next chapters.

There are other offices within the Department of Education that conduct research and development on education issues, and there are other federal agencies that also do so, but each has a much narrower mission than OERI. For instance, the National Science Foundation supports work on mathematics and science education, and the Department of Defense supports some basic research on learning and considerable work on the applications of technology to training. Within the Department of Education, the Office of Special Education and Rehabilitative Services supports work on retardation, specific learning disabilities, and physical impairments, and the

Office of Bilingual Education and Minority Languages Affairs funds some R&D within its areas of responsibility. But only OERI's mandate spans all subject areas; all grade levels, including preschool and postsecondary education; and all providers of education, including parents, private schools, and employers.

HISTORY

Federal sponsorship of education research began in 1867 with the creation of the Office of Education (USOE). Its mission (An Act to Establish a Department of Education, 1867) was to:

> collect such statistics and facts as shall show the condition and progress of education in the several States and Territories, and of diffusing such information respecting the organization and management of schools and school systems, the methods of teaching as shall aid the people of the United States in the establishment and maintenance of efficient school systems.

For its first nine decades, USOE's research activities were primarily restricted to the routine collection and dissemination of statistics, and the federal investment in education research was minimal.

Centers, Laboratories, and the Educational Resources Information Center

The Cooperative Research Act of 1954 first authorized USOE to provide funds for field-initiated research, primarily at universities, much as other federal agencies were doing for research in the natural sciences. The budget for this work was $1 million in 1955, but grew rapidly, particularly in the mid-1960s: $17 million in 1965 and $70 million in 1966 (U.S. Department of Health, Education, and Welfare, 1969b).

Under the Cooperative Research Act, individual projects were funded through proposals initiated from the field, with little opportunity for federal officials to shape a national research agenda (Guthrie, 1989). This approach eventually led to concerns about the fragmented and noncumulative nature of the many studies. Furthermore, the project approach was not closing the gap between research and practice and was not attracting the range of disciplinary talents believed necessary for advancing the field. A *system* for improving the performance and productivity of educational processes was still lacking.

These concerns led to the development of three major initiatives to upgrade the USOE's research and development (R&D) activities during the mid-1960s. The first was the establishment of national R&D centers for conducting large-scale, long-term programmatic work directed toward solving education problems. The second was the creation of regional educational laboratories to move research results into practice through development and demonstration of new curricula and teaching approaches and dissemination activities. The third was the creation of an information system for the dissemination of research results—the Educational Resources Information Center (ERIC). All three institutions exist today, although their activities have changed somewhat over the years. (Their current activities are discussed below.)

The congressional authorization of national R&D centers in 1963 was the first attempt to overcome the shortcomings within the education R&D system by organizational changes. It was believed that an institutional approach would provide the "critical mass" of effort—a forum for research-ers from a variety of disciplines to investigate contemporary problems in education. The R&D centers were to provide the intellectual leadership in a chosen field of work through a program of basic and applied research, supplemented by development work and dissemination activities (National Institute of Education, 1976). The centers were also supposed to serve as a mechanism for ensuring that education R&D was responsive to federally identified needs (Guthrie, 1989).

As the first R&D centers were created, federal priorities for education research had not been developed. As a consequence, the ten original cen-ters, established between 1964 and 1966, proposed their own missions. By 1966, the federal appropriation for the ten centers was $6.6 million (U.S. Department of Health, Education, and Welfare, 1969b).

Educational laboratories were created in response to the report of a national Task Force on Education, chaired by John Gardner, which had conducted a sweeping examination of American education. The task force concluded (President's Task Force on Education, 1964:34) that the research was a necessary component for change, but

> the efforts of the past ten years have not brought about the far-reaching changes that one might wish, partly because neither the efforts to innovate nor the arrangements for disseminating innovation have been on a scale adequate to the need.

The task force recommended the development of a "system designed for continuous renewal, a system in which reappraisal and innovation are built in" (President's Task Force on Education, 1964:33). It also proposed the creation of "at least a dozen major laboratories and perhaps two or three dozen more that are specialized or less ambitious in scope." Activities of the proposed laboratories were supposed to expand on those of the existing centers in three major ways: greater emphasis on demonstration and dis-semination activities, the use of experimental schools and testing of innova-tions in regular schools, and provision for in-service teacher education as an integral part of the program.

Shortly after the release of the Gardner report, the Elementary and Secondary Education Act of 1965 was passed, and the proposed laboratories were authorized. From their inception, however, there was little consensus on the appropriate role for the laboratories, their geographic orientation (regional or nationwide), the type of services they were to provide, or the appropriate mechanism for evaluating their activities. Nonetheless, 17 months after the passage of ESEA, contracts had been awarded for the establishment of 20 laboratories (U.S. Department of Health, Education, and Welfare, 1969a).

The Educational Resources Information Center (ERIC) was proposed as a mechanism for disseminating federally sponsored R&D: information on individual projects and programs was accumulating as a result of expanded research, but teachers and school administrators were largely unaware of this body of knowledge. Patterned after the Clearinghouse for Federal Scientific and Technical Information, ERIC was to be an information retrieval system that would abstract, index, store, retrieve, and disseminate research information. All USOE-sponsored research was to be included. In 1966 the USOE provided $2 million for ERIC's operations with 12 clearinghouses (National Institute of Education, 1976). Like the laboratories and the centers, ERIC was soon a target for critics of federally funded R&D in education: users complained that the system concentrated on quantity rather than quality, information was difficult to access, and requests were often delayed (Trester, 1981).

The National Institute of Education

The Elementary and Secondary Education Act of 1965 proved to be a major milestone in federal sponsorship of education and education R&D. It authorized unprecedented levels of federal financing: appropriations for field-initiated research, centers, and training within the USOE leaped from $19.3 million in fiscal 1964 to $100 million in fiscal 1966 (U.S. Department of Health, Education, and Welfare, 1969a).

The Office of Education was reorganized in response to the increased funding and new research programs. A separate Bureau of Research was established in "recognition of the need for concentrated expertise in the use of research for systematic improvements in education" (Ianni, 1965:14). However, the projected budget growth did not occur during the late 1960s, and this proved particularly debilitating to the network of 20 regional educational laboratories that had just been established. Federal funding was discontinued for five laboratories in 1969 and for four more in 1971 because of budget limitations and dissatisfaction with their performance. Centers, too, were affected by the budget squeeze: federal appropriations declined from $14.7 million in fiscal 1968 to $10.7 million in fiscal 1970 (National Institute of Education, 1976).

It was within this inauspicious climate that the National Institute on Education (NIE) was created in 1971. The legislation (Public Law 92-318, 1972) charged NIE with providing "leadership in the conduct and support of scientific inquiry into the education process" and with the building of "an effective educational research and development system." The preamble to the legislation declares (General Education Provisions Act, Sec. 405):

> It is the policy of the United States to provide every person an equal opportunity to receive an education of high quality regardless of race, color, religion, sex, national origin, or social class. . . . To achieve equality will require far more dependable knowledge about the processes of learning and education than now exists or can be expected from present research and experimentation in this field.

The mandated focus on equity led NIE to focus much of its work on those groups facing the greatest educational and social barriers to success— the poor, racial and ethnic minorities, and women. The problems of these groups were some of the hardest issues facing educators and the least amenable to quick and easy solutions, and NIE was frequently criticized for its ineffectiveness in satisfying the needs of these populations.

From its inception, NIE was rarely free of turmoil. Many supporters of education in Congress and throughout the country expressed concern that President Nixon was using NIE as a ploy for reducing the federal government's commitment to the costly education initiatives of the Johnson administration. Inadequate levels of funding hampered NIE's ability to sponsor major, long-term research projects that many people believed were key to illuminating major education problems. Six directors and four acting directors in 13 years did not allow a strong, consistent leadership to be established. Moreover, as a research agency dealing with education—a poorly understood and profoundly value-laden social enterprise—NIE was always vulnerable to charges that its research programs were influenced by the political and ideological concerns of the administration, congressional sponsors, and agency managers (Sproull et al., 1978). As the U.S. General Accounting Office (1987) noted, members of Congress and presidential administrations politicized NIE by frequently intervening in the determination of its research priorities and activities.

Although its mission was conceived on an ambitious scale, the NIE was always a rather small federal agency. In 1973 NIE's budget was $136 million; in the next year the budget had been drastically reduced to $65 million, and it never again rose above $80 million. In comparison with NIE's $65 million, in 1974 the Agriculture Research Service had a budget of $205 million, the National Science Foundation had a budget of $567 million, and the National Institutes of Health had a budget of $1.86 billion.

NIE inherited both staff and programs from the Office of Education and the Office of Economic Opportunity. Those programs—including career education model development, the experimental schools program, the tuition voucher experiment, and satellite broadcast of instruction—represented, roughly $79 million of the fiscal 1973 budget and $26 million of the following year's budget. After covering the ongoing commitments to the laboratories, centers, and ERIC, there was relatively little in the budget for new initiatives.

The Office of Educational Research and Improvement

When the Office of Education was replaced with a Department of Education in 1979, the Office of Educational Research and Improvement (OERI) was also created. OERI was originally seen as a "holding company" for NIE, the National Center for Education Statistics (NCES), Library Programs, and some other discretionary and dissemination activities. OERI was to provide some overall guidance and coordination, but to allow the main entity to operate semi-autonomously.

OERI's mission was specified in the authorizing legislation, (Public Law 96-88) which begins with the following:

Sec. 405 (a)(1) The Congress declares it to be the policy of the United States to provide to every individual an equal opportunity to receive an education of high quality. . . . Although the American educational system has pursued this objective, it has not attained the objective. Inequalities of opportunity to receive high quality education remain pronounced. To achieve the goal of quality education requires the continued pursuit of knowledge about education through research, improvement activities, data collection, and information dissemination . . . the Federal Government has a clear responsibility to provide leadership in the conduct and support of scientific inquiry into the educational process.

(2) The Congress further declares it to be the policy of the United States to—

(A) promote the quality and equity of American education;

(B) advance the practice of education as an art, science, and profession;

(C) support educational research of the highest quality;

(D) strengthen the educational research and development system;

(E) improve educational techniques and training;

(F) assess the national progress of this Nation's schools and educational institutions, particularly special populations; and

(G) collect, analyze, and disseminate statistics and other data related to education in the United States and other nations.

OERI was reorganized in 1985. The restructuring eliminated the semi-autonomous operating units, including NIE, and placed their functions in five OERI offices: the Office of Research, the Center for Education Statistics, Programs for the Improvement of Practice, Library Programs, and Information Services. This organizational structure has remained with only two modest changes. Management of the R&D centers and field-initiated research was assumed by the Office of Research; the laboratories were managed under Programs for the Improvement of Practice; NCES remained intact as the new Center for Education Statistics, a short-lived appellation; and ERIC was administered by Information Services. In 1988 the Hawkins-Stafford School Improvement Amendments authorized the Fund for the Improvement and Reform of Schools and Teaching (FIRST), and a separate office was created within OERI to administer the program. In 1990, the Office of Information Services was abolished and its activities distributed to the remaining offices: ERIC was transferred to the Office of Research, and most publication activities were placed in the Office of Assistant Secretary.

ORGANIZATION AND ACTIVITIES

OERI is currently organized into six offices: the Office of the Assistant Secretary, the Office of Research, Programs for the Improvement of Practice (PIP), the National Center for Education Statistics (NCES), the Fund for the Improvement and Reform of Schools and Teaching (FIRST), and Library Programs; see Figure 3-1. OERI's offices and major activities are described and briefly critiqued in the rest of this chapter; a number of concerns that apply to several offices or activities are discussed in Chapter 4.

It is important to note that very little R&D is conducted within OERI. The agency plans the work to be done, solicits and reviews proposals, and monitors progress. Most of the work is performed by university-operated centers, free-standing nonprofit laboratories, the ERIC clearinghouses, and scholars and educators across the country in universities, professional associations, state agencies, local school districts, and nonprofit organizations.

The National Advisory Council on Educational
Research and Improvement

OERI is advised by the National Advisory Council on Educational Research and Improvement. Five specific functions of the council are described in its authorizing legislation (General Education Provisions Act, Sec. 405(c)(3)):

(1) advise the Secretary and Assistant Secretary on the policies and activities carried out by the Office;
(2) review and publicly comment on the policies and activities of the Office;
(3) conduct such activities as may be necessary to fulfill its functions under this subsection;
(4) prepare such reports to the Secretary on the activities of the Office as are appropriate; and,

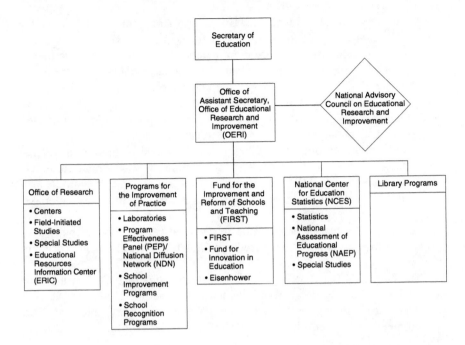

FIGURE 3-1   Organization, Office of Educational Research and Improvement, 1991.

(5) submit, no later than March 31st of each year, a report to the President
    and the Congress on the activities of the Office, and on education,
    education research, and data gathering in general.

The council is composed of 15 members appointed by the President
with the advice and consent of the Senate. The nominees are to be selected
to "ensure that the Council is broadly representative of the general public;
the education professions, including practitioners; policy makers and researchers; and the various fields and levels of education" (General Education Provisions Act, Sec. 405(c)(1)). The members serve staggered 3-year
terms.

For at least the last 3 years, the council has had few or no active
education researchers or social scientists among its members. None of the
1989, 1990, or 1991 council members is listed in the directories of any of
the following associations: American Educational Research Association,
American Psychological Association, American Economics Association, American
Political Science Association, and American Sociological Association. In
addition, none was found in *Who's Who in American Education*.

The council's annual report is its formal mechanism for transmitting advice to OERI, the President, and Congress. According to the council's fiscal 1989 annual report, its first meeting focused on OERI's current literacy activities and the second focused on members' visits to innovative literacy programs in Miami. The report makes nine recommendations, primarily aimed at preventing school dropouts, including the following (National Advisory Council on Educational Research and Improvement, 1989): "retention of students to graduation should be a primary policy objective of elementary and secondary schools" and "restructuring should focus on the goal of seeing students through to graduation." Only one of the recommendations is explicitly directed to OERI: "the Office of Educational Research and Improvement [should] fund research into learning styles for middle and secondary schools that incorporate cooperative learning strategies and make learning a shared experience . . ." Only one other recommendation specifies research: "research [should] be undertaken into programs that assist dropouts to reenter school or otherwise complete the requirements for their diplomas."

The council's fiscal 1990 annual report indicates that its first meeting centered on school leadership and discussed the members' visit to the National Center for Educational Leadership in Cambridge, Massachusetts. The second meeting focused on dissemination strategies. No recommendations were included in this report.

Office of the Assistant Secretary

The assistant secretary of the Office of Educational Research and Improvement oversees agenda setting, the budget process, staffing of the agency, contracts and grants, publications and communications, general administrative functions, and congressional relations. The Office of the Assistant Secretary provides support for all these functions. In fiscal 1991, the office had about 88 employees and a program budget of $623,000. This small budget was mostly used for some of the printing expenses and to establish an electronic network linking the laboratories, centers, and the agency.

The assistant secretary of OERI is appointed by the President with the advice and consent of the Senate. There is a history of frequent turnover among the heads of OERI and its predecessor agency, NIE. As noted above, there were six directors confirmed by the Senate and several interim ones during NIE's 13-year existence; the average tenure of service by the confirmed appointees was just 19 months. During the 11-year life of OERI, overlapping the last 5 years of NIE's existence, there have been five assistant secretaries confirmed by the Senate; the average tenure of service by the confirmed appointees was 28 months. Altogether, only 3 of the past 11 confirmed directors and assistant secretaries have served for more than 2 years. There was more continuity of leadership at the deputy and associate director levels at NIE in the 1970s, but from 1980 to 1986 at least 16 people served in the five top positions immediately below the director or assistant secretary (U.S. General Accounting Office, 1987).

The assistant secretary is required by law to publish proposed research priorities in the *Federal Register* every 2 years, invite comments and suggestions, allow 60 days for public response, reconsider the priorities, and then publish the final priorities. OERI's agenda is also influenced by a large number of standing advisory groups. These include the Laboratory Review Panel, the Fund Board of the FIRST program, the Technical Review Board of the National Assessment of Educational Progress (NAEP), and the Schools and Staffing Survey Technical Review Board. For NCES alone, there are 38 advisory groups with a total of 779 members, operating at an annual cost of about $3 million. Each laboratory has a governing board, and each center and ERIC clearinghouse has an advisory committee. In addition, prior to contracting for major R&D activities, OERI is required to publish a preliminary announcement of the competition and solicit advice before releasing the formal announcement.

It is one thing for a federal agency to set an agenda and another for it to secure congressional authorization and funding for the planned activities. OERI's proposed budget, prepared by the assistant secretary, is reviewed and revised by the Department of Education, the Office of Management and Budget, and the President's Domestic Policy Council before being incorporated into the President's budget and submitted to Congress. Since OERI is a very small agency and seldom perceived to be involved with issues of major importance, the President rarely defends its budget vigorously. Most members of Congress also accord OERI's budget little importance for the same reasons and because few constituents contact their Representatives or Senators about OERI. As a result, most of the substantive input on OERI's budget is provided by a few Senators and Representatives and their staff.

Congress influences OERI's agenda in several ways. It mandates new programs, such as the Rural Education Initiative for the laboratories, Star Schools, and the Javits Gifted and Talented program. It mandates specific studies, such as the 1980s Chapter I Assessment and the new National Assessment of Vocational Education. Congress also expands or contracts existing activities by increasing or deceasing their annual budget with directives in the appropriation reports or with "earmarks" in the budgets. For instance, the appropriations reports have regularly provided directives about funding levels for centers, laboratories, ERIC, and field-initiated research. Yet the assistant secretary does have moderate discretion over implementation of the authorized programs. Although Congress regularly specifies the minimum funding levels for the R&D centers and laboratories, it rarely specifies the number of centers and laboratories, their focus, their activities, or how they are to be managed.

Office of Research

The Office of Research administers most of the research supported by OERI except for the collection and reporting of nationwide statistics, which is managed by NCES. The Office of Research supervises the 25 national R&D centers, field-initiated research (when funding is available for it), ERIC, some discretionary research, and various special projects, which currently include the National Board for Teacher Standards, follow-up activities to the "education summit," School Year Extension Commission, National Writing Project, and education reform evaluation.

In fiscal 1991 the Office of Research had about 69 employees and administered programs with a total budget of $51.7 million, of which only $4.9 million was for discretionary research activities. It has subunits for higher education and adult learning, learning and instruction, schools and school professionals, education and society, and ERIC.

National R&D Centers

As noted above, the centers and laboratories were first created in the mid-1960s in response to concerns that the research being conducted by university faculty members failed to address national priorities, was of small scale and not cumulative, and was not being applied to education practice. Since their inception the R&D centers have engaged primarily in basic research, applied research, and development; in contrast, the regional laboratories have engaged primarily in development, demonstrations, dissemination, and technical assistance. This division of labor is not mandated by law, but it has prevailed, with variations, since the 1960s.

OERI's authorization specifies that the agency shall support "research and development centers established by institutions of higher education, by institutions of higher education in consort with public agencies or private nonprofit organizations . . ." The number and substantive focus of the centers has generally been left to the discretion of the assistant secretary, although there have been occasions when Congress has encouraged or mandated the establishment of a center on a specific topic. The number of centers has grown from 11 in 1966 to the current 25:

Center on Families, Communities, Schools, and Children's Learning
Center on Education in the Inner Cities
Center for Research on Educational Accountability and Teacher Evaluation
Center on Adult Literacy
Center on the Educational Quality of the Workforce
Center on Organization and Restructuring of Schools
Center on Science Teaching and Learning

Center on Assessment, Evaluation, and Testing
Center on Cultural Diversity and Second Language Learning
Center for the Study of Writing and Literacy
Center on Student Learning
Center on For Research on Teacher Learning
Center on Postsecondary Teaching, Learning, and Assessment
Center for Policy Research in Education
Center for Research in Mathematical Sciences Education
Center on Education Finance and Productivity
Center on Literature Teaching and Learning
Reading Research and Education Center
Center for Research on the Context of Secondary School Teaching
Center on the Learning and Teaching of Elementary Subjects
Center for Technology in Education
Center on Educational Leadership
Center on School Leadership
Center for Research on Effective Schooling for Disadvantaged Students
Center on the Gifted and Talented

All the centers operate with 5-year contracts or cooperative agreements; 17 of the current 25 were awarded in 1990. OERI's funding of each center averaged $861,000 in fiscal 1991: this is a very small sum for a R&D center. For example, the National Science Foundation and the National Institutes of Health fund some individual projects at higher levels than OERI funds its centers.

The low levels of funding have hindered the centers' ability to create and sustain a "critical mass" of diverse staff working in close proximity. This lack of concentrated work has been exacerbated by OERI's encouraging consortia of universities to bid on the centers. In most cases, the work of a center is now conducted at two or three separate institutions. The principal investigators at the centers, excluding the directors, work an average of only one-quarter of their time on center studies. Much of their work is devoted to individual research on topics related to the center's mission, rather than to team projects. Large-scale or long-term studies have not been common during the past decade, though there have been some.

The R&D centers have been the subject of several policy assessments and organizational reviews since their establishment in 1964. Most of the evaluations were performed by panels who conducted site visits, interviewed staff, reviewed pertinent agency documents, and talked to people in the education research community. These reviews affirmed the original concept of the educational R&D centers—that is, institutions conducting large-scale, long-term, mission-focused programs of research—but found problems in staffing, needs assessment, the nature of the work undertaken, and the impact of research on schools. Most of them also noted that the early intentions for the centers have been compromised by failure to fund them at the levels originally anticipated.

In 1973 the U.S. General Accounting Office issued a report on products developed by both the centers and the laboratories—books, audiovisual materials, and publications on procedures and organizational structures that could be used in schools. The study focused on products from 3 of the 9 centers and 5 of the 11 laboratories in existence at that time. The report did not distinguish between findings applicable to the centers and those applicable to the laboratories, apparently because GAO found little difference between the two. The major findings were quite negative: the institutions had developed some products and disseminated them to the intended users—particularly products for the training of teachers—but the suitability and impact of the products was in doubt; the objectives of the products were often ambiguous, and they seemed to have been developed with little concern for potential marketability; the evaluations of the products' effects in the classrooms were generally so weak as to be inconclusive; and little interest in the products had been generated among commercial publishers. The report concluded that the Office of Education's own policies and frequent changes in management were responsible for much of the problems, and the report recommended greater consultation with commercial publishers in determining market needs and stricter regulations for the testing of innovative products.

In 1975 a group of ten consultants, headed by Ronald Campbell, was commissioned by NIE to conduct a 3-month review of its funding policies. By that time NIE had switched from institutional funding of the centers and laboratories to a "program purchase" arrangement: each institution had to prepare proposals for clusters of activities. Funding decisions were made in respect to each cluster, with little consideration to the overall plan of each institution. The Campbell group report (Campbell, 1975:79) suggested that:

> [NIE] review and revise all present policies that contribute to the present situation, where it is substantially supporting a relatively large number of special institutions, of diverse quality, with varying lengths of contract terms, subject to uncoordinated NIE management and review, and inconsistently related to NIE priorities.

The group recommended a thorough evaluation of each center and laboratory, and that NIE fund a "smaller number of institutions . . . with improved quality and relevance of effort . . . NIE must give priority in planning and procurement to dealing holistically with each" (Campbell, 1975:71). The group suggested that each center have a single mission and stable funding for 3-5 years at a minimum of $3-$4 million per year ($7-10 million, in 1990 dollars) and close ties to NIE through periodic review and evaluation.

The Campbell group also identified several strengths and weaknesses of the centers. The group observed that university-based centers constituted an important structure for supporting basic social science related to educational issues and that such work should not be judged by its immediate application to solving educational problems. In contrast, it noted that the norms of universities, where all but one center were located, were in many ways unsuited to the demands of specified objectives and rigid timelines that accompany most federal R&D funds. It warned that problems in education are often millennia old and not likely to be solved quickly. It also stated (Campbell, 1975:18) that "pressures for rapid development and evidence of 'impact' have probably forced many centers to neglect basic research . . ."

In the 1976 reauthorization of NIE, Congress mandated the establishment of a 15-member Panel for the Review of Laboratory and Center Operations. The panel members visited all 17 laboratories and centers, met with NIE's policy-making council and interviewed members of the educational R&D community. In its final report, the panel "endorsed the concept of R&D centers and regional educational laboratories and affirmed the importance of maintaining and improving the stability and quality of the existing institutions" (Panel for the Review of Laboratory and Center Operations, 1979:6). The panel agreed that past federal support policies were partially accountable for weaknesses in the centers' work. Cuts in NIE appropriations and the provision of federal funds under the program purchase policy rather than on an institutional basis "tended to dilute laboratory and center institutional missions, unduly favor federally determined priorities, compromise planning capabilities, and encourage some institutions to become educational 'job shops'" (Panel for the Review of Laboratory and Center Operations, 1979:v).

The panel recommended that NIE enter into long-term institutional agreements with seven of the nine existing centers and seven of the eight laboratories. To enhance the setting of priorities, centers were to be primarily responsible for establishing priorities in pursuit of their missions, after consulting with scholars, practitioners, and NIE staff. To ensure stability and accountability, the panel recommended a 5-year funding agreement, renewable for an equal period on condition of a favorable external review in the third year of the institutional agreement.

Despite that recommendation, beginning in 1985 the R&D centers were generally regarded as 5-year projects. In a few cases, awards were for just 3 years and for as little as $0.5 million dollars annually. As contracts expired, OERI changed the foci of subsequent centers, precluding the continuation of much of the prior work. Of the 12 centers operating in the early 1980s, 6 were terminated and 5 were included in the 1985 competition; 3 were awarded to new bidders and 2 were awarded to incumbents. Of the 6 centers that were newly established in 1985, 2 were terminated in 1990, 2 were awarded to new bidders in the 1990 competition, and only 2 were awarded to incumbents. Of all 13 centers operating during the latter half of the 1980s, 3 were terminated, and 8 were included in the 1990 competition; 3 were awarded to new bidders and 5 were awarded to incumbents.

Unlike the R&D centers established in the mid-1960s, there has been no effort to institutionalize the current centers. In the 1960s the federal government helped build facilities for a few centers; expected the centers to be large in size, scope, and funding; encouraged them to pursue new initiatives during the course of their contracts; and committed to long-term support. None of that is currently the case.

Yet despite tight funding and the limited life spans of many centers, some centers have managed to pursue a sustained program of research. For 25 years the Learning Research Development Center at the University of Pittsburgh, operating what OERI now calls the Center on Student Learning, has been a leader in the applications of cognitive science to education. For a similar period the Center for the Study of Evaluation at the University of California at Los Angeles, operating what OERI now calls the Center on Assessment, Evaluation, and Testing, has worked on testing, assessment, and evaluation. The Reading Research and Education Center at the University of Illinois has played a major role in improving reading instruction for 15 years. Two successive centers at Johns Hopkins, spanning 22 years, had been leaders in research and development on cooperative learning, but both have been terminated by OERI.

In addition, a few OERI centers are administered by larger education R&D institutions, also called centers, that have several different projects under way simultaneously, funded by various federal agencies and foundations. At these locations, notably the Wisconsin Center for Education Research and the Learning Research and Development Center, institutionalization was achieved under the earlier policies of the Office of Education and NIE and has since been maintained with diverse sources of funding. Even if either was to lose its OERI-funded centers, it could continue on as a leader in education R&D.

Field-Initiated Research

The Office of Research manages a small field-initiated research program. From 1983 through 1985 OERI did not announce support for field-initiated proposals, but some proposals were received anyway, and a very few of those were funded. OERI's 1986 authorization mandated that a minimum of $500,000 be used to support "meritorious, unsolicited proposals" each year. Since then Congress has never appropriated more than $1.3 million annually for field-initiated research.

In recent years OERI's field-initiated research program has represented 2-5 percent of the agency's R&D budget. In contrast, the National Science Foundation (NSF) invests about $1.9 billion in field-initiated research, approximately 94 percent of its R&D budget, and the National Institutes of Health (NIH) invests about $4.2 billion, about 56 percent of its R&D budget. (Data on field-initiated research are not available from the Agriculture Research Service, the other agency with which we frequently compare OERI.)

In fiscal 1990 OERI funded 12 field-initiated studies at a total cost of $785,166. The funded topics included early language and literacy activities in the home, academic learning and critical reasoning, success factors associated with first-generation Mexican immigrant high school students, and the role of family values and behaviors in educational performance and attainment. Most of the grants were for $50,000–$75,000 and, in accordance with the legislation, none was for more than an 18-month period.

In fiscal 1991 OERI funded another 12 field-initiated studies at a total cost of $967,862. The topics for study included methods of assessing staff development projects, factors that lead to graduation or drop out among Native American students, assessment methods for accurately measuring the new mathematics education goals, and the provision of equity to minority students in small rural school districts. Most of the grant awards ranged from $75,000 to $85,000.

In each of the past several years, OERI's small field-initiated research program has attracted about 200-300 applications. Some OERI staff have suggested that many of the unfunded proposals were of low quality, although they have acknowledged that good proposals went unfunded. Other observers have pointed out that it is difficult to get good investigators to apply when there is so little money and so few awards. OERI funds about 3-5 percent of the proposals it receives; in contrast, NSF and NIH fund roughly 30 percent of the proposals they receive.

Field-initiated research has been crucial to advances in science. Several of the examples of important research and development cited in Chapter 2 were the direct result of such work, undertaken with funding from NIE or other federal agencies and private foundations.

Educational Resources Information Center

The Educational Resources Information Center (ERIC) was originally established to provide access to the large number of unpublished reports being generated by the Cooperative Research Program. Within 3 years journals were also covered. ERIC is an information retrieval system designed to index, abstract, store, retrieve, and disseminate information about education. Most of the work is performed by subject-matter clearinghouses located throughout the country and a central processing facility in Maryland. Each clearinghouse covers a broad topic area and is responsible for identifying, indexing, and abstracting appropriate documents for input into the ERIC database.

The database primarily covers reports from federally funded education research and development projects and published articles on education culled from as many as 800 journals. Papers presented at conferences, curriculum materials, and other documents are also covered selectively. The ERIC system currently references a total of more than 750,000 documents and journal articles. In addition to the database responsibilities, each clearinghouse also produces reports, interpretive summaries, syntheses, digests, and other publications in its field. Most of these are designed to distill a large body of literature into a small and user-friendly format. Unlike most literature search systems, ERIC makes available the full text of most unpublished documents, by microfiche or photocopy.

The number and foci of the clearinghouses has varied over time. All the clearinghouses are up for renewal in 1992. There are currently 16 clearinghouses, with the following areas of concentration:

adult, career, and vocational education
counseling and personnel services
educational management
elementary and early childhood education
handicapped and gifted children
higher education
information resources
junior colleges
languages and linguistics
reading and communication skills
rural education and small schools
science, mathematics, and environmental education
social studies/social science education
teacher education
tests, measurement, and evaluation
urban education

There are also five adjunct clearinghouses, each with funding from other than the regular ERIC budget. They cover literacy education, art education, consumer education, Chapter 1 programs, and U.S.-Japan studies.

The ERIC database can be searched by computer through several commercial vendors, including BRS, DIALOG, and OCLC, all of which provide access to many different information systems. Most microcomputers, with a $150 modem, can be used for the on-line linkage. About 500,000 ERIC searches were conducted on-line in 1990. Utilization studies indicate ERIC is the second or third most heavily used on-line system in the country—after Medline and sometimes Nexis (Tenopir, 1991). Several thousand universities, schools, and libraries also have ERIC on CD-ROM or hard copy, but there is no way to estimate how many searches are done with those resources. Approximately 90 foreign countries also use ERIC products. In addition, the clearinghouse received 90,000 telephone and mailed inquiries during 1990: 17 percent were from professors and researchers, 15 percent from primary and secondary school teachers, 14 percent from school administrators and school board members, 14 percent from librarians, 8 percent from students, 8 percent from parents and the general public, and 25 percent from all others (Office of Educational Research and Improvement, 1991).

Despite the high use of ERIC, there are complaints about the system. Teachers and administrators say the searches are difficult to conduct and the information caters to the needs of researchers. They also find that the searches often identify hundreds of citations, and it is difficult to judge which are the most authoritative. Many users complain that the system concentrates on quantity rather than quality. Researchers complain that the coverage of journals is not as thorough as they would like, that input of new citations often lags, and that ERIC does not cover most books.

Most of these complaints are common to other electronic index systems—both federally operated and commercially operated ones—although the relative severity varies from system to system. It is an inherently difficult task to provide diverse users with well-targeted access to a huge literature base. When we asked five National Research Council reference librarians who regularly use several electronic retrieval systems about ERIC, they indicated it was above average on ease of use, scope of coverage, and ability to find desired or useful citations; average on avoiding a large number of unwanted or useless citations; and slightly below average on the time lag in indexing materials and on duplication of citations.

The complaint that there is much low-quality material in ERIC is probably true, but there is reason to think the problem is not as severe as many think. Documents of no merit to one category of user, say, researchers, can be of considerable merit to other categories, say, teachers and parents. ERIC was originally created, in part, to index all reports from the Office of Education's contracts and grants for education R&D, and it generally does that regardless of the apparent quality of the documents. In the past few years ERIC has become increasingly selective in indexing documents that are sent to it from other sources; it now rejects about one-third of them. It has comprehensively indexed articles in a small number of journals and selectively indexed articles in other journals that are scanned. When there is a high level of selectivity, there is considerable risk that some useful materials will be omitted. ERIC does publish selective bibliographies and reviews of the literature. They are popular, but some users never learn about them, and others prefer to examine the original sources.

Several enhancements to ERIC have been suggested by users, review committees, and the ERIC staff. Most could improve the system at a modest cost. For example, ERIC indexes education-related articles from about 800 journals, but this is done with minimum coordination; no one person is in charge of this part of the operation. As a result, some new journals are not reviewed for their utility, and established journals are not periodically examined to determine whether their current status should be changed. As the budget of ERIC dropped by almost 50 percent from the late 1970s to the late 1980s (in 1990 constant dollars), fewer and fewer journals have been indexed comprehensively, and users cannot tell which are indexed comprehensively and which are indexed selectively. Some of the leading journals in the various social sciences are not even being scanned for important education-related articles. For example, since 1986 the *American Economic Review* has published articles on the future supply and demand of teachers, the effects of state mandates on student performance, the teaching of economics in high school, the effects of student aid on college enrollment, and the relation of schooling to wage trends—and none was indexed by ERIC. Over the same period the *Psychological Bulletin* has published major reviews of the research literature on memory and information processing, gender differences in verbal ability, gender differences in mathematics performance, the structure of vocational interests, and the effect of divorce on the well-being of children—and none was indexed by ERIC.

Like most similar electronic information systems, ERIC does not make the full text of cited documents available electronically. The on-line and CD-ROM searches generally provide only citations and abstracts. A notable exception is the full-text coverage of the *ERIC Digests*—brief annotated bibliographies and reviews of the literature prepared by the clearinghouses. For unpublished documents, microfiche copies are available at 900 depository libraries in the country, and microfiche or photocopies can be ordered from the ERIC Document Reproduction Service. For journal articles, users have to retrieve the journal from a library, or they can order photocopies of some from a commercial vendor. It is widely thought that the next generation of reference information systems will provide full-text information. ERIC has begun probing this frontier by working with a commercial vendor who may provide the full text of "key" ERIC documents on CD-ROM.

Another enhancement currently being explored by ERIC is the possibility of an international English-language equivalent of ERIC. ERIC currently indexes some British, Australian, and Canadian documents and journal articles. A concordance of the thesauruses used by the retrieval systems in those three countries and the United States is being prepared. In addition, there is a commitment among these countries to move towards an uniform format so that the data in each country's system can be shared by the others. Expanding ERIC's coverage to non-English documents would be more difficult because bilingual staff would be needed to index and prepare English-language abstracts. Yet some other federally funded information retrieval systems, such as Medline, regularly index major foreign journals.

Although ERIC is a state-of-the-art literature search system, such systems are only one of many new forms of electronic communication. ERIC does not provide electronic mail and bulletin board capabilities, linking teachers to researchers and other teachers with specific interests for the exchange of queries and information. ERIC does not provide direct access to the NCES databases; nor does ERIC provide electronic access and retrieval of curriculum modules, teaching aids, and other materials for use in classrooms. An electronic communication mechanism has recently been established for the nation's university faculties through the National Science Foundation's Internet, now being upgraded to the National Research and Education Network (NREN), which provides electronic mail, access to digital libraries and databases, and remote use of scientific sensing instruments. None of these services is available to teachers and administrators except in a few statewide and local experiments.

Programs for the Improvement of Practice

Programs for the Improvement of Practice is responsible for fostering the development of innovative programs and approaches, disseminating them to teachers and administrators, and assisting with their incorporation into practice. It supervises the ten regional laboratories, the Program Effectiveness Panel and the National Diffusion Network, the Javits Gifted and Talented Program, the Leadership in Educational Administration Development program, the Mid-Career Teacher Training program, Educational Partnerships, the Star Schools Program (which uses satellite broadcasts to enrich local school instruction), and the School Recognition Programs. It also convenes and supports the Urban Superintendents Network. In fiscal 1991 the office had about 87 staff and program budgets totaling $75.2 million.

Regional Laboratories

Regional laboratories were established to bridge the gap between research and practice (National Institute of Education, 1983b). OERI's authorization (Public Law 99-498, 1986) specifies that it shall support "regional educational laboratories established by public agencies or private nonprofit organization to serve the needs of a specific region of the Nation under the guidance of a regionally representative governing board . . ." Over the past two decades, the number of regional laboratories has ranged from six to the current ten:

> Appalachia Educational Laboratory
> Far West Laboratory for Educational Research and Development
> Mid-continent Regional Educational Laboratory
> North Central Regional Educational Laboratory
> Northwest Regional Educational Laboratory
> Pacific Regional Educational Laboratory
> Regional Laboratory for Educational Improvement of the
>   Northeast and Islands
> Research for Better Schools (mid-Atlantic region)
> SouthEastern Regional Vision for Education
> Southwest Educational Development Laboratory

The laboratories operate with 5-year contracts, and all were awarded in 1990. OERI's funding of each laboratory, including special money for rural initiatives, averaged $3.0 million in fiscal 1991. A few of the laboratories have been quite entrepreneurial, raising substantial funding for special projects from other federal agencies and foundations and charging for some services provided to schools. This has allowed them to considerably expand the activities that would have been possible with OERI funding.

Over the years the laboratories' activities have gradually shifted some, from applied research and large-scale development to technical assistance work with schools and, more recently, to dissemination activities and assistance to state agencies. These shifts resulted from NIE decisions to have research done primarily by the centers and field-initiated investigators, from cuts in the laboratories' budgets that almost precluded large development projects, from legislation in 1979 prohibiting the Department of Education from engaging in curriculum development (Public Law 96-88), and from the directive of the 1985 contract competition specifying (National Institute of Education, 1984:12):

> [the laboratories should use] an improvement approach of working with and through an even wider range of client organizations than is now the case . . . particularly . . . organizations that provide improvement assistance directly to schools and classrooms, and State-level decision makers.

The first shift cost the laboratories some national visibility that results from large development projects—such as the Career Exploration and Planning Program that has been commercially distributed for 15 years and the Comprehensive School Mathematics Program, which anticipated the mathematics standards promulgated by the National Council of Teachers of Mathematics (1989).

Since the initial recommendation in 1964 from the Gardner Task Force to create "at least a dozen major laboratories," (President's Task Force on Education, 1964:iii) subsequent groups have been charged with evaluating the role of the laboratories in supporting change in education. These evaluations have been based on information gathered during site visits to the laboratories; interviews with staff in NIE, state agencies, and local school districts; and the review of the relevant literature and other documents. In general, the evaluations have found the laboratories to be an important instrument of the federal education R&D strategy, but they have also identified several problems.

Francis Chase, Dean of the School of Education at the University of Chicago, was asked by the Office of Education to conduct a review of the operations of the laboratories only 9 months after the first laboratory contracts had been signed. Twenty laboratories were starting up or in operation and were receiving sharp criticism from persons in and outside the educational establishment. The criticism focused on the appropriate number of laboratories, their purpose and orientation, the degree of overlap with the R&D centers, and the appropriate mechanism for evaluating their activities. Chase (1968) concluded that despite their newness, most of the laboratories that were operational at that time had developed reasonable goals, built the nuclei of promising staffs, and already made some contributions. He observed, however (Chase, 1968:3):

> [only a small number] have moved with any definitiveness to supply the need for programmatic research, rigorous 'field testing' of research findings, or the engineering of components for the 'systems' approach to education . . . [and] several laboratories are engaging in dubious activities and have become the prisoners of mistaken concepts of regionality, of self-defeating attempts to address themselves to everyone's perceptions of needs, and of 'entangling alliances' of various kinds.

Chase warned that in the haste to establish the laboratories, insufficient consideration had been given to mechanisms for avoiding duplication among the laboratories, for assuring coordination with other existing educational institutions and agencies, and for making the laboratories adequately responsive to both the Office of Education and their respective regions. Despite these problems, Chase thought the laboratories, as originally conceived, were a necessary component for the reform and strengthening of the education enterprise.

In the late 1960s Elwin Svenson studied the laboratories' relationships with state education agencies. Relying on intensive interviews and examination of records, he found the relationships ranged from close and mutually trustful to nonexistent (Svenson, 1969). He determined that state education agencies were open to working with the laboratories on needs assessments, product development, and dissemination, and they had the best perceptions of laboratories when there had been considerable two-way communication and cooperation, but many were not well informed of the laboratories' resources and activities. He also found that consultation with the state education agencies made it more likely the laboratory products would be adopted for use in the schools.

In the late 1960s and early 1970s Chase continued to study the laboratories in the context of the larger education R&D enterprise. He reported (Chase, 1970:300) finding "several characteristics and tendencies which promise to speed up needed improvements in education." These included an increasing tendency on the part of the laboratories to concentrate efforts on well-defined objectives, an emphasis on developing learning systems that strive to address all elements likely to affect the results, engagement in a continuing process of modification and refinement, and the building of organizational links to facilitate the flow of research knowledge into practice. Chase recommended that funding be increased to annual budgets of $3-10 million per laboratory ($12-40 million in 1990 dollars) and that conditions be established that would permit moderate autonomy with accountability.

In a 1972 report to the House Select Subcommittee on Education, Chase concluded that significant progress had been made in the preceding 5 years by the federal education R&D system in developing theories of planned change, training personnel for that purpose, and coordinating the activities of multiple agencies. He suggested further progress could be hastened by creation of a national agency to identify the most urgent educational needs, establishment of an agenda for addressing those needs, and coordination of efforts addressed to carrying it out. He supported President Nixon's proposals for establishment of what became the National Institute of Education. Chase reiterated that long-term and systematic research is valuable, but is seldom supported by legislators, executive branch officials, practitioners, and parents who are eager for immediate results.

The Campbell report (1975:58,70) also made some observations specific to the laboratories:

> Laboratories seem to us a unique structure, poised between the university and the service-delivery system of education for a variety of purposes . . . .
>
> Failure of the laboratories to reach some goals held for them at the outset seems to us chiefly a failure of the government to guide and encourage them towards those goals, not a failure of the concept. The concept of a specialized, separate . . . [institution] in touch with schools but able to retreat from direct service to test ideas and develop new programs still seems distinctive and sound and worthy of extensive support.

The Campbell report also suggested that the program purchase approach to funding the laboratories and centers was dysfunctional and should be replaced with institutional support for those with favorable performance evaluations.

The report of the Panel for Review of Laboratory and Center Operations (1979) also proved important to the laboratories future. It recommended long-term institutional funding agreements for most of the laboratories and centers, with systematic monitoring to assure accountability. This reinforced an earlier recommendation from the Campbell group. Following considerable discussion with members of Congress and their staffs, NIE's program purchase funding approach was replaced with 5-year commitments for both laboratories and centers.

In 1982 U.S. Department of Education staff conducted a service delivery assessment of the laboratories to determine how practitioners perceive the quality and usefulness of their activities and to identify barriers to more extensive use of research products in the classrooms. The investigators found that all laboratories served state education agencies, intermediate service agencies, and local education agencies, with state education agencies being the primary clients. They reported cooperative and effective relations with the laboratories, a marked improvement from Svenson's 1969 study. Most clients who could estimate laboratory impact rated it positively (Wade et al., 1982).

A Laboratory Study Group was assembled to advise NIE on the 1985 competition for laboratories, the first competition for all the laboratories since the mid-1960s. The group concluded that the laboratories should offer a range of services, but (National Institute of Education, 1983a:ii,iii):

focus resources for concentrated impacts . . . emphasize transformation and delivery of research in forms that are useful for improving education policy and practice . . . [and] foster cooperative educational improvement activities among various constituent groups in their regions.

It recommended more communication and coordination among the laboratories and centers, a system of assessment and accountability for the laboratories, an immediate 50 percent increase in federal funding, and exploration of opportunities for cost sharing among laboratories and their clients.

The most recent assessment of the laboratories was conducted by the Laboratory Review Panel, established in 1987 and chaired by Christopher Cross shortly before he was appointed assistant secretary of OERI. The panel was established to help OERI plan the 1990 competition for laboratory contracts. The panel reviewed the laboratories, commissioned several papers, and met with representatives of the laboratories and their governing boards. Its report (Cross, 1989) recommended a critical reexamination of the relationships among all of OERI's main institutional components—laboratories, centers, ERIC, and the National Diffusion Network—and encouraged improved communication and coordination among them. The panel also suggested that OERI not require the laboratories to work primarily "with and through" state and intermediate service agencies, as specified in the 1985 laboratory request for proposals, but be allowed more flexibility in their service delivery strategies. A redistribution of funds was proposed to provide greater support to those laboratories serving regions with the most students. An evaluation of the laboratories' impact was recommended. And OERI was encouraged to rigorously encourage competition for the new laboratory contracts to be awarded in 1990.

In 1991 OERI awarded a contract to evaluate the laboratories' effectiveness. The contractor is to undertake three tasks: (1) examine the effectiveness of the laboratories' processes for assessing the needs in their respective regions; (2) study the effectiveness of laboratories' arrangements for collaboration with other providers of applied research, development, and improvement assistance; and (3) assess the adequacy of the outcomes of particularly significant laboratory activities. The evaluation is to be completed within 3 years.

The laboratories have probably been more disdained and more beloved than any other OERI and NIE institution. Researchers often criticize the laboratories, claiming they do mediocre or poor work. These judgments cannot be based on a systematic assessment of the laboratories' work, since none exists, and they may be colored by professional jealousies: the laboratories employ few researchers and have gradually gained an increased proportion of the NIE and OERI R&D budgets. Staff within OERI generally find the laboratories less responsive to the agency's needs and directives than are the centers, but this is at least partly a consequence of their congressionally mandated regional governance.

At the same time, the laboratories also have many supporters. A recent national survey of school districts' use of education R&D found that almost half the districts had used products or services of the laboratories during the past 16 months. When respondents were asked to list "one R&D resource from any source . . . that has been particularly useful," more respondents cited resources from the laboratories than from any other source: 171 from the laboratories, 120 from state education entities, 106 from ERIC, and 96 from the National Diffusion Network (National Center for Education Statistics, 1990). Satisfaction, of course, does not constitute clear evidence of effectiveness in improving the quality of education, but it is important in any service industry, and the laboratories are now primarily service providers.

Taken as a whole, prior reviews and recent evidence suggest that the laboratories are weaker and less effective institutions than originally hoped, but stronger and more effective than their detractors have claimed. Since their founding in the mid-1960s, there have been proposals to make the laboratories national institutions (each serving the entire country), and, conversely, to establish a laboratory in each state (see Guthrie, 1989). If laboratories are primarily to do development and demonstration work, a few national laboratories, each with a distinctive focus, would permit larger efforts, with a wider range of staff expertise, but this arrangement would result in less contact with school districts across the country. If the laboratories are primarily to assist local districts and schools with improvements and reform, then state laboratories would enhance the close ties and face-to-face interactions so important to this work, but they would have smaller staffs and less breadth of expertise—unless there were huge increases in the budgets.

Program Effectiveness Panel and National Diffusion Network

The Joint Dissemination Review Panel and the National Diffusion Network (NDN) were established in the early 1970s to judge the effectiveness of innovative programs and to help disseminate those that are found effective. In 1987 some changes were made to the panel's procedures, and it was renamed the Program Effectiveness Panel (PEP). The current authorization (Public Law 100-297, 1988) states:

> The Nation Diffusion Network shall be a national program that recognizes and furthers excellence in education by—
>
> (1) promoting the awareness and implementation of exemplary educational programs, products, and practices to interested elementary, secondary, and postsecondary institutions throughout the Nation; and
>
> (2) promoting the utilization of the knowledge, talents, and services of local staff associated with various educational excellence recognition efforts. The National Diffusion Network shall be designed to improve the quality of education through the implementation of promising and validated innovations and improvements in educational programs, products, and practices, and through the provision of training, consultation, and related assistance services.

PEP has approximately 60 members, all with expertise in program evaluation. About one-third are U.S. Department of Education staff; the rest are from universities, school districts, professional associations, and other organizations involved in education R&D. The panel serves primarily as a mechanism for validating the effectiveness of educational programs developed by schools, universities, and other nonprofit organizations. It reviews evaluation data collected by the developers and determines whether to certify a program or process as effective in respect to its stated objectives.

Applicant programs must first be nominated for PEP review by one of the nine assistant secretaries in the Department of Education, who makes a preliminary assessment of the program's evidence, conformity with "program office requirements," and conformity with PEP guidelines. If the program was developed with funds from the department, the assistant secretary of the funding office generally makes this preliminary assessment. If not, the assistant secretary of OERI does so.

Each submission is examined by a randomly drawn subpanel of six reviewers, who generally conduct their work by mail. The subpanel members primarily review the evidence presented in the application. They do not visit the demonstration sites or otherwise collect data on the programs, but they may ask that additional information be requested from the developer when it is important for making judgments about the submitted claims.

The subpanel judges each submission on "whether the program is efficacious and transferable to other educational settings" (Public Law 100-297, 1988). It scores the applications on the basis of the results achieved by the program (0-50 points), the strength of the evaluation design used to assess the results (0-40 points), and the potential for similar results being achieved if the program were to be used by others (0-10 points). To be approved, a program must earn a median score of at least 40 points on the program results criteria and a median of at least 70 points on all three criteria.

About 20-30 new submissions are reviewed each year, and 47 percent have been approved over the past 4 years. Approved programs are considered "proven exemplary educational programs and practices." Since 1987 approval has been effective for 6 years.

Recertification and approval for another 6 years is possible. The requirements for recertification are: continued evidence of program effectiveness (0-50 points), evidence of success in dissemination (0-25 points), and evidence of success in program implementation and retention (0-25 points). Programs must earn at least a median of 70 points on all three criteria. Not all programs apply for recertification. Only about 5-10 apply each year, and 72 percent have been successful during the past 4 years. A few programs have undertaken substantial additional development work before recertification, and OERI's FIRST office programs have sometimes provided financial support for that work.

All PEP-approved programs become National Diffusion Network programs. NDN helps disseminate programs in three ways. First, a brief description of the program and contact information is printed in a comprehensive guide to NDN programs; small topical guides are also sometimes published. Second, NDN funds one or more facilitators, located in every state and certain territories, to assist local schools in defining needs, examining alternative NDN programs, and adopting programs. Some states supplement these funds so that the facilitators can conduct awareness conferences, assist local school districts with start-up costs, and provide technical assistance, monitoring, and evaluation during implementation of NDN programs. Third, the developers of approved programs are eligible to compete for NDN funds to assist in their efforts to publicize the program, train staff at adopting sites, and provide other technical assistance. These are called "developer demonstrator" or "dissemination process" projects. The criteria for funding are "a workable plan for disseminating the program," "program's approach is innovative," and "program is accurate and up-to-date" (Public Law 100-297). About 12 new programs apply each year, and over the past 4 years 69 percent of new applicants were funded. Funding now averages about $75,000 annually for 4 years. Renewal grants for another 4 years are also available. About 28 applications for renewal are received each year, and over the past 4 years 81 percent of the applicants have been successful.

Since NDN's inception in the early 1970s, almost 500 programs have been approved, but nearly half of them are no longer providing services. The active programs address a broad range of educational needs. There are programs for preschools, grades K-12, and out-of-school adults. Some of the programs provide information, several are complete curricula, some offer training and professional development, and others assist in school restructuring.

There have been a few studies of PEP's predecessor, the Joint Dissemination Review Panel (JDRP), and of NDN. They have generally found that JDRP and NDN do help to put innovations into the schools, but that enduring improvements in student outcomes are seldom achieved.

In the second year of JDRP and NDN, the Stanford Research Institute was asked to conduct a major study of functions, costs, and success at achieving adoptions. It found major strengths in the validation process conducted by the JDRP, the linking activities of the facilitators, and the training and technical assistance provided by the developer demonstrators. Concerns were raised about insufficient guidelines for the JDRP applications, poor interface between NDN and state education agencies, inadequacies in the disseminated materials, problems in maintaining the integrity of the innovations, lack of good data on student impacts, and low adoption rates in urban schools (Emrick et al., 1977; Hall and Alford, 1978).

In the early 1980s a study was conducted of several educational dissemination strategies sponsored by the federal government. The authors concluded the NDN was the only federal delivery system that provided all the elements that appeared necessary for effective dissemination of exemplary programs (Crandall and Loucks, 1982; Huberman and Crandall, 1982). Strengths of NDN were seen to be the quality control provided by JDRP, the opportunities provided to schools for exploration of alternatives, and the face-to-face assistance that developer demonstrators provided to adopters. Weaknesses identified were relatively low adoption rates in urban schools, a general lack of follow-up training and technical assistance after adoption, and frequent failure to institutionalize the changes. In many sites the only evidence of effects on students were teachers' reports. When more formal data were available, about one-half of the sites showed substantial student gains.

The U.S. General Accounting Office (1981) studied the Title I reading projects disseminated by NDN. It found some success, but low adoption rates, which were attributed to unconvincing evidence about the effects of allegedly exemplary programs and a lack of state incentives for local schools to demonstrate improvements in educational outcomes. The recommendations suggested NDN be required to provide complete information on program effects and costs.

PEP and NDN have been laudable attempts at quality assessment and dissemination of innovations, but there are serious weaknesses and opportunities for improvement. Innovations can earn PEP certification of effectiveness when they have been assessed in only a few sites, on only a few outcomes, and with no follow-up measurement of impact after termination of the "treatment" (Ralph and Dwyer, 1988). In addition, the guidelines to applicants and the review process focus exclusively on whether there is adequate evidence to substantiate positive claims of the developers. There are no instructions requiring submission of available evidence on possible disadvantages. For instance, if an innovation is tested for effects on students' skills and interests in reading, and the data show increased skills but decreased interest, the applicant is not required to report the latter. Developers' desire for NDN assistance would make them inclined to exclude such information, and the 15-page limitation for the application makes it almost impossible to provide full disclosure of a program's effects.

Although many researchers find that PEP standards fall short of rigorous evidence, many of the developers find them a major challenge. Sometimes the developers are not well trained in evaluation and do not understand how to meet the standards. PEP has published guidelines with extensive examples and has a contractor who will provide developers with technical assistance, but program evaluation involves complex skills that novices are not likely to master quickly. In other cases the developers are well-trained and experienced researchers, but they find it very difficult to secure the funding needed for the several years of data collection that is required for rigorous evidence of program effects in schools. NDN has no funds to assist with this work. Although some funds are potentially available through the FIRST office (described below), the maximum duration of grants from that office has been 3 years, which is often less than the time needed to accumulate strong evidence of program impact. It is feared, however, that if the PEP standards are raised substantially, innovation may be stifled, and developers will bypass PEP and disseminate their programs privately, with no quality assurance.

NDN's support for dissemination of innovative programs has used a two-tier approach: funding for facilitators to alert a statewide audience to the NDN programs and funding for developers to provide detailed information, materials, training, and follow-up support. The evaluations cited above and other studies show that adoption of discrete innovations generally does not have a large and enduring impact on the quality of schooling (Fullan, 1991; Louis and Miles, 1990; Sarason, 1990). Many education experts now believe that substantial improvements require reform of the schools: coordinated changes across subject areas and grade levels and in the organization, management, and operation of a school. There is an important role for innovations in school reform, but only in the context of broader changes. NDN generally does not support such broad changes and operates independently from state and laboratory efforts that do so. The exceptions are the few NDN programs that involve processes designed to achieve school reform and some enterprising state facilitators who have forged strong linkages with other reform activities.

Fund for the Improvement and Reform of Schools and Teaching

The Fund for the Improvement and Reform of Schools and Teaching (FIRST) manages several programs designed to support local school-based reforms that are expected to have national significance. The programs include FIRST's namesake, the Fund for the Improvement and Reform of Schools and Teaching, the Fund for Innovation in Education, and the Eisenhower National Program for Mathematics and Science Education. All three of the programs were established in 1988. In fiscal 1991 the office had about 18 staff and a budget of $46.4 million.

There is a widespread perception that the FIRST office is controlled more by the Secretary of Education than is the case for other offices within OERI, and this appears to be true. All the FIRST office programs are authorized and appropriated as Department of Education programs, not OERI programs. They are managed within OERI because of administrative decisions made by the secretaries, and one of the programs includes discretionary funds for the secretary.

FIRST programs are directed toward promoting school-level changes. The Schools and Teachers Program provides grants to state agencies, districts, and schools, to increase the educational opportunities and performance of elementary and secondary school students. The Family-School Partnership Program awards demonstration grants to school districts with a substantial portion of low-income students for projects that help teachers to cooperate more effectively with parents, help parents support the education of their offspring in the home setting, and evaluate family involvement programs.

The Fund for Innovation in Education supports efforts in identifying and disseminating innovative educational approaches. It provides grants in four areas: comprehensive health education, computer-based education, technology education, and general innovation. The latter category includes funds to be used at the discretion of the Secretary of Education. Since 1990 those funds have been used primarily for work directed at achieving the National Education Goals.

The Eisenhower National Program for Mathematics and Science Education supports innovative projects of national significance that enhance access to, and the quality of, mathematics and science education. Priority is given to strengthening state and local programs funded under the much larger Eisenhower State formula funds.

FIRST office projects are generally funded for 1-3 years for $50,000–$150,000. As the examples in Chapter 2 indicate, this is considerably less time than has usually been necessary to develop and evaluate "reforms of national significance." The primary exception would be cases in which applicants use the funds to finish or refine prior developments, but there is no reason that the programs should support only that work.

The FIRST office has established an informal collaboration with NDN. FIRST encourages its awardees to submit their innovative programs and processes to PEP and NDN. In addition, it has provided funding to some NDN programs for additional development and testing.

Most of the activities supported by these programs are not R&D, as commonly understood by those who monitor R&D activities. The "D" refers to developments built on research-based knowledge (U.S. Office of Management and Budget, 1990), but neither the legislation nor the administrative guidelines specify that the proposals under FIRST are to make use of relevant research.

National Center for Educational Statistics

Since the establishment of the Office of Education in 1867, the federal government has been the major source of statistical information on education in the United States. Most of this work is now conducted by the National Center for Education Statistics (NCES). NCES had about 139 staff and a budget of $63.4 million in fiscal 1991.

NCES is authorized under Section 406 of the General Education Provisions Act of 1986 (Public Law 99-498), which specifies:

> The general design and duties of the National Center for Education Statistics shall be to acquire and diffuse among the people of the United States useful statistical information on subjects connected with education (in the most general and comprehensive sense of the word) particularly the retention of students, the assessment of their progress, the financing of institutions of education, financial aid to students, the supply of and demand for teachers and other school personnel, libraries, comparisons of the education of the United States and foreign nations, and the means of promoting material, social, and intellectual prosperity through education.

NCES conducts a number of data collection programs to provide information on the status of U.S. education. These include annual collection of data on elementary and secondary schools, annual collection of data on higher education, several special studies of schools, the National Assessment of Education Progress, and a few large-scale longitudinal studies of students' progress through school and into the workplace. NCES, in conjunction with NSF, also supports most of the nation's activities in international studies of student achievement.

Many of NCES's long-established and well-known programs have been described in "Monitoring the State of Public Education" (in Chapter 2). Important improvements have recently been made to some NCES programs, and many new programs are currently being implemented. A few of these are described here.

A new National Household Education Survey was conducted in 1991 and will be done annually starting in 1993. It will collect information on children's school readiness and educational activities, the role of the family in students' learning, school safety and discipline, and adults' participation in adult and continuing education. An Early Childhood Longitudinal Study is also being planned to follow a cohort of young children, examining how their health, family, and educational histories affect their success in school. The Common Core of Data survey will soon include expanded data on school finances, in response to recommendations made by the Council of Chief State School Officers. Since 1990 NCES has annually surveyed all private schools.

Since 1983 the National Assessment of Education Progress (NAEP) has collected some data on school characteristics as well as students' knowledge and skills, but recently it has begun to collect more extensive data on schools' policies, objectives, services, programs, and practices and on teachers' training, experience, and instructional practices. This expansion permits analyses of how those characteristics are associated with student achievement. In 1990 the sampling for NAEP was also expanded, on a trial and voluntary basis, to provide reliable data on eighth grade mathematics skills for individual states. If the procedure is permanently adopted, it will permit states to monitor their own achievements, compare their results with other states, and observe state trends over time.

Preparation for the Third International Mathematics and Science Study is under way. Improvements will include collection of more detailed information on the curriculum and instruction received by the tested students and some innovative assessment procedures will be tried.

Early planning is under way for an assessment of postsecondary student learning. A longitudinal study of college students, the Baccalaureate and Beyond study, will follow graduates for at least 12 years to examine their progression through graduate school and into the workplace. Special emphasis will be given to participation in public service professions, including teaching.

NCES's operations were widely criticized in the 1970s and early 1980s. One major study (National Research Council, 1986) confirmed problems identified in several prior reviews. The accuracy of NCES's data on the status of education in the United States was compromised by heavy reliance on state administrative records, which were generated by incomparable procedures and with frequently poor quality control; NCES lacked appropriate operating standards for a statistical agency; and the agency was trying to do more than could be done well with its level of funding and staffing. The study also found chronic delays in the reporting of the data and conceptual obsolescence in some of the data series.

Since that report NCES has upgraded or replaced several data collection efforts, added several new data series, and diligently sought the advice of statisticians and researchers. Legislation in 1986 modified NCES's status, partly removing it from the direct authority of the assistant secretary for OERI (Public Law 99-498). As of June 1991 NCES was supposed to be headed by a Commissioner of Educational Statistics, appointed by the President with the advice and consent of the Senate, who will serve for a 4-year term, but the appointment process has not yet been completed. Separate contracting and staffing authority was offered in the legislation, but the Secretary of Education chose not to implement that option. NCES does have independent report review and clearance authority. The arrangement, however, is the result of internal negotiations and agreements, not of a statutory mandate, and the Department's Office of Public Affairs must approve all printing.

These changes were accompanied by a tripling of NCES's budget between fiscal 1987 and fiscal 1991. There is a widespread perception that NCES has improved its operations dramatically over this period. One business association wrote the committee that "NCES has matured well over the last several years and its data collection activities have been much more useful to a variety of stakeholders . . ." This opinion is shared by many researchers and professional associations, and it has been affirmed to the committee by congressional research agency staff. Few observers would give NCES a perfect grade, and those who must analyze data collected over many successive years still suffer from the pre-1987 problems, but there is nearly unanimous agreement that the data and reporting of NCES have markedly improved.

Library Programs

The Office of Library Programs provides grants to support operations of state libraries, local public libraries, college and university libraries, and "libraries of public and private organizations" (U.S. Department of Education, 1990). It is widely acknowledged that the library programs do not fit well within the mandate of OERI and were placed there by historical accident. The difficulty in relocating the programs is that there is nowhere else in the Department of Education that is a logical fit for the programs. The office has about 53 staff and a fiscal 1991 budget of $142.2 million, more than one-third of the total for OERI. Only about $350,000 of the budget is used to support research activities in library science.

OPERATIONS AND FUNDING

OERI's operations involve the numerous functions typical of any federal research agency. The committee focused its examination on three areas that came to its attention as being troublesome: staffing levels and opportunities for professional development; procurement of centers and laboratories; and the review and clearance of OERI reports.

Staffing

In the fall of 1991 OERI had a staff of 472. Of those, 287 were program professionals who solicit advice for research agendas, plan research, prepare requests for proposals, supervise and participate in the review of proposals, negotiate the substantive work of grants and contracts, monitor the latter, disseminate research results, and maintain liaison with professional organizations and the public. Only about three dozen of those staff members regularly conduct research, and most of those spend more than one-half of their time on managerial activities. The 472 staff are distributed among OERI offices as follows:

Office of Assistant Secretary	88
Office of Research	69
Programs for the Improvement of Practice	87
FIRST	18
NCES	139
Library Programs	53
Other (special councils and panels)	18

Some staff in OERI claim there has been a serious staffing shortage over the past few years, but others disagree. A study by the U.S. General Accounting Office (1987) found that between fiscal 1980 and fiscal 1986, the staffs at NIE and NCES declined 26 percent, and their program budgets declined 59 percent (in constant dollars). Between 1986 and 1991, OERI's data indicate that the staff increased by 13 percent and the program budgets increased by 47 percent (in constant dollars).

The ratio of program budget to staff has definitely increased over the past 5 years, but it had decreased substantially over the prior 6 years. In considering these numbers it should be noted that the staff salaries and expenses are covered in a "salary and expenses" budget, which is entirely separate from the program budget. The salaries and expenses budget is based primarily on the number of staff, their average grade levels, and their anticipated office expenses.

Many factors affect the number of staff needed for a given program budget. They include the extent and nature of the activities undertaken, whether they are new or routine, and the quality of the staff. According to the Office of Management and Budget (personal communication), there are no formal standards by which to judge the staffing levels of federal agencies. Over a period of years the responsibilities and activities of a federal agency usually change some, even though the agency retains the same mission. Without an intensive examination, which the committee was not able to conduct, it is not possible to judge whether OERI, as a whole, now suffers a serious staffing shortage.

There have been allegations that the staffing problem at OERI is not one of numbers, but rather one of quality. Many observers outside the agency find the staff to be unimpressive, as a group, although individual exceptions are frequently noted (Kaestle, 1991). One outside researcher wrote to the committee:

> Establishing research priorities, drafting substantively sound requests for proposals, and effective monitoring of grants and contracts all require an understanding of the conduct and substance of educational inquiry. We have worked with a variety of project monitors, and the differences among them have been striking.

There does seem to be widespread agreement within the agency that there have been inadequate professional opportunities for the staff to remain up to date and involved with the research community. Some effort has been made recently to improve this situation, but a tight salaries and expenses budget has limited what can be done.

In contrast to OERI as a whole, data for NCES provide compelling evidence of substantial understaffing. In the early and mid-1980s, NCES's budget ranged from $12 to $14 million, and the allotted staff positions ranged from 107 to 155. In fiscal 1989, 1990, and 1991, the budgets jumped to $31 million, $40 million, and then $60 million, while the allotted staff positions were 133, 128, and 138, respectively. Even after accounting for inflation, the budget tripled between the mid-1980s and 1991, but the staff levels remained close to the average for the early and mid-1980s.

The budget increases at NCES have also been accompanied by major increases in administrative responsibilities. The National Assessment of

Educational Progress used to involve a single contract with one institution. It now includes a National Assessment Governing Board, a NAEP review panel, agreements with more than 30 states for the state-level data collection on a trial basis, and an evaluation of that trial. NCES has added many new studies, including a Household Education Survey of preschool and adult education, a Schools and Staffing Survey of the teaching work force, a National Postsecondary Student Aid Study, a longitudinal study of beginning postsecondary students, and a National Adult Literacy Survey. NCES has also expanded its involvement in international studies of education. In fiscal 1985 NCES had a total of 57 projects; in fiscal 1991 there were 167.

There have been a few changes that reduced NCES's staffing needs. For instance, beginning in 1985 most of the editing and production of NCES's reports were transferred to another office within OERI, reducing NCES's need for 4-7 staff positions. However, the total workload of NCES has obviously increased dramatically since the mid-1980s.

Among federal statistical agencies, NCES now has the lowest ratio of staff per $1 million of program budget. The Bureau of Labor statistics has 8.6 staff per $1 million of program budget, the National Center for Health Statistics has 6.9, and NCES has 1.9. Only one other federal statistical unit has a ratio of less than 6.0 staff per $1 million program budget: the Bureau of Justice Statistics, which manages a small number of data collections that have remained mostly unchanged for many years.

As indicated above, program budget is not used to pay staff, but rather for outside work performed under contracts and grants. Thus, for a given set of activities, as the staff available to do the work increases, the needed program budget decreases. For instance, the Bureau of the Census does much of its work internally, with higher staff levels and lower program budgets than would be needed if it contracted out most of its work (its ratio is 15.3 staff per $1 million of program budget). But when the ratio of the staff to program dollars declines below a certain level, staff members must spend nearly all their time monitoring contracts, and that type of work does not attract the skilled researchers and statisticians who are needed for planning and analysis. This has now become the case at NCES.

As a result of the rapidly expanding responsibilities and constrained staffing levels, NCES is again developing one of the problems for which it was severely criticized in the early and mid 1980s—the delayed release of data and publications. Because of the nature of the work flow, longer delays can be expected in the coming years if staffing levels are not increased promptly.

Decisions about federal staffing levels are made in a complex manner. There is a single salaries and expense budget for all but two offices in the Department of Education. Each assistant secretary proposes numbers; the Office of Planning, Budget, and Evaluation revises and totals them; the Secretary of Education makes further changes; the Office of Management and Budget makes recommendations to the President; and then the President submits a salary and expenses budget to Congress. Usually that budget is enacted by Congress with few changes (unlike the program budgets, which are often modified by Congress). After passage of the budget, the Secretary of Education makes a final allocation of the positions and dollars to the assistant secretaries, who in turn allocate them among their offices. Since NCES comprises less than 1 percent of the Department of Education's budget, its growing staff needs are easily overlooked.

Procurement

Rules and regulations guiding OERI's procurement process are found in several documents: legislative authority for OERI is provided in Section 405 of the General Education Provisions Act (GEPA), which was amended by Section 1401 of the Higher Education Amendments of 1986. The Education Department General Administrative Regulations (EDGAR), Title 34, specify the requirements for implementing grants. Procedures for awarding contracts are described under the provisions of the Federal Acquisition Regulations. Individual programs are also affected by specifications in their authorizing legislation.

Under OERI's current authorization, the Secretary of Education may enter into "grants, contracts, and cooperative agreements with institutions of higher education, public and private organizations, institutions, agencies, and individuals" for the purpose of "supporting scientific inquiry into the educational process" (General Education Provisions Act, Sec. 405(b)(3)(A)(i)).

The secretary is required to publish proposed research priorities in the *Federal Register* every 2 years, followed by a 60-day waiting period for receiving public comment and suggestions. In addition, when planning award competitions, the secretary must first "solicit recommendations and advice regarding research priorities, opportunities, and strategies from qualified experts, personnel of the regional education laboratories and of the research and development centers, and the Council, as well as parents and other members of the general public."

Funding of the Centers and Laboratories

In the mid-1960s the centers and laboratories were created to be large-scale institutions conducting research and development and dissemination activities over an extended period of time, much like the Atomic Energy Commission laboratories. When NIE was created, it quickly switched from funding institutions to funding various programs of activity that were proposed by those institutions. The rationale for the program purchase policy had at least two parts. First, the top researchers recruited to NIE believed many of the centers and laboratories inherited from the Office of Education were ineffective relics of the past; they sought more control over their activities and hoped to eliminate some of the institutions. Second, it was thought that NIE staff could better judge the merit of proposals for programs than the merit of proposals for institutions, and more effectively monitor program progress, because all proposals in a given area of activity would be handled by one or two people with considerable expertise in that area. Center and laboratory staffs feared that the program purchase policy would fragment their efforts and threaten their survival. During that policy's short life from 1973 to 1976, fragmentation did occur, but the institutions survived. Two centers and two laboratories experienced substantial reductions in their NIE funding, but one center and two laboratories experienced substantial increases.

The program purchase policy was renounced by the NIE board in 1976. The Campbell (1975) report, commissioned by the board, had recommended a return to institutional support. The center and laboratory directors had also vigorously expressed their displeasure with the policy to members of Congress, and the 1976 reauthorization of NIE suggested a return to institutional support. The reauthorization also mandated the Panel for the Review of Laboratory and Center Operations (1979), which strongly favored institutional support, with periodic evaluations, for those centers and laboratories that had already demonstrated high quality and productive work.

Despite the quick demise of the program purchase policy, neither NIE nor OERI really returned to long-term institutional support for the centers or laboratories. Rather, NIE muddled along for a few years, halfway between a policy of program purchase and one of institutional support, and then in the early 1980s began planning a competition for the institutions. Since 1985 the centers and laboratories have had to compete for funding every 5 years. The centers have essentially become 5-year projects, with the foci of their activities determined by OERI and with many having little past or future. In contrast, the laboratories have regained a semblance of institutional support over the past decade. Although they also had to compete in 1985 and 1990, only one incumbent laboratory was defeated in those two rounds. Laboratory awards are now almost three times larger than those of the centers, and the laboratories are funded with contracts, which allow them to receive a fee for general and administrative costs in excess of their direct expenses, permitting accumulation of some capital for new initiatives and lean times. The centers, on the other hand, are funded with grants and cooperative agreements that do not permit such a fee.

Peer Review

The 1985 competitions for center and laboratory awards were the first since the 1960s and raised concern in Congress and the research community about how expertly and fairly they would be conducted, particularly since the multiple 5-year awards would make them the largest competitions in the history of the Department of Education. Judging by most accounts, the competitions in 1985 appear to have been administered commendably (Finn, 1986; Garduque and Berliner, 1986; Moorman and Carroll, 1986). A similar assessment is generally made of the 1990 competitions (Sroufe, 1991).

Planning for the 1985 competitions began with public hearings in 11 cities. To encourage a fair and open competition, grants of $15,000-$25,000 for planning and proposal preparation were awarded to 25 potential laboratory bidders and 36 potential center bidders. A total of 125 researchers, educators, and public representatives sat on 12 panels to review the proposals. Site visits were made to all bidders whose proposals were judged promising.

Planning for the 1990 center competition included several study group meetings, commissioned papers, a blue-ribbon panel to review the prior planning work, and the services of 130 reviewers. Planning for the 1990 laboratory competition included a review of the laboratories' self-evaluations and peer evaluations, establishment of an external laboratory review panel to advise on the competition, several commissioned papers, meetings with representatives of the major educational associations, and open hearings in three cities. Twenty-five people reviewed the proposals.

The one element of these competitions that has been subject to some continuing criticism is the manner in which the peer review was conducted. For that reason, the committee examined the peer review process in more detail.

Peer review of scientific merit has formally used at least since 1665, when the Royal Society required peer review of articles prior to their publication in *Philosophical Transactions*. Peer review of proposals for federally funded R&D work began in the United States with establishment of the National Advisory Cancer Council in 1937 and became commonplace as federal funding for science expanded rapidly in the 1950s (Chubin and Hackett, 1990). It is now used by many federal agencies when evaluating proposals for both field-initiated and institutional research, most prominently by NSF and NIH. However, some agencies, particularly within the Defense Department, rely instead on internal reviews by program managers.

At OERI the selection of awards is determined by the process and principles of peer review "except where such peer review procedures are clearly inappropriate given such factors as the relatively small amount of a grant or contract or the exigencies of the situation" (General Education Provisions Act, Sec. 1401(d)(3)(B). According to OERI (Chalker, 1990:19):

> One of the main functions of a peer review panel is to ensure that decisions are informed by sound advice from multiple perspectives. Therefore, panels may include a mix of researchers, policy makers, practitioners, and members of the general public including individuals representing business and industry.

The inclusion of people other than researchers in the review of R&D proposals is not unprecedented. Although NSF uses scientists almost exclusively, it should be noted that 94 percent of its budget goes to basic research, not applied research or development. And NSF's Education and Human Resources Directorate does include teachers and other practitioners in the review of proposals for mathematics and science education research and development activities. At NIH there is a two-tier review process. The first review is done by an initial review group, composed of scientists with national stature in a particular discipline. The second review is done by the national advisory council for the particular institute. These councils are composed of 12 or more members drawn from both the scientific and lay communities. They review the initial judgments of the proposals and make recommendations for funding in light of program relevance and relationship to the institute's overall mission. In practice, the councils make few changes in the priority rankings from the initial review (Chubin and Hackett, 1990).

Education researchers generally suggest that practitioners be involved in defining the priorities for education research, but that researchers alone should advise on which proposals should be funded. A compromise sometimes offered by researchers is a two-tier system, with teachers and administrators first judging the practical merit of proposals and then researchers judging the technical merit.

OERI used a different two-tier system for the 1985 center and laboratory competitions. The first stage assessed the merit of proposals, with review panels composed mostly of researchers and practitioners familiar with research. The second stage was an oversight review of the first stage and advised the agency on opportunities for collaboration across proposals that could produce cumulative and coherent work, with a panel composed mostly of practitioners and policy makers. Although no changes in the decisions of the first-stage reviewers were suggested, OERI found this two-tier process cumbersome because the second stage reviewers often found it difficult not to second-guess the technical reviewers' decisions (Moorman and Carroll, 1986).

For the 1990 competitions, OERI moved to a single-tier process with panels of mixed expertise. Among the 130 reviewers of the proposals were local educators, state legislators, parents of Chapter I students, and representatives of local and state education associations, teacher unions, and the media. It is estimated that only about one-fourth to one-third of the reviewers were researchers. In these panels, all participants judged both technical and programmatic merit. Since one-third or less of the reviewers of the center proposals were researchers, two-thirds of the judgments about technical merit were made by people with little expertise on those matters.

Heterogeneous review panels have been criticized by researchers as constituting external review instead of peer review by scientists. It is said that such panels include a predominance of people with no knowledge of research, and these people are likely to select proposals on the basis of personal preferences, interest group loyalties, and political allegiances, rather than scientific rigor. Given the ratio of researchers to others, this criticism appears to have some merit, but if review panels were comprised entirely of researchers, it could be argued that the selection of proposals would be biased towards their interests, disregarding the concerns of teachers, school administrators, and policy makers.

Report Review and Clearance Procedures

The Department of Education operates a report review and clearance procedure that applies to most of its subunits, including all of OERI except NCES. The Publication and Audiovisual Review System specifies that most reports and speeches prepared by department staff must be reviewed and cleared "to safeguard ED resources from waste, fraud, abuse, or misman-agement" (U.S. Department of Education, 1989). Several criteria are to be considered when deciding whether a report "is necessary," including "consistency with ED's mission and goals" and "conformity with legislation, regulations, and policy." The clearance procedure requires sign-off by the head of the originating office, by the assistant secretaries in the department with responsibilities related to the substance of the report, and by the director of the editorial policy division of the department's Office of Public Affairs. This policy would allow the department to prevent the release of a report, even if well researched and documented, if it failed to support a department policy. The department's June 1989 *Public Affairs Handbook* even specifies that clearance is required for written speeches that:

> [are] not prepared or delivered on official time, and even if no compensation is involved, and which:
>   1. Deal with subject matter related to any Department program, even if the author or speaker is not identified as an employee of the U.S. Department of Education; or
>   2. Identify the author or speaker as an employee of the Department of Education, regardless of whether the subject matter is related to a Department program.

The committee's conversations with more than a dozen OERI staff who have gone through the department's report clearance process suggest that it has been politicized on several occasions during the past decade. Political sensitivities within the department have resulted in many hours of negotiations, several delays, occasional modifications, and a few withdrawals, but apparently no outright suppressions. Some staff have been dissuaded from undertaking analyses on subjects sensitive within the department, and some have downplayed results that might be unwelcome by the department. These critical views are not shared by all the OERI staff with whom we talked, but the vast majority reported instances of difficulty. The responses indicate that the problems were generally more severe during the early 1980s, more severe with official OERI reports than with papers prepared by staff members for professional meetings and journals, and more severe for reports that deal with policy matters or characterize department programs.

Several OERI staff suggested there is merit in a nonbinding review by assistant secretaries in the department with responsibilities related to the substance of the report—they had received many helpful comments. Virtually all acknowledged that there is a need for a report review process, at least for official OERI reports and presentations, but most thought it should be conducted by OERI and should focus on scientific quality and editorial style, not consistency with department policy.

The National Science Foundation, as an independent cabinet-level agency, has full authority over its reports. The Bureau of Labor Statistics, despite being housed within the Department of Labor, also has such authority. At the National Institutes of Health (NIH), most reports are reviewed and cleared within the individual institutes, but a few, particularly those on politically sensitive issues, are forwarded for review by the director of NIH, the Assistant Secretary for Health, or the Secretary of the Department of Health and Human Services.

Funding

NIE was established to enhance the federal role in education R&D, yet within a year its budget began spiraling downward. That trend continued when NIE's functions were assumed by OERI, reaching a low point in 1989 (Figure 3-2). The total decline between 1973 and 1989 (in constant 1990 dollars) was 88 percent. When the budgets of NCES are aggregated with those of NIE, the low point was in 1986, with an 84 percent decline. In contrast, over the same period, there was a 24 percent constant-dollar increase in total federal R&D expenditures and a 7 percent constant-dollar increase in total budget of the Department of Education (Figure 3-3). Since the low points, OERI budgets have increased (in constant dollars), mostly due to substantial increases for NCES's statistical activities and NAEP. Figures 3-2 and 3-3 reflect OERI funds for the centers, laboratories, field-initiated research, ERIC, NCES, and special studies and demonstrations; they do not include the FIRST office programs or the library programs, which are administered by OERI, but involve very little research or research-based development.

For many years, the congressional appropriation committees have determined the annual levels of support for the centers and laboratories by "directives" in the hearing report that specify amounts of funds to be given

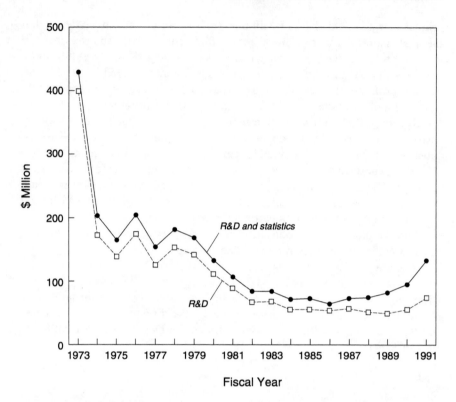

FIGURE 3-2   Funding for the National Institute of Education and the Office of Educational Research and Improvement, 1973-1991 (in 1990 constant dollars). SOURCE: Unpublished data from the Office of Education Research and Improvement.

to the centers (as a group) and to the laboratories (as a group). This has not been welcomed by the OERI administrators and many researchers in the field. The administrators prefer more discretion over the distribution of resources, and researchers hope such discretion would result in a larger portion of OERI funds being available for field-initiated research.

Researchers, watching resources for field-initiated work dwindle, have blamed the loss on the set-asides of funds for the laboratories and centers, which have taken up increasingly large percentages of the budgets. Some observers suggest a quite different view: that the centers and laboratories, especially the latter with clients spread across the country, have provided most of the constituent support for NIE and OERI, and without their efforts, the agencies would have disappeared. Both views may be correct.

The centers and laboratories, however, have also suffered from the declining budgets: in 1973 NIE provided $80 million for their operations (in

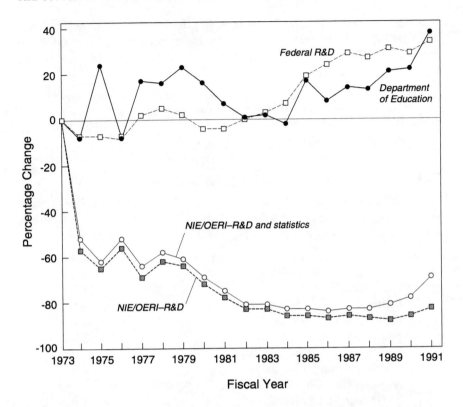

FIGURE 3-3 Percentage change in funding for all federal R&D, all activities in the Department of Education, and NIE/OERI, 1973-1991 (in 1990 constant dollars). SOURCES: Data on federal R&D from National Science Foundation (1991a:Table 29); data on Department of Education from Congressional Research Service (1991:Table B.1); data on NIE/OERI from the Office of Educational Research and Improvement, unpublished.

1990 constant dollars); by 1979 that had declined to $52 million; and in 1991 the amount was $47 million. For individual laboratories and centers, the effect has been more dramatic because there are now twice as many of them as there were in 1973.

The budget cutting has also been reflected in congressionally requested studies. For instance, in the mid- 1970s Congress directed NIE to conduct a nationwide study of the administration and effectiveness of compensatory education. The equivalent of $34 million (in 1990 dollars) was appropriated for the 3.5-year study. In 1990 Congress directed OERI to conduct a nationwide study of school reform efforts—a much broader topic—but just $9 million was made available for the 3.5-year study.

These budget cuts have had a marked effect on the work and products of OERI. A U.S. General Accounting Office report (1987:2) that reviewed the work of NIE, NCES, and the department's Office of Policy, Budget, and Evaluation concluded:

> During the past decade, the production of federally sponsored research, statistical, and evaluative information on education has declined notably . . . so much so that the availability of up-to-date information to disseminate to teachers and other practitioners may be threatened.

OERI's 1991 Budget

OERI's budget for fiscal 1991 totaled $379.5 million. Slightly more than one-third of it was for R&D, statistics, and NAEP. The distribution was as follows (in millions):

Research, development, and dissemination		$78.4
National research centers	$20.7	
Regional laboratories	24.9	
ERIC	6.6	
Field-initiated research	1.3	
Education reform evaluation	2.9	
National Institute of Literacy	4.9	
Education summit follow-up	4.9	
National Board for Professional Teacher Standards	4.9	
Other	7.3	
NCES (statistics and NAEP)		59.6
School Improvement Programs		99.3
Libraries Programs		142.2
Total		$379.5

The 1991 OERI budget was a 21 percent increase from the prior year's level of $314 million. There were modest additions for many line items, but the big increases were for NCES, the addition of follow-up activities from the education summit, and the National Board for Professional Teacher Standards.

Comparisons with Other Fields

The U.S. Office of Management and Budget (OMB) and the National Science Foundation are responsible for collecting and reporting data on federal and national expenditures for R&D. They use definitions that are somewhat narrower than those used for the data in Figures 3-2 and 3-3 for OERI. According to the National Science Foundation (1991a:3):

Research is systematic study directed toward fuller scientific knowledge or understanding of the subject studied.

Development is systematic use of the knowledge or understanding gained from research, directed toward the production of useful materials, devices, systems, or methods, including design and development of prototypes and processes.

These definitions exclude all dissemination activities and routine statistics collection, both of which have long been considered important parts of NIE, NCES, and OERI activities. Although one might argue with the appropriateness of the NSF definitions, they are important because they provide a basis for comparisons across agencies and industries. In 1991, only an estimated $58.1 million of OERI's $380 million budget was spent on R&D as defined by OMB and NSF—just 15 percent of the total. In addition, although OERI is the Department of Education's lead agency for education R&D, in fiscal 1991 it accounted for only one-third of the department's R&D.

The U.S. Office of Technology Assessment (1988:164) recently reviewed federally funded R&D for technology applications to education. It noted the following about the Department of Education:

Education's limited spending for R&D in the area of educational technology is not surprising when one looks at the overall low priority granted education research in general. Barely half of one percent of the Department of Education budget goes to research. By comparison, the Nation spends about as much annually on health care as on education, but it spends 60 times as much on health research. The military, where R&D has been increasing at an average increase of 7.8 percent per year since fiscal year 1984, devotes about 12.8 percent of its total DoD obligation to research.

A U.S. General Accounting Office (1988) report compared the Department of Education's R&D funding between 1980 and 1987 with that of other federal departments and agencies. Seven major departments and agencies showed declines in R&D budget obligations similar to the Department of Education, while five experienced increases. When observing the budgets for statistical activities, all but one agency experienced declines, but the decline for NCES was larger than the average. Program evaluation budgets, excluding the Department of Defense, showed declines, and the Department of Education's decline was similar to the average.

OMB and NSF collect and report federal R&D expenditures across agencies by 16 budget function categories, such as national defense, health, and transportation. Because each agency reports R&D expenditures in a maximum of 3 of the 16 functions, the data are not comprehensive. There is an "Education, training, employment, and social services" function, which has a subcategory of "Research and general education aids." None of the substantial investments in education R&D by NSF or the Department of Defense is included, because they are precluded from reporting in that budget function. In 1991 the subcategory of education had projected R&D expenditures of $140 million by the Department of Education and $106 million by the Smithsonian Institution (National Science Foundation, 1991b), the only two institutions tabulated for that subcategory, and clearly little of the Smithsonian budget is actually used for education R&D. For these reasons, NSF's budget function data are inadequate for monitoring federal expenditures in education R&D.

Occasionally, comprehensive analyses across agencies have been undertaken to estimate federal expenditures in a given area. OMB conducted a special survey for the National Education Goals Panel in the summer of 1991 and estimated that the federal government spent $310 million on education R&D in that year (National Education Goals Panel, 1991). This committee undertook a similar analysis, talking to budget office personnel and key program administrators and examining listings of funded projects. We estimated total expenditures in 1991 to be $364 million. Most of the difference in the two totals result from estimates for education R&D by the Department of Defense, with the OMB estimate being considerably lower.

Despite the shortcomings in the budget function data, they are the best available for making comparisons across broad areas of research such as education, health, and agriculture. And there is reason to think they work better for most functions than they do for education. For instance, the budget function data for health are only 8 percent lower than data from NIH's own comprehensive analysis. Given the manner in which the budget function data are generated, they will almost always underestimate the total federal investment in a specified area.

Table 3-1 presents data for several broad areas that correspond with the budget functions. It shows federal funds for R&D in each area, total federal expenditures for all activities in each area, and all expenditures in the country for all activities in each area.

Federal expenditures for education R&D are one-third those for R&D in agriculture and transportation and only 4 percent of federal expenditures for R&D in health. Because the data for education R&D are from comprehensive analysis across agencies and the data for the other areas are from NSF's budget functions and therefore underestimates, the disparities are even greater than they appear from these data.

The low investment in education R&D is not a function of the federal government's overall involvement in this area. It invests less than 1 percent of its total education expenditures on R&D, but it invests 3.2 percent of its total transportation expenditures on R&D, 6.9 percent of its total

TABLE 3-1 Expenditures by Area of Activity for Federal R&D, Total Federal Expenditures, and All National Expenditures, Fiscal 1990 (in billions)

Area of Activity	Federal R&D[a]	Total Federal Expenditures[b]	All National Expenditures
Education	$ 0.3[c]	$ 38.7[d]	$ 365[e]
Agriculture	1.0	14.5	100[f]
Transportation	1.0	30.9	163[f]
Energy	2.7	4.9	406[g]
Space	5.8	14.6	n.a.
Health	8.3	60.9	616[h]
Defense	39.9	303.3	328[i]
All activities	63.8	1,368.5	5,464[j]

NOTE: n.a., not available.
SOURCES:
[a]National Science Foundation, 1991a:Table 1 (for all areas of activity except education).
[b]*Budget of the United States Government*, 1992, Part 4:Table A-2 (for all areas of activity except education).
[c]National Education Goals Panel, 1991:Exhibit 79.
[d]National Center for Education Statistics, 1991b:Table 338. Table shows total federal expenditures for education of 50.4 billion; we excluded $12.1 billion for research programs in all disciplines at universities and related institutions, except the estimated $0.3 billion for education R&D.
[e]National Center for Education Statistics, 1991b:Table 29.
[f]U.S. Department of Commerce, 1992, Part 4:Table 699 (fiscal 1988).
[g]U.S. Department of Commerce, 1992, Part 4:Table 951 (fiscal 1988).
[h]U.S. Department of Health and Human Services, 1991:Table 1 (fiscal 1990).
[i]U.S. Department of Commerce, 1992, Part 4:Table 541 (fiscal 1990).
[j]National Center for Education Statistics, 1991b:Table 29. (Total is gross national product.)

agriculture expenditures, and 13.6 percent of its total health expenditures; see Figure 3-4.

The low investment in education R&D also is not a function of total national expenditures for each activity. Federal education research is just 0.1 percent of total national expenditures for education. Federal transportation research is almost 0.6 percent of total national expenditures on transportation; federal agriculture research is 1.0 percent of total national expenditures on agriculture; and federal health research is 1.3 percent of total national expenditures on health care; see Figure 3-5.

By all the above comparisons, federal funding for education R&D lags far behind federal funding for R&D in other broad areas of activity. From Table 3-1 one can compute that only one-half of 1 percent of all federally funded research and development is directed to education.

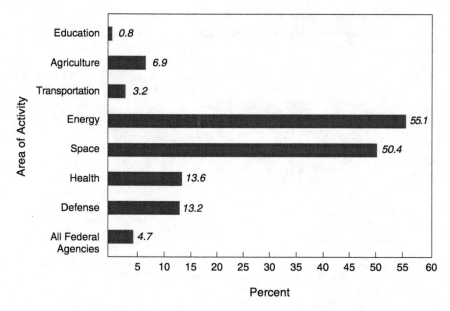

FIGURE 3-4   Federal R&D in selected areas as a percentage of total federal expenditures in each area, 1990.

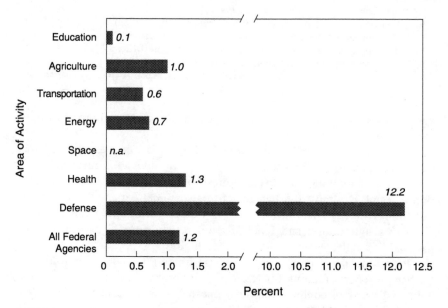

FIGURE 3-5   Federal support for R&D in specified areas as a percentage of total national expenditures in each area, 1990. NOTE: n.a., not available.

Other Funding of R&D

There are no data on total nationwide expenditures for education R&D, including expenditures by private organizations and state and local governments. NSF is responsible for monitoring national expenditures for R&D, but it does not do so for education R&D. As a consequence, it is difficult to assess how the declines in OERI's and NIE's support for education R&D may have been magnified or offset by trends at other levels. The data show that there has been a large decline in federal support for education R&D over the past two decades, and incomplete information suggests that there have been small and moderate increases in support from several other sources.

A comprehensive analysis of total federal expenditures for education R&D in 1975 found a total of $1.1 billion (in 1990 constant dollars) (National Institute of Education, 1976). Somewhat less comprehensive analyses conducted by the Office of Management and Budget for the years 1974, 1975, and 1976 indicated federal expenditures of $1.1 billion, $1.0 billion, and $1.3 billion, respectively (in 1990 constant dollars). The above-noted 1991 analyses suggest the federal total is now only $310 to $364 million. All data on funding levels are based on OMB's and NSF's narrow definitions of R&D.

Only four federal agencies invested more than $5 million in education R&D and their activities are briefly noted below. The Department of Education is the largest funder, spending about $193 million in 1991. Of that amount, OERI accounts for only an estimated $58 million. The largest share of the department's funding, an estimated $94 million, is for the Office of Special Education and Rehabilitation Services, which conducts R&D on various learning disabilities, special education approaches, and the handicaps of children and adults. Smaller amounts of R&D are accounted for by R&D on Chapter 1 programs ($10 million), international education and foreign language ($3 million), bilingual education ($3 million), and other subjects. Some of this work is administered by the respective program offices, but some, particularly evaluations of demonstration efforts, is handled by the department's Office of Planning, Budget, and Evaluation.

The National Science Foundation spent an estimated $54 million in education R&D, mostly through its Education and Human Resources Directorate. It supports work on the teaching and learning of mathematics and science; the applications of advanced technologies, particularly computers, to science and mathematics education; the development of improved curricula, materials and strategies for primary and secondary school instruction in mathematics, science, and technology; improvements in undergraduate college instruction in mathematics, science, and engineering; and studies of science, mathematics, and engineering education.

The Department of Health and Human Services supported about $39 million of education R&D in 1991. Its efforts focused on the biology of learning, cognitive processing, the relationships between health and learning, and the education of health professionals.

The Department of Defense funded an estimated $16 million of education R&D in 1991, according to the OMB data; the committee's estimate is $75 million. The department supports psychometric research; basic research on cognition, learning, and problem solving; computer-assisted learning through intelligent tutoring, simulations, and other means; and the development of computerized expert systems to assist in complex decision making.

In April 1991 President Bush announced a wide-ranging America 2000 education reform strategy. It proposed world-class standards and national achievement tests; several efforts to improve teaching and leadership in schools and recognition and rewards for excellence; the promotion of school choice; one-time $1 million grants to 535 schools that the undertake specified reforms; cooperation with the new New American Schools Development Corporation (see below); and job skills training and continuing education for adults. Substantial funding increases have been proposed for each area of effort except the latter two. Legislative proposals in support of the program appear bogged down because there is considerable disagreement in Congress over the advisability of national achievement tests, school choice, and the one-time grants to 535 schools.

There is widespread anecdotal information indicating that many state departments of education and large school districts have added research staff over the past 20 years, but the information also suggests that these personnel are primarily used for routine student assessment programs and evaluations of local demonstrations. NSF surveys indicate that state agencies spent $26 million of state funds on education R&D in fiscal 1973 and $21 million in fiscal 1988 (both in 1990 constant dollars) (National Institute of Education, 1976; National Science Foundation, 1990).

These state agency expenditures do not include substantial state support for thousands of faculty in public colleges and universities who spend a portion of their time doing education research. This is not the release-time paid by foundation and federal research awards, but rather the part of faculty members' normal weekly activities that is expected to be devoted to scholarly pursuits. There is similar private support for the scholarly activity of faculty in private colleges and universities. Lieberman (1991) estimated that the two accounted for about $300-$400 million worth of education research. The committee was not able to determine how this amount may have changed over the past several decades. Most of this university-supported work is believed to be discipline oriented, rather than problem oriented, because promotion and tenure are judged primarily by contributions to the disciplines. The work is also thought to involve mostly small-scale studies, because universities have very limited funds to support the research assistants, original data collection efforts, and data processing that large-scale studies usually involve.

State education policy centers have been created in about 25 states during the past several years. Their purpose is to help inform the policy-making process with nonpartisan research. Most operate on a very small scale: in 1990 only four had an operating budget in excess of $100,000 (McCarthy, 1990). University funds and foundation grants are their main sources of support.

Foundation support for education research has increased modestly from 1981, the first year for which totals are available. It rose from $20 million then (in 1990 dollars) to $36 million in 1990, according to the Foundation Center's database. The latter figure is less than 1 percent of total foundation spending for that year.

Professional education associations are reported to have expanded their R&D staffs over the past two decades, but aggregate data are not available. Most of these associations rely substantially on federal and foundation funds to support their research and development activities, and thus they contribute limited additional funding for those activities.

Several major business associations became involved with education reform during the 1980s and have commissioned or conducted education policy studies. Their interests vary, but they generally focus on work force preparation, business-school partnerships, and the Job Training Partnership Act programs. Together, the work does not appear to exceed $10 million annually, and a substantial portion is funded by foundations and corporations. The latter has not previously been a common source of funding for education research.

The New American Schools Development Corporation (NASDC) was created recently by business leaders at the request of President Bush. NASDC hopes to raise $200 million from private sources for a one-time 5-year effort to "create and test designs for schools that achieve national education goals and meet world class standards for all students" (New American Schools Development Corporation, 1991:13). NASDC is deliberately seeking ideas from sources not traditionally associated with education. Though some have interpreted NASDC as a "vote of no confidence" in OERI, the President apparently sees it as a supplemental "jump start" effort (Alexander, 1991:27). The administration's fiscal 1992 and 1993 budget requests have sought to increase funding for OERI's research, statistics, and school improvement efforts.

Whether NASDC will succeed remains to be seen. Only about $40 million of the $200 million has been committed over the past 9 months. NASDC officials say they have not really started their fundraising, but some corporate leaders have voiced reluctance to contribute. Equally important, the ambitious goals of NASDC are on a very tight schedule. The designs are to be developed during the first year; implemented, tested, and refined during the next 2 years; and then disseminated to local communities during the following 2 years. The examples of education development efforts cited in Chapter 2 suggest that much more time would be needed to achieve NASDC's goals. At the end of 5 years there is likely to remain much need for fine-tuning the models, rigorous testing of them, and supporting their adoption.

Private organizations, such as Bell Laboratories and the Educational Testing Service, undoubtedly invest in education R&D, but again there are no aggregate data. Commercial textbook and software publishers may also do so, but their work has long been criticized for lagging far behind advances in research knowledge.

Several professional associations of educators and scholars have recently become heavily involved in curriculum improvement efforts. The National Council of Teachers of Mathematics developed objectives for mathematics curricula and assessment that have been well received and widely endorsed. Project 2061 of the American Association for the Advancement of Science is developing several alternative approaches to teaching science. Whittle Communications has announced the Edison Project to invent new schools that will then be operated privately around the country. All of these undertakings are development efforts, not research, and it is unclear how much they have been based on research findings or will use research in refining their work and testing it.

There has been some conjecture that because of increases in nonfederal funding of education R&D, the federal role now can be considerably reduced. The committee finds no evidence for that conjecture. Solid evidence indicates that total federal investment in education R&D has declined by $700 million (in 1990 constant dollars) since 1975. Although there are some indications that school districts, professional associations, business organizations and foundations have increased their support of education R&D, the spotty available evidence suggests these increases almost certainly fall short of the amount of the decline in federal support. The evidence also suggests that the expanded nonfederal support is directed towards local testing and assessment programs and some limited topics of research, rather than the broad spectrum of research and development that has traditionally been the mission of OERI and NIE.

4

Appraisal of OERI

Although the Office of Educational Research and Improvement (and its predecessor, the National Institute of Education) has contributed much to education research and development (see Chapter 2), several pervasive problems have impaired the agency's effectiveness. Some of these problems span the various offices and activities and others span history. Several problems are inherent in the nature of education and education research; others are amendable to policy and administrative correction.

MISSION AND OBJECTIVES

Mission

OERI's legislated mission statement asks the agency to be almost everything for everybody. Since funding has always been less than needed, the agency tends to spread its resources thinly among many endeavors. OERI has regularly responded to pressures to do so—sometimes readily and sometimes reluctantly—after confrontations with irate interest groups, the executive branch, and members of Congress. The result is manifest throughout the agency: from 1980 to 1991 the number of centers more than doubled while the budget for them (in constant dollars) decreased by 21 percent; the field-initiated research program now provides grants for a maximum of 18 months, with virtually no chance of a renewal award; and the FIRST program funds more than 100 school-based reform efforts that are supposed to be of national significance, but for only 1- to 3-year periods for only $50,000 to $150,000. An official of a business organization wrote to the committee: "What is needed is a vision and mission articulating direction, priorities and goals. In business it is called a strategic plan."

OERI's mission statement does not state that the agency's governance, operations, and activities should involve a working partnership between research, schools, employers, families and policy makers. Although the agency has made efforts to involve these groups in its work, the enthusiasm for doing so waxes and wanes over time. Some assistant secretaries have deliberately sought to involve the various groups; others have seemed almost oblivious.

It is doubtful that the problems with OERI's mission statement have, by themselves, seriously compromised the agency. Rather, these problems, in concert with several others (discussed below), have seriously affected OERI.

Continuing Controversy About Education

Controversy has surrounded federally funded education R&D ever since the Office of Education was founded in 1867. There have been conflicts over the appropriateness of federal activity in education R&D, the agendas pursued, the specific activities undertaken, the distribution of funds among various potential performers, and the utility of the enterprise (Kaestle, 1991; Sproull et al., 1978). The controversy has variously involved the Congress, the President, the education community, researchers, federal administrative agencies, and factions within OERI and NIE.

Some controversy results from the sheer numbers of potential users of education R&D: 535 members of Congress; the administrators of several federal agencies; 50 governors, state legislatures, and state departments of education; hundreds of intermediate state agencies; numerous education associations; 15,000 school districts; 83,000 public schools and 26,000 private schools; almost 3 million teachers; and 32 million parents of school-age children. These potential users place varying and sometimes conflicting demands on the enterprise.

Education itself has been a battleground of interest groups since at least the 1870s (Peterson and Rabe, 1983; Ravitch, 1974), and the conflicts naturally spill over onto research issues. There are several reasons for those conflicts. Americans put great faith in education as a means to upward mobility and a good life: they believe it can make a difference, they expect it to, and they are upset when it does not achieve that goal. Americans also hold deep-seated and differing values about both the goals and the means of education. When research findings or innovative programs contradict values and beliefs, the results are often dismissed, and the enterprise that produced them is criticized. For instance, an elementary school mathematics curriculum that encourages children to explore, conjecture, and challenge is considered by many scientists as an important investment for the future of science, but some parents see it as lacking discipline and encouraging disrespect.

Research has repeatedly been caught up in disputes over the value of intelligence and standardized achievement testing, the relative advantages of phonics and whole-language approaches to teaching reading, the need for school desegregation, the effects of mainstreaming handicapped students, the merit of bilingual education, and the importance of small class sizes. Few groups welcome a study, however well designed, that might undermine their beliefs, their prerogatives, or their jobs.

Widespread disagreement about education and education R&D was also apparent in comments the committee received in respect to this study. Many suggestions were offered for improving education R&D, but only one, improving linkages with practice, was offered by more than 25 percent of the people we heard from. Most people think improvements are needed; few agree on what those improvements should be.

However extensive the problems caused by these disagreements and conflicts, they make education research all the more important. Consider the observation of Albert Shanker (1988), president of the American Federation of Teachers:

> We believe that in an enterprise such as education, which is often fraught with conflicting values, opinions and politics, research is the best hope we have of distinguishing between fads and facts, prejudices and informed judgments, habits and insights. Without systematic inquiry, development, and testing, we will continue to have the same babble of arguments and practices concerning what works or ought to work. Without good research, we will continue on an endless cycle of mistakes and the loss of successful insights and discoveries. Without good research, there will continue to be an endless reinvention of mousetraps, the same rehashing of controversies, and, in the end, the same faltering school system.

A History of "Politicization"

The National Institute of Education was born in the midst of political maneuvering. It was proposed by President Nixon, a Republican, at a time when he was simultaneously proposing cuts in federal funding for many social and education programs to a Democratically controlled Congress (Sproull et al., 1978). Political conservatives, wanting to limit federal involvement in the nation's life, were generally against the institute. So were many liberals, who were unwilling to trade federal support of local school programs for education research. Senator Warren Magnuson, a powerful member of the Senate Appropriations Committee and chair of the subcommittee responsible for the Department of Health, Education, and Welfare, was angered by Nixon's proposals to cut $3 billion from that department and sought to extract revenge through NIE.

Ever since, there has been a widespread perception that NIE and OERI have been inappropriately and dysfunctionally politicized. The examples of politicization, however, vary markedly depending on who is citing them. Members of Congress and their staffs frequently charge that the administration's ideological and political agendas have skewed the appointment of top administrators, the selection of topics to be studied, the determination of how the topics are to be studied, the awarding of contracts, and the editing of reports and timing of their release. For instance, it is claimed that there was little research on the educational effects of dual-earner families during the Carter administration (for fear that the results might impair the women's employment opportunities, which were supported by that administration) and little research on women's equity issues during the Reagan administration (because excellence, rather than equity, was that administration's focus). In their turn, members of the administration frequently charge that Congress has politicized the research by favoring constituency desires rather than substantive merit, by large set-asides for the laboratories and centers, by mandating specific centers and studies, by limiting the focus of some congressionally mandated studies (such as the lack of examination of student achievement in the 1980s Chapter I study), by pushing other pet projects with threats against OERI's appropriations, and by making "big cases" over trivial complaints from constituents.

Staff within OERI frequently repeat the above charges and contribute additional ones. They allege that in the early 1980s the agency hired a number of people who were politically connected but not qualified for doing the programmatic work. Many staff also allege that the report clearance process in the Department of Education has been used against OERI reports that fail to support the department's positions on various issues.

Some researchers complain that those who hold views unpopular with the members of proposal review panels are precluded from funding, and that various interest groups have distorted OERI's agenda. Organizations of professional educators frequently complain that OERI (and NIE) has been the pawn of the researchers and ignored the needs of practitioners. Education writers complain of political coloring of research reports, especially those on issues of major concern to the administration.

The perceptions of politicization are not limited to people in Washington. One state department of education official wrote to our committee:

> To us, the fundamental problem has been political. The Congress and sundry administrations have routinely been at odds over what should be researched. Hence, there has been minimal funding for research except the

> rather diffuse, short-term agendas . . . Unless there is a fundamental structural change to obviate this nonproductive arrangement, progress is unlikely.

Most of these charges are difficult to investigate. But given their sheer number, some are probably true.

While Congress was pushing down the ceiling of NIE's budget during the mid-1970s, three groups could have been of help to the agency. The main education associations of teachers, administrators, and school board members actively supported some proposals for federal assistance to education, but were little interested in education research at that time. The American Educational Research Association, the primary organization of education researchers, had little inclination or skill in marshalling political support. The third group, the Council for Educational Development and Research (CEDaR), was an association of the laboratories and some centers. It presented the case for institutional R&D, mobilizing satisfied client school districts and state agencies to support its cause, and succeeded in convincing Congress to establish floors under the appropriations for those institutions. When the ceiling on NIE's budget caved in, the floors sagged but did not collapse, and almost everything else was flattened.

Ever since there has been feuding between university researchers who want to do field-initiated research and CEDaR. The former variously accuse CEDaR of single-handedly determining the budget for the entire agency through its minions in Congress, destroying support for field-initiated research, and securing "pork" for its member institutions. However, the above-cited events are not consistent with the accusations. The budget for the laboratories and centers declined by 35 percent (in constant dollars) between 1973 and 1979. There also is ample historical evidence that Congress was uneasy about field-initiated research by the mid-1960s, well before the formation of CEDaR (see Chapter 3—"History"). The numerous reviews of the laboratories and centers over the past two decades have almost uniformly suggested that institutions such as these are needed, and though the general performance has not been as high as hoped, it has not been universally dismal. CEDaR responds to its critics by accusing university researchers of failing to present a credible case for the support of education R&D and of weakening the entire enterprise with criticisms of CEDaR, the laboratories, and sometimes the centers.

Thus, for almost three decades, charges of politicization have swirled around NIE and OERI. Many people view the agency as politicized, and that perception inevitably affects the credibility of its work. The diversity of the allegations, however, does suggest that these charges are partly a function of the dissension that often accompanies education. Over and over again, what one group views as leadership, other groups view as politicization.

GOVERNANCE

The National Institute of Education was created as a separate agency within the Department of Health, Education and Welfare (HEW), to consolidate education research and development activities, give responsibility for management of these activities to professional scholars, and to provide higher status for the work. Its director, appointed by the President with the advice and consent of the Senate, reported to the Assistant Secretary for Education, who was also in charge of the Office of Education and starting in 1974, the newly established National Center for Education Statistics.

A National Council on Educational Research was created by legislation to set overall policies for NIE. The House bill had provided for an advisory council, but the Senate bill and the resulting legislation called for a policy-making council, apparently because a few Senators sought to ensure NIE's independence from the Assistant Secretary (Sproul et al., 1978). The 15 members were appointed by the President, with the advice and consent of the Senate, and served 3-year staggered terms. The first council was comprised of five university presidents or chancellors, two university professors, three businessmen, one state superintendent of instruction, one state education administrator, one school district superintendent, one school principal and a graduate student. It was chaired by Pat Haggerty, chairman of the board of Texas Instruments. The council was to prescribe the director's powers and duties, advise the assistant secretary and the director on program development, recommend improved methods of collecting and disseminating educational research findings, conduct studies necessary to fulfill its own functions, and submit annual reports to the Institutes's activities and on education and educational research in general (Public Law 92-318, 1972).

In the 1976 reauthorization of NIE, Congress specified that the council was to be "broadly representative of the general public; of the education professions, including practitioners and researchers; and of the various fields of education, including preschool, elementary and secondary, postsecondary, continuing, vocational, special, and compensatory education (Public Law 94-482).

With the creation of the Department of Education, OERI was established as an umbrella organization to house NIE, the National Center for Educational Statistics (NCES), Library Programs, and some discretionary and dissemination activities. The National Council of Educational Research was retained, but as before, had authority only over OERI.

In 1985 the Secretary of Education reorganized OERI to make the semi-autonomous units become line offices and replaced the policy-making council with a National Advisory Council on Educational Research and Improvement. This was done to reallocate authority for these activities to the secretary, minimize duplication, improve coordination, expand links with practitioners, and generally improve the quality of the work (Bennett, 1985). The 1986 reauthorization of OERI supported these changes (Public Law 99-498). The council was appointed exactly as before, was composed of essentially the same types of representatives, and they served for the same 3-year staggered terms. The responsibilities were also essentially the same, with two exceptions. The council no longer was to prescribe the duties of the head of NIE (or OERI), and in all the other areas it was to provide advice to the Secretary of Education and to the Assistant Secretary of OERI, rather than determine policy.

A few years later Congress modified the governance of the National Center for Educational Statistics (NCES) providing it with a commissioner serving a 4-year term, appointed by the President with the advice and consent of Congress. Congress also offered NCES the option of independent staffing and procurement authority, but the Secretary of Education chose not to implement these options (see Chapter 3—NCES).

It is not clear which governance structure—the policy-making council of NIE or the advisory council of OERI—has been most effective. There is widespread agreement that the advisory council has not been influential within OERI or outside of it. The policy-making council, under both Republican and Democratic administrations in the 1970s, was generally considered competent and hardworking, but it was unable to help NIE gain the support of educators, the public, or Congress. In the early 1980s it was considered less distinguished, more politicized, and even less effective in securing support. Most researchers believe that NIE conducted more good research and achieved more important progress in knowledge in the 1970s than did OERI in the 1980s, but this judgment may be skewed by the larger constant-dollar budgets for NIE in the 1970s and by the fact that the contributions of research often take a decade before they are obvious, making OERI's contributions less discernable at this time.

The two most prominent federal research agencies—the National Science Foundation (NSF) and the National Institutes of Health (NIH)—have different governance structures, although in actual practice the differences are not great. NSF has a policy-making board, the National Science Board, which is comprised of persons eminent in the fields of "science, engineering, agriculture, education, research management or public affairs." The members are appointed by the President, with the advice of the board and with the advice and consent of the Senate. The members serve 6-year staggered terms. Former directors of NSF believe the board has expanded their power, not diminished it, by forging some consensus among scientists, building public and congressional support for the agency, and buffering it from dysfunctional politicization.

At NIH, each institute has an advisory council of 12-18 members, appointed by the Secretary of Health and Human Services in consultation with the institute director, who serve 4-year terms. Two-thirds are selected from "among the leading representatives of the health and scientific disciplines (including not less than two individuals who are leaders in the fields of public health and the behavioral or social sciences) relevant to the activities of the [institute]." The remaining one-third are selected "from the general public and shall include leaders in fields of public policy, law, health policy, economics, and management." One of the important functions of these councils is to engage the communities of researchers and practitioners in discussions of R&D needs and to build agreement as to what should be the priorities. Though these councils are not policy-making, there is a tradition of their advice being heeded by the institute administrators.

There are advantages and disadvantages to both policy-making boards and top-level advisory councils. Policy-making bodies are more prestigious and, all other things equal, generally more powerful. For that reason, distinguished and accomplished people, especially those still interested in having an impact, are more likely to accept appointments to a policy-making board and to take their responsibilities seriously.

However, a policy-making board raises the issue of accountability. After being appointed, it does not have to answer to anyone, particularly if the members are appointed for fixed terms: some people believe this gives the board the necessary independence to stand above the fray of constituent politics and to do what is best for the nation; others believe it encourages elitism and irresponsibility.

A policy-making board, unlike a top-level advisory council, appears to impinge on the normal executive branch prerogative of proposing federal programs and activities, but the actual effect is modest since the President is still free to submit whatever budget proposals he or she chooses and to sign or veto legislation. Some fear that a policy-making board can create a dangerous imbalance in the powers of the President relative to the Congress. This could happen only if the President submits budgets contrary to the policies of the board, and Congress implements the proposals of the board, and even then the President would still retain the veto power.

As a consequence, a policy-making board within the federal government does not usurp the power of a vigilant President or the Congress, but rather becomes a third party that informs and may influence both. Its impact ultimately is dependent on decisions by the executive and congressional branches. Thus, in actual practice, a policy-making board has little more power than an advisory council, only that which comes from its greater stature and ability to attract more prominent members. And if a board runs amuck, the President and Congress can thwart or abolish it through the normal legislative process.

This analysis presumes the policy-making board focuses mostly on agenda-setting activities. If it becomes involved in determining the administrative procedures of the agency, problems could go unchecked by the President or Congress, because such matters are not easily visible to either branch and are time-consuming to counter with legislation.

In addition to policy-making and advisory bodies, there is another option—to use neither. Critics of both types of bodies point out that they can become highly politicized and captured by special interests, are unlikely to recommend bold new approaches, and inevitably require funds for support staff and travel that could be used for other purposes. There is some merit in all of these points, but there are countervailing considerations. Whatever the risks of a group becoming politicized or captured, they are less likely than the risks with one or two political appointees whose jobs depend on their decisions. A diverse and accomplished group of people, appointed with a balance of power between the executive and congressional branches of government, and whose jobs do not depend on their decisions, are balanced and buffered in a way no one assistant secretary can be. Group governance may mitigate against bold redirections of an agency, but that doesn't mean the agency would be precluded from funding such work. And the costs of boards and advisory councils for an agency the size of OERI are usually considerably less than 1 percent of the budget; a board or council does not have to improve the productivity of the agency by much to recoup its cost.

Another key issue in the governance of OERI has been the roles played by the top administrators. Seven of the ten former top administrators of OERI and NIE held their positions for less than 2 years. The rapid turnover appears to be due to several factors. As mentioned above, education and education R&D have historically been very contentious, and this conflict takes a toll on top administrators. The job requires considerable skill as a researcher, manager, and politician, and many of the appointees have been inexperienced in one or two of those areas. The declining budgets have alienated agency staff, minimized the discretion of top administrators, and contributed to an impression of failure. In addition, the assistant secretary of any highly visible government agency must respond to the diverse and sometimes conflicting demands of the President, Congress, and the public.

Although assistant secretaries throughout the federal government do not last longer, on the average, than the heads of OERI and NIE, tenure in major federal research agencies has been much longer. As noted in Chapter 3, during the 13-year life of NIE there were six Senate-confirmed directors; since 1985, when NIE was dissolved into OERI, the agency has had three confirmed assistant secretaries. That total of nine over 19 years compares with six directors at NSF, five at NIH, and three at the Agriculture Research Service.

Each new director or assistant secretary of OERI (and NIE) has sought to make his or her mark by pursuing a distinctive agenda, but most have not remained long enough to enact more than a small portion of it. For example, in 1978 the NIE director identified complex learning skills as a priority area: she commissioned papers to identify key questions for further research, convened a conference at which the papers were reviewed by researchers and practitioners, and then organized the first grant competition in that area of research. Of the more than 90 proposals that were received and reviewed by panels of experts, 30 were judged worthy of being funded. But then, in 1981, a newly appointed director—who did not regard complex learning skills as a priority area—decided not to fund any of the proposals.

Most of the directors and assistant secretaries do remain long enough to reorganize the agency. It is not clear whether the reorganizations are due to a persisting belief that there are structural solutions to the problems of educational research or due to the lack of opportunities for discretion in other areas of managing the agency.

Surely one of the big surprises to new board or council members and incoming assistant secretaries is how little discretionary funds are available for establishing new programs. Of the $300-400 million dollar budgets of OERI, an assistant secretary is likely to have substantial discretion over only $5-10 million. Most of the $46 million in the FIRST office is for specified purposes, except for part of the $26 million in the Funds for Innovation in Education, which is essentially the discretionary fund of the Secretary of Education. The $142 million in Library Programs is set by specifications in the authorizations. The $45 million set-aside for the centers and laboratories is authorized with broad language that potentially allows considerable discretion, but the centers and laboratories operate under 5-year contracts or cooperative agreements, and the appropriations' reports occasionally include directives for these institutions. NCES operates with a long list of projects that have been negotiated with Congress.

New ideas, of course, can be proposed for future budgets, but there is an 18-month lead time, competing proposals from other agencies, and budget ceilings. Newly authorized programs often have to wait another year for their first appropriation. By then most assistant secretaries have left their positions, and unless there is a strong board or council to follow through, there is little chance of the agency providing leadership.

A few federal agencies have top administrative officers with a fixed term of appointment. The director of NSF is appointed for a 6-year term. The commissioner of the Bureau of Labor Statistics is appointed for a 4-year term, and there is a long history of reappointments. The commissioner of NCES was recently given a 4-year term. The head of Congress's Office of Technology Assessment has a 6-year term, and the head of the General Accounting Office has a 12-year term. None of these agencies is perfectly analogous with OERI, but in each case the terms of office have been used to encourage sustained professional management of research and to minimize the opportunities for politicization. In those federal research agencies without terms of office, there is usually a tradition of long tenures by the top administrators: tradition can be effective, but it cannot be legislated.

The most common terms of office are 4-year and 6-year periods. The former allows each President to make an appointment. The latter does not, and the timing of the appointment, relative to the President's term, fluctuates.

There are some potential problems with terms of office. They reduce accountability to the executive branch and do not necessarily increase accountability to whatever board or council may exist. In addition, an incompetent can linger on for several years, although a precaution against this would be to allow removal by the President with the advice and consent of the Senate. In actual practice, the problems apparently have been few, and the practice has grown slowly over the years.

Another governance issue of growing concern is the appropriate position of NCES. Through the 1970s and most of the 1980s it was a relatively small entity with an annual budget of about $15-30 million (in 1990 constant dollars). In fiscal 1990 the budget was $40 million, in 1991 it was $60 million, and large increases are projected for the next few years. Some people believe that NCES will soon become the tail that wags the dog, although others predict that NCES may soon implode from understaffing (see Chapter 3). It has been suggested to the committee that NCES be taken out of OERI and placed in tandem with it under an assistant secretary. The advocates of this suggestion fear that the politicization and instability in OERI will corrode NCES. That is possible, but there is little assurance of less politicization or more stability in the tandem structure: in both cases, NCES would answer to a political appointee. The proposed structure was used for NIE and NCES during the early 1980s—years that are widely thought to be the darkest for both—though not necessarily because of the structure.

FUNDING

The funding history of OERI and NIE has been a bruising downhill slide that has inevitably extracted a heavy toll on the agency. As indicated above, new directors have quickly become criticized and demoralized. Careful agenda setting became futile; "quick fixes" replaced thoughtful investments; and few sustained research and development activities could be maintained. Resources were spread so thinly that mediocrity was virtually assured. Individual researchers, with less political clout than institutions, were squeezed out. Agency staff focused on required administrative functions and survival strategies rather than fulfilling the agency's substantive mission. Top-flight personnel often shunned working in the agency.

Dramatic budget cuts have forced OERI (and NIE) to do less—much less. Basic research, aimed at discovering new phenomena, is barely funded. In 1973 the average center budget was $6.0 million (in 1990 dollars); it is now $0.9 million. The average laboratory budget was $6.4 million (in 1990 dollars); it is now $3.0 million. The centers and laboratories formerly developed major innovations—such as Student Team Learning and the Comprehensive School Mathematics Program—but they rarely can do such work now. The laboratories used to do considerable work directly with schools and teachers, but they now do more work with state agencies and improvement assistance organizations. In the 1970s NIE provided support for the graduate training of minority and women researchers, but there has been very little such support in the 1980s. In the 1970s NIE funded research and demonstrations on how to effectively disseminate innovations and change schools, but in the 1980s OERI funded little such work.

Each of OERI's programs of research is now generally limited to a dozen senior researchers affiliated with a single R&D center. There is little money for special projects to supplement the work of the centers. As a consequence, virtually all of OERI's support for research on a given topic is committed to the small number of researchers affiliated with one center. Other researchers studying those topics are almost precluded from OERI support for 5 years, until the center competes again for support.

Two critical types of R&D activity have been severely underfunded at OERI. First, the agency invests very little in field-initiated research. For several years prior to 1986, OERI did not fund any field-initiated research. Now only $1.3 million, or 2 percent of its R&D budget, is for this purpose. Field-initiated research is research whose topics and methods are suggested by scholars around the country, rather than in response to requests by an agency for specific work. It harvests the insight, creativity, and initiative of researchers widely dispersed across the country, and it has been a major contributor to knowledge and technology in all fields of science. NIH invests 56 percent of its R&D budget in field-initiated research and NSF devotes 94 percent (data are not available for the Agriculture Research Service). As best as we can determine, it has been congressional action that has constrained field-initiated research at OERI by imposing set-asides on virtually all of the agency's primary appropriation and specifying very low levels of support for this work.

The second underfunded critical type of R&D activity is basic research. Basic research in education is aimed at expanding understanding of the fundamental aspects of human development, learning, teaching, schools, and their environmental contexts; such research generates new views of what exists and new visions of the achievable. (In contrast, applied research is aimed at expanding knowledge of the means to achieve specific objectives.) In 1989, the last year for which data are available, only $1.9

million of OERI's R&D budget was allocated to basic research—just 5.5 percent. By comparison, at the Agriculture Research Service, 46.6 percent of the R&D budget is allocated to basic research; at the National Institutes of Health, 59.8 percent; and at the National Science Foundation, 93.5 percent. Overall, federal government, excluding the Department of Defense, invests 40.6 percent of its R&D budget in basic research (National Science Foundation, 1991a)

In the late 1970s a National Research Council report (1977b) *Fundamental Research and the Process of Education*, recommended that the federal government "increase . . . the proportion of the federal investment in education research and development designated for fundamental research" and that NIE "take immediate steps to implement a policy of strong support for fundamental research relevant to education." Soon after that report, support for basic research at NIE increased substantially for a few years (Timpane, 1982). During the early years of the 1980s, the entire Department of Education invested about 11 percent of its R&D budget on basic research; since 1986 it has spent only about 2 percent (National Science Foundation, 1991a).

Basic research has been slighted at OERI primarily because Congress, teachers, administrators, and the administration have repeatedly urged that the agency quickly solve the pressing problems in schools. Since basic research seldom yields practical applications in less than a decade, the agency has responded to demands for solutions by focusing on applied research, development, and dissemination activities. This is an understandable short-term response, but it is akin to eating one's seed corn. As indicated in Chapter 2, several of today's most promising innovations in education have been heavily influenced by findings from basic research in cognitive science—work that was conducted not only by education researchers but by investigators in several of the behavioral and social sciences. Basic research in computer science and mathematics was also critical to some of the described innovations.

COORDINATION AND COOPERATION

It was hoped that the creation of NIE in 1972 would serve to improve coordination among several programs that had been inherited from the Office of Education—centers, laboratories, ERIC, career education model development, experimental schools, researcher training, field initiated research, and dissemination activities (National Institute of Education, 1973a). NIE did move, during its early years, to coordinate work on several key topics. Most noticeably, it engaged in major efforts, with distinguished outside scholars, to plan programs of research in high-priority areas that coordinated the work of centers, field-initiated studies, and various special projects. Nevertheless, agenda setting in federally funded education research has generally been erratic and unsystematic. There has been limited coordination of efforts and communication of findings among the various units in OERI and NIE, among the various offices in the Department of Education, and among the several other federal agencies that support education R&D activities. The committee was frequently told that there is a need for OERI's activities to be better coordinated with those of other federal, state, and local agencies.

Each office in OERI generally prepares its budget materials with little advance program planning or consultation among the offices. A few years ago there was an agreement to develop a consultative process, but it was never implemented. Though budget proposals are requested at about the same month each year, there is little advance planning, and each office rushes to prepare its budget documents. Staff do sometimes seek out counterparts in other offices for help in planning studies, reviewing draft reports, and participating on proposal review panels, but this is usually done informally and on the basis of personal contacts, primarily among those in the Office of Research, Programs for the Improvement of Practice, and NCES. The FIRST Office and Library Programs are more isolated.

For more than two decades the national R&D centers and regional laboratories have had partly overlapping responsibilities of research, development, demonstration, and technical assistance—with the centers emphasizing research and the laboratories mostly engaged in the latter three. There was some cooperation in the preparation of the 1985 and 1990 competitions for laboratory and center awards. After granting the awards, however, there was little follow-up cooperation. Although the centers do research that could be of use in the laboratories' development and technical assistance work, the laboratories seldom work closely with the centers. Conversely, although the laboratories have extensive contacts with state departments of education and local school districts, the centers seldom seek their advice about the needs of those organizations. NCES regularly queries the laboratories and centers when planning its data collection activities, but the Office of Research does not regularly contact the laboratories when planning its activities; the Programs for the Improvement of Practice also does not regularly communicate with the centers when planning its activities, although there have been some recent efforts to correct this situation. After the 1990 competition for laboratories and centers, OERI did not circulate copies of the winners' proposals to the other winning institutions until requested to do so at a joint meeting of the laboratory and center directors.

The lack of coordination of the laboratories and centers is long-standing. One new center director noted to the committee:

the relationship of Centers to Labs . . . is a matter that puzzles us and continues to do so after the recent meeting in Washington of Center Directors and Lab heads. When we asked about how this relationship works, we received polite smiles. Apparently there is some history here that people would rather not get into. We remain uncertain about how we [a new Center] are to relate with Labs or even whether we are to relate to them at all.

A few instances of long-term cooperation between a center and a laboratory have produced notable results. The Learning Research and Development Center and Research for Better Schools, both located in Pennsylvania, collaborated on the development of individually prescribed instruction. The Far West Laboratory and the Center on Teaching at Stanford developed a series of minicourses widely used for in-service teacher development.

There is also a lack of coordination between the dissemination and technical assistance work of the National Diffusion Network (NDN) and that of the laboratories. The NDN state facilitators generally know the needs and wants of teachers and principals in their respective states better than the laboratories, but the laboratories seldom benefit from this knowledge. NDN state facilitators are still primarily involved in disseminating innovations, although it is now well understood that innovations alone, without broader reform in the schools, seldom have substantial and lasting effects. The laboratories are increasingly assisting districts and schools with systemic reform, but without regular input from the NDN facilitators.

Some of the lack of coordination has been due to internal administrative action or inaction, but some has been a result of external forces. The diversity of interest groups concerned with education and continuing conflicts over mission (Sproull et al., 1978:219) have prevented the agency from focusing its limited resources on a few high-priority matters. For instance, in 1989 the Office of Research prepared several options for the 1990 competition of the centers and recommended one that proposed using the limited available funding for only five substantial centers. The Undersecretary of the Department of Education selected an option with 12 centers, and after receiving comments from the public and Congress, OERI held a competition for 17 centers.

Within the Department of Education there are two units in addition to OERI that conduct substantial research and evaluation: the Office of Planning, Budget, and Evaluation (OPBE) and the Office of Special Education and Rehabilitation Services. Historically, the three have operated with little coordination in planning, little sharing of information on the work each is sponsoring, and little knowledge of what each has learned. A letter to the committee from a researcher suggested: "There needs to be much closer linkage between research and major educational programs supported by the federal government—by taking small steps to investigate and validate specific program procedures before large and costly efforts, that are difficult to 'fine tune' are put in place."

The lack of cooperation has been exacerbated by the 1970 "Cranston Amendment" (Public Law 91-230), which prevents other offices in the Department of Education from having OERI do work for them—but does not prohibit other departments, such as the Departments of Labor and Agriculture, from doing so. This amendment was precipitated by the department's prior commingling of some funds from different appropriations, which was perceived as an attempt to circumvent the intent of Congress.

There is also very limited coordination and cooperation between the special technical assistance dissemination efforts of the various program offices in the department—such as the Chapter 1 Technical Assistance Centers, the Regional Drug-Free Centers, and the Education Evaluation Bilingual Assistance Centers—and those of the laboratories and centers, with the exception of ERIC, which receives materials from many of these sources. The problem has recently been recognized by the department's regional inspector general (Nestlehutt, 1991:1-2), who identified 43 different programs that "provide technical assistance, assist in program evaluation, perform training and research, and disseminate data and information . . . [and] evidence uncoordinated growth that fails to ensure an effective and efficient issue of Department resources." An inventory conducted by OERI found 12 separate technical assistance programs, supporting 135 projects or institutions at an annual cost of $90 million. Means for coordinating these various activities are currently being considered.

As noted above, the National Science Foundation, the Department of Defense, and the Department of Health and Human Services also fund considerable education R&D. There has generally been little communication among those agencies and little monitoring of their activities. When the National Education Goals Panel recently wanted to know how much the federal government spends on education R&D, the Office of Management and Budget had to do a special survey (National Education Goals Panel, 1991). That survey collected data on funding levels, but not on the nature of the work undertaken. As a letter to the committee noted: "At the present time OERI has no capability to even know what research is being undertaken outside the purview of the agency, much less to develop educational applications for it." One assistant secretary of OERI did establish collaborations with a few other federal agencies concerned with education issues, but these were achieved only after some effort, and it remains to be seen whether they will continue in the future.

For at least 20 years there have been limited attempts to coordinate related activities in different federal agencies. There is a Federal Interagency Committee on Education with a mandate to coordinate all education activities sponsored by federal agencies. For a while it monitored early childhood education research closely, but it no longer does so. There is also a Federal Coordinating Council for Science, Engineering, and Technology (FCCSET) that has a Committee on Education and Human Resources. It recently conducted a detailed survey of federal agency activities in mathematics and science education activities, including research activities within that domain.

Most knowledgeable observers suggest that despite the appeal of attempts to coordinate related activities in several federal agencies, the forces working against such efforts are strong (Kaestle, 1991). The agencies are competitors for federal funding, each is reluctant to give up its prerogatives, and the task of coordination is usually assigned to a mid-level staff member. Unless a high official is leading the effort, it appears to have little effect. Observers also note that some duplication is not a waste of resources because it allows replication. Yet it is clear that funders could benefit from knowing what their counterparts are supporting, and that users would benefit from access to the best information and assistance available from all sources.

SUSTAINED EFFORTS

The Office of Technology Assessment's recent report (1988:167-168,171,184) on R&D for technological applications for education provides a good discussion of the importance of sustained efforts in R&D work:

The Department of Education has had an off and on love affair with technology. Where research support has been consistent, as in support of children's television programming in the late 1960s through the 1970s, or long term as in support for technology in special education, important milestones were reached. These are exceptions. Most research projects did not have opportunities to proceed from laboratory research through to development of products and processes, much less to testing in the classroom, with real students and teachers.

In the 1970s, the Department supported quite a few projects lasting 5 or more years . . . During the 1980s few projects received comparable long-term support.

. . . [The 1987-88 plans] fall short of focused, long-term commitments called for by the National Governors' Association, the National Task Force on Educational Technology, and the National School Boards Association .

. . . Significant improvements in education can be made if sustained support is made available for development of new tools for teaching and learning. The private sector, while a contributor to this effort, does not have the primary responsibility or appropriate vision for making this a priority. States and localities do not have the capacity.

OERI's overall record of support for sustained efforts is somewhat better than this indictment, but hardly exemplary. Five of the current ten laboratories have existed since 1967. Their responsibilities and modes of operation, however, have been altered some by OERI and NIE over the years. For instance, in the 1960s and 1970s, they undertook mostly applied research and development work. In the late 1970s and early 1980s they did considerable work with schools and teachers. In the mid-1980s they were directed to work more with state agencies and improvement assistance organizations. Then in 1990 that mandate was relaxed.

Only 2 of the current 25 OERI centers are direct descendants of the 10 that existed in 1973: the Center on Student Learning at Pittsburgh's Learning Research and Development Center and the Center on Assessment, Evaluation, and Testing at UCLA's Center for the Study of Evaluation. Of the 12 centers that existed in the early 1980s, 6 were eliminated when their contracts expired in 1985, and 3 were awarded to new bidders. Of the 13 centers whose contracts expired in 1990, 3 were terminated, and 3 were awarded to new bidders.

Despite the rapid changes in leadership and frequent reorganizations in OERI and NIE, underlying stability has sometimes been maintained. For instance, Virginia Koehler Richardson managed a program on research in teaching at NIE for a decade. She notes (quoted in Kaestle, 1991:20):

> To propel a research agenda through all that change . . . requires some real stability on the part of the people that are there . . . and different kinds of rhetoric . . . changing wording, incorporating some of the newer notions, and just ensuring that people felt that research on teaching was a worthwhile endeavor . . .

It was never easy, and when the agency was threatened with extinction in the early 1980s, "burnout" and "exhaustion" drove her to academia.

Instability often results in mediocrity. Most of the research-based innovations that are currently available to educators provide only modest improvements, partly because of the complexity of human learning and behavior, but also partly because these innovations are seldom subject to successive iterations of research, development, and testing aimed at strengthening effects, assuring effectiveness in a wide range of settings, enhancing market appeal, and minimizing costs. Funding for such work is rarely available, and universities often do not consider the second and subsequent iterations to be scholarly work.

One notable exception is the repeated cycles of work used in developing Student Team Learning, then Cooperative Integrated Reading and Composition, and finally Success for All at two successive R&D centers at Johns Hopkins—the Center on Social Organization of Schools and the Center on Elementary and Middle Schools. Each program built on and extended the prior one (see Chapter 2). The first of these became one of the most widely adopted of all NDN programs; the second also gained PEP certification and is being disseminated through NDN; the third is now in the demonstration stage. Despite these accomplishments, the centers that produced them were closed down by NIE and OERI in 1985 and 1990.

The need for several iterations of research, development, and testing is not peculiar to education innovations. It is common in all fields of science and technology. It took almost 50 years of research and development to achieve a satisfactory vaccination for polio. The story of flight involves repeated cycles of research, development and failure; then research, development, and short-lived successes; followed by research, development, and unacceptably expensive successes; and, finally, decades latter, research, development, and commercial success. There has never been that kind of focused persistence in education R&D.

After interviewing many of the former top officials in OERI and NIE, Kaestle (1991:19-20), tried to articulate how to balance the need for stability with the need for response to emerging issues and opportunities:

> Good stability means supporting some carefully selected, sustained work on subjects of central importance, where answers are not likely to be forthcoming quickly or cheaply. Good stability is having ongoing committees of the best scientific people as a balance against fads and politics and as a way to build credibility for the accumulating knowledge base. On the other hand, good instability means having the capacity to respond to new leaders' interests and philosophies and to shifts in national concerns, to be able to weed out weak work after a period of evaluation, and to be ready to grab innovative ideas and push new insights when it seems warranted. To make these decisions is difficult; to structure agencies to accommodate both values is even more difficult.
>
> One of the most difficult problems is how to foster the right kind of stability and the right amount of change. The issue would be simpler with more money, but it would not vanish. It is difficult, our narrators indicated, to create conditions in which you have the conditions for sustained work and professional control at the same time you allow for new players, responsiveness to changing public concerns, support for renegade scholars and paradigm-busters, and the capacity to terminate outdated or incompetent work.

A state department of education official wrote to the committee, supporting the need for sustained efforts: "Educational innovation is difficult and risky. We need a stable system of R&D programs so that risk is not only tolerated, but also valued and encouraged."

As the nation moves from innovation to comprehensive reform, the need for sustained efforts becomes even more important. As Elmore and McLaughlin (1988) have observed:

Reform of the basic conditions of teaching and learning in schools requires "steady work". . . . Lags in implementation and performance are a central fact of reform . . . the time it takes for reforms to mature into changes in resource allocation, organization, and practice is substantially longer than the electoral system that determine changes in policy.

QUALITY ASSURANCE AND ACCUMULATION OF RESULTS

OERI has a checkered history in respect to quality assurance. As noted in chapter 3, OERI has permitted practitioners to evaluate the technical merit of research proposals when they often have no training or experience suitable for the task, and it has allowed researchers to pass judgment on the programmatic merit of applied research and development proposals even when they have little expertise needed for doing so. The Program Effectiveness Panel (PEP) often judges programs as "proven exemplary" on the basis of evaluations in only a handful of sites, on only a few outcomes, and with no follow-up assessment 1 or 2 years after termination of the "treatment." PEP also does not examine possible disadvantages of applicant programs.

There have been several "reviews" of the centers and the laboratories, but never a comprehensive evaluation of either set of institutions that examined their products, services, and impact. Although the centers and laboratories develop innovative programs and processes, they are not required to have their effectiveness appraised by PEP or any other independent authority.

OERI's internal report review processes have varied by office and over time. Sometimes external and internal peer review have been required; at other times only the approval of the office head or the assistant secretary has been needed. In addition, many staff claim, with a few others disagreeing, that the Department of Education's clearance procedures sometimes result in politically motivated changes to OERI reports or delays in their release.

Quality assurance is essential in any research agency, not only for the sake of valid results, but also for credibility and support from Congress and other users. Weiss (1980) has noted that just as good research can enlighten policy makers, invalid results can "endarken" them, misinforming policy decisions. In addition, if policy makers become aware of low-quality work, support for the research enterprise is likely to suffer.

OERI supports reviews and syntheses of the R&D literature by several means. The centers and laboratories conduct reviews—sometimes to provide summaries to scholars and practitioners, and sometimes to inform their future work. The centers usually publish their reviews in journals, and the laboratories often print and distribute theirs to the state and local education agencies with whom they work. The ERIC clearinghouses commission and publish reviews on various topics, usually oriented towards informing teachers, administrators, and policy makers of the practical implications of various bodies of research. And OERI staff have prepared some major reviews of the literature which have been published as agency reports.

OERI has not made much use of another mechanism used by several federal agencies for synthesizing and judging available evidence on a given topic. That mechanism is the expert committee assembled to examine the available evidence on disputed topics and determine what is established and what is not yet known from the evidence.

The Environmental Protection Agency (EPA) has a standing Science Advisory Board that reviews and judges the scientific bases of all proposed standards and regulations of the agency. A National Research Council study (1977a) found that the board had helped the agency improve the accuracy and reliability of its scientific determinations and provided political legitimization for the agency. Though the board languished during the early 1980s, it has since become a significant actor in EPA decision making; it has 67 members, 14 staff, and produced 43 reports in 1988 (Jasanoff, 1990).

Since the 1960s the Food and Drug Administration (FDA) has used numerous committees to review the evidence on disputed matters, finding them valuable because of the technical expertise provided and the social legitimation that comes from using independent scientists (Jasanoff, 1990). The FDA has also contracted with a professional association to review the safety of certain food additives. The latter of these two undertakings involved an expert panel that examined and discussed the available literature on the topic, prepared an interim report that was released publicly, invited written comments and held an open meeting for responses, and then prepared the final report (Federation of American Societies for Experimental Biology, 1977, 1985).

Since 1977 the Office of Medical Applications of Research at the NIH has held almost 100 consensus development conferences to evaluate the effectiveness and safety of medical interventions and to improve the translation of biomedical research results into knowledge that can be used effectively by health care providers. The topics of the conferences are those that have provoked controversy, for which considerable scientific evidence is available, and that are or should be of significant interest to health care practitioners. Considerable preparation work is done before the conference, but the expert panel meets for only 2.5 days with a public audience. An interim report is read to the audience on the morning of the third day, comments are received, and then final revisions are made by the panel.

OERI usually refers to "dissemination;" NIH often refers to "technology assessment and dissemination." Several of NIH's major health promotion campaigns over the past decade, such as those for breast cancer screening and the National Cholesterol Education Program, have been partly based on the findings of NIH's consensus development conferences. Almost all the conferences are now reported in the *Journal of the American Medical Association*, and heavy media coverage has accompanied release of the reports.

Consensus processes are difficult, time consuming and expensive. If they are not done well, they can easily fall into disrepute. An evaluation of NIH's early conferences in 1979 and 1980 found they elicited substantial media coverage, but usually had only a small effect on clinical practice. NIH subsequently made several changes to improve the impact of conferences on practice. A recent Institute of Medicine report (1990) reviewed the NIH consensus development process and recommended more input from practitioners during the planning of the conferences, more thorough preparation for the conferences, experimentation with new means of facilitating the group decision making, and adequate financial support.

Although OERI and NIE have supported reviews of R&D literature, they have rarely summarized and synthesized what has been accomplished under their own funding. There are several obvious questions to ask when judging the work of OERI and NIE: What has been learned? What has been developed? What has been disseminated? What has been changed? There are thousands of final reports from projects, laboratories, and centers, but hardly any efforts to aggregate them across providers and over years. As a result, the agency is not able to explain its accomplishments to Congress, professional associations, the public, or itself. Two useful exceptions are unpublished staff papers summarizing what had been learned from NIE-sponsored studies on assessment between 1977 and 1983 (Rudner et al., n.d.) and on teaching and learning between 1978 and 1982 (Wirtenberg, 1982). A recent staff publication by Fox (1990) discussed how education research has been used in education policy making, but it does not clearly indicate which of the cited examples are based on work sponsored by OERI or NIE. Ironically, none of the three documents is indexed in ERIC or available in OERI's library.

OERI and NIE have not created a depository of their own institutional memory. As a consequence, future staff, researchers, and practitioners will have no way of easily learning from the agency's past successes and failures. The learning communities of the future will either have to plow through millions of pages of documents or proceed without the benefits of some lessons learned during the 1970s and 1980s.

LINKAGES WITH PRACTICE

Contrary to popular perception, OERI and NIE have worked hard and creatively at establishing good linkages between research and practice. They have published hundreds of documents for practitioners, including *Increas-*

ing Achievement of At-Risk Students at Each Grade Level; *Women and Mathematics: Research Perspectives for Change*; *Science Education Programs that Work*; *Good Secondary Schools—What Makes Them Tick*; *Violent Schools, Safe Schools*; *Dealing with Dropouts: The Urban Superintendents' Call to Action*; *Profiles of Successful Drug Prevention Programs*. OERI and NIE have long mandated that the centers and laboratories engage in developments that make research useful to teachers and administrators. They have administered ERIC, a state-of-the-art document search service that is widely used throughout the country. They have operated the Program Effectiveness Panel (PEP) and the National Diffusion Network (NDN). And they have funded regional laboratories to provide states, districts, and schools with a range of services aimed at improving education.

In the 1970s NIE funded several innovative efforts aimed at enhancing dissemination and building the capacity of local education agencies to benefit from education R&D work (Hutchins, 1989). The Research Development and Utilization Program had "linker" agents to assist districts identify potentially useful R&D products and agencies that could help in the adoption process (Louis et al., 1981). The Research and Development Exchange, begun in 1976, had all the laboratories and one center work collaboratively on dissemination and technical assistance efforts (Hutchins, 1989). The Local Problem Solving Program assisted schools in developing the ability to adapt existing innovations to their particular needs, develop their own innovations, and undertake change in a systematic manner (Hutchins, 1989). The Experimental Schools Program provided substantial funding to a few local schools districts that agreed to undertake locally initiated comprehensive change (Doyle, 1976; Herriott and Gross, 1979). And the State Capacity Building Program funded state education agencies to develop stronger links between research and practice (Louis et al., 1984). In the 1980s OERI increasingly involved teachers, administrators, and policy makers in the setting of research agendas and review of proposals, in hopes that the research would better address their needs.

Some of these innovative efforts were failures. Others have been successes, but were terminated because of declining budgets. Despite much experimentation and hard work, linkages between education research and practice have generally been weak. Of all the suggestions made to the committee about how to enhance the utility of education research and development, improving linkages with practitioners was cited most frequently.

Why have there been persistent problems in linkages? Some of the answers have to do with the nature of research and development and how NIE and OERI has tried to make it available to practitioners—these can be thought of as supply-side problems. Some of the answers have to do with the nature of the teaching profession and schools—these can be thought of as demand-side problems. As one person who wrote the committee noted:

we need a much closer working relationship between researchers and practitioners. As researchers become more involved in the issues of practice and the problems of change, they develop more valid information for program improvement; as educational professionals engage in the community of inquiry, they become better prepared to design the schools and educational programs of the future.

On the supply side, several aspects of education R&D and dissemination activities have made them difficult to use or otherwise unattractive to teachers and administrators. Research reports are difficult to read and interpret, many innovative programs have been either ambiguous or overly rigid, and many allegedly effective programs have had only modest effects.

Original research reports are unlikely to be of much use to teachers. There often are many studies on a given issue, and teachers do not have time to locate and read them (Cox et al., 1985; Rackliffe, 1988; Sawyer, 1987). The reports are usually highly technical and difficult for non-researchers to read (Billups and Rauth, 1987; Rackliffe, 1988). The research often seems out of touch with the reality of schools according to many teachers and administrators who met with the committee. Some studies frequently appear to contradict other studies, and it can be a complex intellectual task to interpret the entire body of research on a topic (Glass, 1976, Hunter and Schmidt, 1990; Light and Pillemer, 1984). A researcher who works closely with practitioners claimed to the committee:

> While the quality and salience of educational research to practice has improved greatly in the last few years, much of it remains irrelevant to anything other than the advancement of the researcher.

Many of the innovations presented to teachers and administrators have been "fuzzy," lacking in a clear rationale, without specific procedures, and without convincing evidence as to their effectiveness. Others have been so specific—in an attempt to be "teacher proof"—that they have demeaned the teachers and undermined their talents and skills. Help in adopting an innovation has usually involved printed materials and 2-3 days of training, with little or no follow-up support after the teachers return to their classrooms. Educators have found many research-based innovations to be "ivory-towerish," implausible, incompatible with their concerns, not easily adapted to their local conditions, and not well tested in the field (Louis et al., 1984).

Most of the innovations disseminated over the past two decades appear to produce only modest results, even under the best of circumstances. And there is a long history of results being less favorable once a program is disseminated beyond the initial demonstration sites (Berman and McLaughlin, 1977).

One potential path for education research to influence teaching is through the curriculum materials used in the classrooms. However, the entire Department of Education is prohibited by legislation (Public Law 96-88) from "Direction, supervision, or control over the curriculum of any educational institution." This has generally been interpreted as precluding the funding of curriculum development efforts unless specifically mandated by Congress, as was the case for a model drug prevention curriculum. As a consequence, OERI's potential impact on curriculum materials must be through utilization of the agency's R&D by commercial publishers, but OERI maintains few links with commercial publishers.

Publishers are rarely consulted when OERI is developing research agendas, and special efforts are not made to provide publishers with the results of OERI's work. One exception is OERI's reading center, which has held several meetings for commercial publishers of reading instruction materials to convey the implications of reading research findings. In the 1970s NIE had a Publishers Alert Service for several years, but dropped it because of limited impact. Publishers wanted to be involved at an earlier stage of development than most centers and laboratories preferred; they perceived the school districts to be not particularly interested in innovative approaches; and they had little interest in "thin market" materials such as those designed for high school principals or students of a specific state (BCMA Associates, 1977).

Most teachers, principals, school superintendents, school boards, and chief state school officers are members of at least one of six major professional associations. Many read their associations' publications, and some attend their annual meetings and special conferences. OERI's linkages with these key professional associations have varied over the years. There has often been an exchange of publications; OERI sometimes has displays and makes presentations at the associations' meetings; and association officials and members serve on the ERIC clearinghouse advisory committees and occasionally on other advisory committees and on proposal review panels. Associations have submitted proposals to OERI, and some have been funded. And a few of the assistant secretaries have held special meetings for association representatives, for the exchange of ideas and to keep them informed of OERI's activities.

Some observers believe that OERI could make more use of the professional associations to assess the research needs of teachers and administrators, to bring the talents of practitioners into the federally funded R&D process, and to disseminate R&D results to practitioners. Other observers are less sanguine about a role for professional associations, pointing out that two of them are unions, and the others—like most professional associations—sometimes put the interests of their members ahead of what might be best for students.

One association representative suggested to the committee: "Associations like ours can be helpful in . . . dissemination of center/lab findings to practitioners . . . since we already have networks in place." The associations could also be used in several other ways. For instance, OERI could ask to schedule sessions at the professional meetings to solicit input on research priorities from the practitioners, to cull their craft knowledge for researchers, and to introduce them to interpreting and using research.

The laboratories, which formerly focused much of their work on individual schools, have moved during the past 6 years to work more with state agencies and improvement assistance organizations. This has been partly because budget declines necessitated reducing the number of contacts, partly because of some congressional complaints that OERI was "meddling in the affairs of local schools," and partly because of a 1985 formal directive from OERI (subsequently relaxed in 1990).

Although Congress determines OERI's budgets, there has been little effort by the agency to incorporate the needs of Congress into its agenda setting. Congress's most obvious need is for timely information in relation to the reauthorization of existing education programs, but OERI has rarely proposed studies for that purpose. The 1985 and 1990 solicitations for centers and laboratories did not direct the institutions to consult with Congress or the congressional research agencies about R&D needs. The specialists in those congressional agencies who do contact the centers or laboratories for help have usually been pleased with the assistance they received. Even those, however, complained that they had no easy way of knowing what the centers and laboratories had done and were doing.

On the demand side of the research-practice linkage problem, there are several constraints. Parents often do not insist on improvements to schools, teachers have been immersed in traditional instructional approaches, schools of education seldom prepare teachers to use research to change schools, teachers work under schedules that leave little time for anything but their immediate responsibilities, and significant improvement of schools requires considerable leadership and coordination.

Recent national surveys find that about 65-69 percent of adults think public schools in the nation deserve a "C" or lower grade, but only 26-27 percent of parents think their children's public schools deserve such grades (Elam, 1990; Elam et al., 1991). That perception may blunt the pressure for substantial improvements in the nation's schools.

Unlike all other professionals, teachers are exposed to traditional methods of their craft for 12 years before they start college—all through their elementary and secondary schooling (D. Cohen, 1987). Before they begin their professional education, they have expectations about how teaching should be done, which makes it difficult for them to consider dramatically different approaches.

The first potential link between research and teaching is during this professional education, but it generally provides little explicit introduction to the contributions of research, where to find it, how to read and interpret it, and how it might be used in teaching. Most of the nation's teachers are educated in regional and state universities at which the faculty have heavy teaching loads and seldom engage in research (Goodlad, 1990; Howey and Zimpher, 1989). Schools of education generally do not strongly emphasize the integration of theory, research, and practice; nor do they focus on the knowledge and skills needed to change schools (Fullan, 1991). They prepare teachers to work in "top-down" organizations with limited opportunities for professional decision making. OERI has had few direct links with these institutions, other than mailing publications and notices to them and using their faculty occasionally when planning research or reviewing proposals. A few OERI-funded centers, however, have established closer relations with the schools of education.

Teachers' work in schools usually involves nonstop instructional schedules throughout the day, with course planning and paper grading carried out after school hours. Teachers spend most of their day isolated from other adults and sources of professional support (Goodlad, 1984; Huberman, 1984; Lortie, 1975). They have very little time and assistance in reflecting on their practice, seeking research-based knowledge, examining new options, and preparing to try them out. A researcher who has worked extensively with schools wrote to the committee:

> Teachers are socialized into a subculture where publicly expressed questions, the essence of research, are seen as threats to authority or signs of weakness. . . to create a demand, a market for research information . . . requires the creation of a culture in the schools that values scholarship.

Most of teachers' work is "on the fly." It is under conditions of uncertainty, enveloped in the press of classroom events, and subject to innumerable contingencies (Brophy and Good, 1974; Jackson, 1968). When teachers are given new curriculum materials, they adapt them rather than adopt them (Berman and McLaughlin, 1975, 1977; Cohen and Ball, 1990; Porter and Brophy, 1988). Teachers need to exercise good judgment and be expert problem solvers, but they receive little preparation for either (Darling-Hammond et al., 1983; Griffin and Barnes, 1986; Hopkins, 1990; Schon, 1983). One writer to the committee noted:

> The universities formulate the constructs of the research agenda and expect schools to carry them out. This has never worked, never will. The constructs have no bearing on the realities of the classroom.

This is an overstatement, but it accurately reflects the views of many practitioners.

Good teaching is a complex activity that does not lend itself to compulsory or mechanical adoption of innovations. New curricula, teaching approaches, and technology can be valuable, but only in the hands of enthusiastic and committed teachers. "Significant educational change consists of changes in beliefs, teaching style, and materials, which can come about only through a process of personal development in a social context (Fullan, 1991)." Collegiality among teachers and direct involvement in improvement efforts are important to successful change (Fullan, 1991).

The implementation of a single innovation seldom substantially improves schooling. Effective reform of schools requires coordinated changes across subject matter, grades, and management practices. Any one teacher's efforts will be of limited significance unless supported widely by the other teachers and the administrators. That needed support is far from assured. Teachers, like others, hold diverse values and beliefs about education. There are few incentives and rewards for outstanding performance in most school systems. And accurately assessing that performance is very difficult (Murnane and Cohen, 1986), because the ultimate goals of education—preparation for the workplace, good citizenship, and personal fulfillment—are multidimensional, diffuse, and long term.

These supply-side and demand-side barriers to linking research and practice create a difficult challenge that could not previously have been comprehensively addressed by OERI or NIE. An understanding of the challenge has evolved only during the past decade (McLaughlin, 1990; Turnbull, 1991). And OERI has never had the funding necessary for confronting it.

5

Recommendations

We have briefly reviewed the need for education reform and the difficulties in achieving it (Chapter 1). We have discussed the various roles of education research and some of its contributions (Chapter 2). We have examined in detail the structure, programs, operations, and funding of the Office of Educational Research and Improvement (OERI) (Chapter 3). Finally, we presented our appraisal of the agency and the environment in which it operates (Chapter 4). In this chapter we first summarize our conclusions and then present our detailed recommendations for OERI.

Education research has been used and useful in far more ways than is commonly thought. Research has contributed new perspectives and conceptualizations of learning, teaching, and schools. It has guided the development of innovative curricula, teaching strategies, special programs, and technologies. Evaluations have assessed the consequences of programs, practices, and policies. And statistics have monitored the status of the nation's schools and warned of impending problems.

Despite the contributions of education research, education reform is difficult to accomplish successfully. Authentic and sustained reform requires the confluence of many elements—appropriate school organization, improved curricula and pedagogy, more public understanding and community support, better teacher education, supportive policies, and the mobilization of adequate resources. In addition, the contributions of research to practice often have not been direct and predictable; rather they have slowly percolated through established policies and practices. Numerous supply-side and demand-side problems impair the linkages between the research and practice.

In answer to the question—How can the Office of Educational Research and Improvement better contribute to the improvement of schools?—the committee has reached a two-part answer: by strengthening the agency's ability to support and achieve benefits from traditional approaches to R&D and by expanding the agency's functions to encourage establishment of learning communities—collaborative relationships between teachers, administrators, and researchers in the pursuit of new understandings and practices that will improve education. The traditional approaches and this new one should not be pursued separately. The fostering of learning communities will need the insights and innovations of the traditional approaches. In turn, the traditional approaches will function better if informed by the needs, craft knowledge, and inquiries of teachers and administrators.

OERI can foster learning communities through support for research, development, demonstrations, and evaluations aimed at encouraging the needed collaborations; through obtaining diverse input into the planning of research and development; and through wide dissemination of its work. However, OERI cannot singlehandedly encourage learning communities. Leadership and support must also come from those who educate teachers, administrators, and researchers; from those who hire them, manage their work environment, and structure the incentives and rewards for outstanding performance; and from national, state, and local policy makers who establish the broad parameters that affect both.

The mission of OERI is inherently difficult, and the committee does not expect that to change. The disagreements and conflicts over education are endless. Probing the mysteries of human learning is not easy. Linking research with practice remains a challenge. And improving schools is always difficult.

But OERI is also faced with many problems that are not inherent in its mission or responsibilities. If these problems are eliminated or reduced, the agency could be more effective. Frequent changes in leadership have caused organizational instability, false starts, abandoned efforts, and unfulfilled agendas. Having the head of any research agency serve at the will of a high political appointee creates the appearance, if not the reality, of politicization. So does requiring a research agency to submit its reports for clearance by a politically controlled public affairs office. Congressional actions have also weakened OERI. In addition to substantial budget cuts through most of the 1980s, set-asides in the appropriations have almost eliminated field-initiated research, and mandated studies have occasionally been politically skewed.

Fragmentation within OERI, and between it and other federal agencies, has resulted in agenda setting with little benefit from what the others have learned and accomplished. The paucity of sustained research has often limited the advance of understanding. The paucity of sustained development efforts has resulted in many innovations that are less effective and more expensive than necessary. Inadequate mechanisms for quality control and accumulation of results have forced practitioners and policy makers to wade through large literatures with little guidance as to what is valid, important, and widely applicable. Weak links with teachers, administrators, and policy makers have often limited researchers' knowledge about the realities of schools and public policy making and denied practitioners the benefits of R&D. Inadequate funding has contributed to most of these problems and undermined OERI's capacity to deal effectively with them.

Along with these conclusions, four caveats should be kept in mind when considering our recommendations. First, much that needs to be done about U.S. education is beyond the responsibilities and authority of OERI. OERI's mission is to expand understanding and assist in the improvement of education. It has no authority over teacher education institutions, state education agencies, school boards, district administrators, principals, teachers, or parents. The agency also is tightly constrained in the extent to which it can promote or induce change. The role of OERI (and its predecessor, the National Institute of Education [NIE]) has always been limited to generating new knowledge, developing new techniques and approaches, disseminating information about both, and assisting interested parties to apply the education research and development.

Second, no two or three of the committee's recommendations, by themselves, are likely to make a big difference. The committee has not found an isolated fatal flaw in OERI. Rather, it has found an agency with a very difficult role, severely constrained resources, and a number of organizational and functional weaknesses. OERI needs to be rebuilt, not merely repaired.

Third, even if OERI is rebuilt, it cannot fulfill the unreasonable expectations that have often been placed on education R&D. OERI cannot provide quick answers to long-standing and complex questions. It generally cannot find simple, universal solutions for problems embedded in diverse causes. And it cannot, alone, reform education in the United States. What OERI will be able to do is respond more fully to needs for education R&D, support the sustained work that is necessary for scientific and technological advances, improve quality control, and better assist teachers and administrators in a quest for improved education.

Fourth, unless there is a substantial increase in OERI's budget, no amount of leadership and organizational change can accomplish what needs to be done. Our recommendations would require a large increase in the agency's budget. If such an increase is not provided, the agency's mission and responsibilities should be dramatically narrowed.

Our recommendations are organized into four groups and numbered accordingly: (A) mission, governance, and agenda; (B) organization and functions; (C) operations; and (D) funding. The committee has made rough estimates of the additional resources needed for most of the recommendations. These estimates are based on the committee's judgments about the intensity of effort that is desirable and its knowledge of the staffing levels used in other federal research agencies to conduct similar activities. Unless otherwise indicated, all estimates are for permanent staff and for annual program expenditures in 1991 constant dollars. The committee has not estimated the increases that will be needed for support services personnel or for the staff and expenses budget, though increases will obviously be needed for both.

MISSION, GOVERNANCE, AND AGENDA

The legislative authorization for OERI directs the agency to "provide leadership in the conduct and support of scientific inquiry into the educational process." That mission is accompanied by a substantial list of specific responsibilities. The authorization also outlines the composition and duties of OERI's 15-member advisory council and prescribes a mechanism for generating and publishing priorities for research.

Our first seven recommendations apply to OERI's mission statement, leadership structure, and mechanisms for setting research priorities. They simplify the mission statement, replace the advisory council with a more representative policy-making board, establish a new mechanism for setting priorities,specify the board's responsibilities for monitoring and reporting on the federal system for education R&D, and provide for a balance in various forms of needed research and development.

A-1 The mission of OERI should be to provide leadership in:
  • **expanding fundamental knowledge and understanding of education;**
  • **promoting excellence and equity in education; and**
  • **monitoring the state of education.**
  The mission should be accomplished in collaboration with researchers, teachers, school administrators, parents, students, employers, and policy makers.

OERI's current mission statement includes a long list of responsibilities for the agency, which drives the agency to try to be everything to everybody. As a result, OERI has spread its resources so thin that there is little chance of fulfilling any of the responsibilities well. The recommended mission statement does not preclude any of the agency's current responsibilities, but it does direct the agency to focus more narrowly if its budget is not sufficient for credible work in all areas or if the subsequently discussed governance and agenda-setting processes suggest doing so.

We have added to the mission statement a reference to expanding fundamental knowledge and understanding in education. Basic research is critical to progress in research (see Chapter 2), and OERI has a long history of giving it short shrift. The Office of Education, in the late 1960s, and NIE, in the early 1970s, provided substantial support for basic research, but OERI has provided very little funding for it: $1.9 million in 1989 (the last years for which data are available), or 5.5 percent of OERI's R&D budget, a far smaller percentage for basic research than prevails in other major federal research agencies.

We have retained from the current mission statement a reference to promoting excellence and equity in education because both are in keeping with the goals of this country. We have also retained a reference to monitoring the state of education because it is essential for knowing what is actually achieved.

OERI's current mission statement does not explicitly indicate that the agency should work closely with the major groups that are importantly involved in, or affected by, education. Although OERI (and NIE) has not been oblivious to this need, at various times it has operated with less participation from some of these groups than would be optimal. Each of the groups included in our recommended mission statement has unique perspectives and expertise that are essential for reforming U.S. education: researchers apply the theories and methods of various sciences in developing new knowledge; educators and parents are the main agents of a child's education; employers are a key "consumer" of education; policy makers determine the distribution of public resources and set the broad parameters for the conduct of education; and students are both the targets of education and key actors in them.

The perspectives and expertise of all these groups needs to be infused into OERI's work. That will not be easy under any circumstances, but it is a critical challenge that must be met by the agency. Some of the committee's subsequent recommendations should help with the task.

This recommendation would not require changes in OERI's staffing or funding levels.

A-2 OERI should support a balanced portfolio of activities: basic research, applied research, statistics, development, evaluation, dissemination, and technical assistance; field-initiated and institutionally based R&D; and long-term sustained efforts and responses to newly identified needs and opportunities. To do so, OERI must substantially expand support for basic research, field-initiated research, and sustained R&D activities.

OERI supports many kinds of education R&D activities. Each makes different contributions, and a mix of them is necessary to fulfill its mandate.

Over the years, the distribution of these activities has skewed away from basic research, field-initiated research, and long-term efforts. This change has been the result of declining budgets, congressionally specified set-asides for specified activities, and decisions of OERI and NIE administrators. Although there is overlap among the three categories of basic research, field-initiated research, and long-term sustained efforts—much basic research is field-initiated, some basic research is part of long-term sustained efforts, and some field-initiated research is part of long-term sustained efforts—each needs to be recognized for its contribution.

In 1989 OERI spent only 5.5 percent of its R&D budget on basic research; in the same year, the Agriculture Research Service spent 46.6 percent of its R&D budget on basic research, NIH spent 59.8 percent, and NSF spent 93.5 percent. Basic research explores the fundamentals of the studied phenomena, generates new views of reality, and proposes new visions of the achievable.

Since 1988 only about 3 percent of OERI's R&D budget has been available for field-initiated research; in comparison, NIH uses about 56 percent and NSF about 94 percent of their budgets, respectively, for field-initiated research. This research permits scholars and others throughout the country to propose topics for research rather than only to respond to announcements prepared by the agency. It also helps train the next generation of researchers by providing assistantships for graduate students throughout the country. Field-initiated research has been a key contributor to scientific and technical advances in all fields.

OERI and NIE have often been criticized for failing to provide sustained support for R&D activities. The actual record is varied, and the criticism is only partly justified, but more sustained efforts are needed. Long-term efforts are needed for advances in basic research as well as for development of new applications. Major advances in the natural sciences and technology applications often have taken a decade or longer.

Without substantially enhanced programs of basic research, field-initiated research, and long-term sustained efforts, OERI will be a feeble partner in the nation's quest for substantial education reform. Research and development require long-term investments.

The staff and budget implications of this recommendation are discussed under Recommendations B-2 and B-3.

A-3 OERI should have a director appointed by the President, in consultation with the agency's board and with the advice and consent of the Senate, for a 6-year renewable term.

Nominees for the directorship should be distinguished researchers, proven managers, and persons with substantial knowledge of U.S. education. The director would be responsible for implementing the agenda developed by a policy- making board specified in Recommendation A-4. Under the delegated authority of the secretary, the appointee would also guide and manage all the agency's activities.

NIE had six Senate-confirmed directors over a 13-year period, and since it was dissolved into OERI in 1985 there have been three confirmed assistant secretaries of the latter agency. During the same 19-year period, there have been six directors of NSF, five at the National Institutes of Health (NIH), and three at the Agriculture Research Service. The rapid turnover at OERI has been dysfunctional to an agency that needs sustained leadership in planning for, investing in, and supporting the long-term efforts that are required for major scientific and technological advances.

There are several precedents for 4- or 6-year terms of office in federal research agencies, though none of them is perfectly analogous to OERI's situation (see Chapter 4, "Governance"). These arrangements have been used to assure sustained professional management and to minimize the opportunities for politicization. They cannot assure either—appointees are still free to quit and both the President and Congress retain discretion over agency budgets. In addition, there are some potential problems with terms of office for the top administrator. They make the administrator less accountable to the executive branch, and an incompetent could linger for years unless there is a precaution against this, such as specifying removal by the President with the consent of the Senate. Nevertheless, we have specified the longest term of office that can reasonably be supported by precedent. We think the potential benefits outweigh the potential risks. Four-year terms are more common and provide each President with an appointment opportunity. When they have been used there often is a tradition of reappointments. Given OERI's history, we fear that there would be few reappointments and 4 years is a short period in the management of R&D.

It should be noted that a fixed term of office does not give the director unlimited discretionary powers. On the contrary, he or she would still be subject to many of the normal management processes and to the full budgetary process that involves the Secretary of Education, the Office of Management and Budget, the Executive Office, and Congress.

This recommendation would not require additional staffing or funding for OERI.

A-4 OERI's agenda setting should be guided by a 24-member policy-making board. At least one-third of the membership should be distinguished researchers who have done work on education issues, complemented by a balanced representation of practitioners, parents, employers, policy makers, and others who have made noteworthy contributions to excellence in education.

OERI currently has a National Advisory Council on Educational Research and Improvement. It is composed of 15 members serving 3-year terms, appointed by the President with the advice and consent of the Senate. Congressional legislation requires the council to be "broadly representative" of several groups. For at least the past 3 years, however, the council has apparently had no active education researchers or other social scientists among its members. The council is also widely considered to have little influence.

NIE had a policy board. Under both Republican and Democratic administrations in the 1970s, it was widely considered competent and hardworking, but was unable to help NIE gain the support of educators, the public, or Congress. In the early 1980s the board was considered less distinguished, more politicized, and less effective.

Three options for OERI's future have been analyzed (see Chapter 4, "Governance"). There are potential advantages and disadvantages to policy-making boards, advisory councils, and administration of the agency without either. With OERI's history of controversy, constant charges of politicization, and fragmentation, bringing focus and stability to the agency is a bigger job than any one person is likely to manage. We have chosen a policy-making board because persons of accomplishment are more likely to agree to serve on such a board and because a policy-making board is likely to be more influential. Our analysis indicates, however, that policy boards for federal agencies have little unilateral power—they must win the respect and support of the President and Congress.

The board we propose would differ significantly from the boards of NIE. It would be larger and more diverse, helping to ensure that its members understand the views of the major groups concerned with education. It would be limited to people who have already proven their ability to make important contributions to research on education or to excellence in education, thus ensuring competence and some common understandings during its deliberations. In addition, as indicated in the next recommendation, the board would not set OERI's agenda on the basis of its member's own predilections, but rather would distill priorities from the needs and capabilities of the country after wide consultation with those concerned about education.

The board we propose is modeled closely on the National Science Board of the National Science Foundation. Most observers believe that this board has served its agency well. But there are no assurances that the same structure will work effectively for OERI: the National Science Board has the advantage of making decisions about astronomy, geodesy, and computer engineering, topics about which only a small number of people have any knowledge; OERI's board would be making decisions related to education, a topic with which almost everyone has prolonged experience and strong opinions. Though there are reasons to be uncertain about the efficacy of the proposed board, the committee thinks it is the best option available for stabilizing and guiding OERI. Its task will not be easy, and its success is not guaranteed, but the alternatives are less promising.

The board members should be appointed by the President, with the advice and counsel of the board, for 6-year staggered terms. For initial appointments to the board, the President should seek advice from professional organizations of those who are involved with education and research on educational issues. The board should be led by a chair, elected by the board members from among their own ranks, for a 2-year renewable term. The OERI board should monitor the health, needs, and accomplishments of OERI's R&D and all federally sponsored education R&D; report periodically to the President and Congress about both; and guide the agenda setting of the agency.

This recommendation will not require additional staff or funding.

A-5 The OERI board should establish a process to develop priorities for OERI's agenda. The process should involve active participation of the various groups concerned with education. These priorities should be set so as to maintain the continuity, stability, and flexibility needed to conduct high quality research and to effect educational change.

The current authorization for OERI requires the Secretary of Education to publish proposed research priorities in the *Federal Register* every 2 years, allowing 60 days for public comment. This process results in the establishment of a new set of priorities every 2 years, which can interfere with the continuity and stability needed for many education R&D activities.

The committee proposes long-term plans, with a limited biennial update. Development of 5-, 10-, and 15-year national research plans have been standard practice at NIH for many years. It would be desirable that the agenda-setting process begin after the director has served for about 1 year— assuring his or her familiarity with the realities of the agency.

OERI's agenda for education R&D must reflect the priority needs of researchers, teachers, administrators, parents, students, employers, and policy makers. Publication in the *Federal Register* is far from sufficient outreach to these groups. OERI did hold some meetings before competing the laboratories and centers in 1985 and 1990, but several of its other programs have not had the benefit of such outreach.

The agenda-setting process must also reflect the capabilities of the education R&D enterprise. Unrealistic objectives of quick fixes to complex problems or universal solutions to problems with multiple causes serve only to disappoint researchers and potential users of their work. Without the integration of needs and capabilities, the productivity, effectiveness, and applicability of the education R&D will suffer.

The board should not impose its own priorities, but rather it should design, oversee, and participate in a process that distills priorities from the needs and capabilities of the country. Preparing priorities that fairly reflect diverse views of all the groups concerned with education will not be easy. Education has been the subject of fierce loyalties and long-standing conflicts. Facts and values frequently clash; needs and capabilities seldom coincide. The priority-setting process will be messy and at times confusing, but only through such a process can there be an agenda that truly reflects the country's needs.

In the context of the previous and following recommendations, this one would require OERI to have about three additional staff persons and $100,000 annually to support the board's priority-setting process.

A-6 The OERI board should publish a biennial report on federally funded education R&D that describes its accomplishments, summarizes the programmatic activities and funding levels throughout the federal government, identifies unmet needs, and makes recommendations for future directions.

For most of the history of OERI and NIE, the board's (or council's) report has not portrayed the extent and nature of federal involvement in education R&D nor reflected on the progress and contributions of research and development to the improvement of education. This has limited its ability to identify needs, chart a course for OERI in light of what other agencies are doing, and illustrate the utility of proposed work. This lack has also deprived the agency of institutional memory, hindered researchers' and practitioner's efforts to build on what has been learned by past efforts, and denied policy makers information on the extent of progress.

OERI and other federal agencies involved in education R&D have done a poor job of describing the contributions of their work (see Chapter 4). There is a need to synthesize—succinctly and saliently—what has been learned from education research, how it has extended prior knowledge, the implications for practice and school reform, the development and assistance activities that have used the research, and the effects of those efforts. This information is important not only for OERI, but for researchers, teachers, administrators, other agencies engaged in education R&D, the President, and Congress.

This recommendation directs OERI's policy-making board to prepare a more ambitious report than is currently the case. The resources needed for some of the data collection are discussed in Recommendation A-7. Additional resources will be needed to analyze the collected data, to assemble information on the accomplishments of federally supported education R&D, and to prepare a written report of that information. This would require about two additional staff members and about $25,000 annually.

A-7 The Office of Management and Budget (OMB), the National Science Foundation (NSF), or the Federal Coordinating Committee for Science Engineering and Technology (FCCSET) should extend data collection programs, in consultation with OERI, to provide annual data on federal agencies' program activities and expenditures for education R&D.

There has rarely been comprehensive information on the programmatic activities and funding levels of education R&D throughout the federal government. For two decades NSF has been responsible for monitoring the extent and nature of R&D in the United States: it collects and reports federal R&D expenditures by agency, fields of science and engineering, and budget functions, as well as several other categories, yet none of these data provide even a rough picture of federal support for education R&D.

In addition to the Department of Education, several other federal departments and agencies sponsor education R&D. NSF, the Department of Health and Human Services, and the Department of Defense have long-standing and substantial involvements in this work. Reasonably comprehensive and current information on federal agencies' education R&D activities is needed to identify existing priorities and unmet needs. The committee has not analyzed which agency would be best suited to collect the needed information nor what specific data should be collected. Determination of those matters should be made during consultations among OMB, NSF, FCCSET, and OERI.

This recommendation will probably require one additional staff person at OERI to coordinate preparation for the consultations and follow-up from them, for a period of 1 or 2 years. The agencies that undertake the data collection will also need some increase in staffing and budget, but if the work can be melded into another data collection effort, only a fraction of one person's time and $25,000-$50,000 for additional expenses will probably be needed.

ORGANIZATION AND FUNCTIONS

OERI currently has six offices: the Office of the Assistant Secretary; the Office of Research, which administers the 25 R&D centers, the Educational Resources Information System (ERIC) and field-initiated studies; Programs for the Improvement of Practice, which includes the ten regional laboratories, the Program Effectiveness Panel and the National Diffusion Network

(PEP/NDN); the National Center for Education Statistics (NCES); Fund for the Improvement and Reform of Schools and Teaching (FIRST); and Library Programs.

The committee recommends several changes in the organization and functioning of OERI to address major deficiencies in the current organizational structure and provide a mechanism for improved integration of research, development, demonstration, dissemination, and school assistance activities.

The reorganization would result in seven to nine major units: an Office of the Director, three to five R&D directorates, NCES, Library Programs, and a Reform Assistance Directorate (see Figure 5-1). Each R&D directorate would include a program of field-initiated research and institutional mechanisms for sustained and integrated programs of basic research, applied research, and development. The Reform Assistance Directorate would be responsible for supporting reform efforts at the state and local level. This unit would include regional Reform Assistance Laboratories, an expanded PEP/NDN, a modified FIRST Program, and a national electronic network system that would incorporate the current ERIC system. It would also support schools of education, state departments of education, and local districts in efforts to make teachers and principals full partners in the quest for school reform. The ten recommendations in this section detail our proposed organizational structure and many changes in the operations and functions of OERI.

B-1 OERI's research and development activities should be organized under several R&D directorates. Direct support for school change should be organized under a single Reform Assistance Directorate. Organization and management practices should forge appropriate linkages and coordination among the all the directorates and the field.

This recommendation is directed at improving three key deficiencies of OERI: fragmentation of its activities; little collaboration between researchers, teachers, and administrators; and the lack of integrated assistance for school reform.

Over time, OERI and NIE have been organized both programmatically (with R&D units for basic skills, equal educational opportunity, and career education) and functionally (such as by research, development, and dissemination). OERI currently is organized partly in each of those ways, with an Office of Research, NCES, Programs for the Improvement of Practice, FIRST, and Library Programs. Some scholars have concluded that prior reorganizations of OERI and NIE had little effect. The committee does not disagree with those conclusions, but believes that the rapidly changing leadership and dwindling resources that accompanied prior reorganizations foredoomed them to failure.

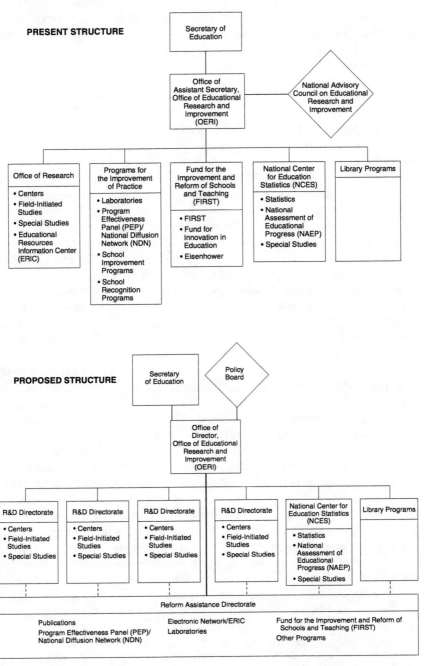

FIGURE 5-1 Present and proposed organization, Office of Educational Research and Improvement.

Under the proposed reorganization, much of OERI's research and a substantial portion of its development activities would be organized within three, four, or five R&D directorates. Each directorate would coordinate R&D centers, field-initiated research programs, special studies, and linkages with the Reform Assistance Division.

The committee is not prepared to specify what the foci of the directorates should be, other than they should be enduring and important problem areas, as determined by our recommended agenda-setting process. One possible organizational arrangement might include four R&D directorates: the social context of education; preparation for schooling; organization and administration of schools; and teaching, learning, and assessment. Another possibility would be to focus the directorates on various subject areas: reading and writing; mathematics and science; and social studies, humanities, and the arts. A third possibility might be three directorates, on preparation for schooling, inner-city schools, and rural schools.

The primary responsibilities of the Reform Assistance Directorate (RAD) would be to provide reform assistance to parents, schools, districts, states, Congress, professional education associations, teacher development institutions, commercial publishers, and employers. It would do so through a broad range of dissemination, liaison, technical assistance, and support activities. This unit would administer OERI's publication activities, the regional laboratories, PEP/NDN, FIRST, and ERIC, with important modifications to all but the first. The regional laboratories would become Reform Assistance Laboratories (see Recommendation B-4); PEP/NDN would be expanded (see Recommendation B-5); the FIRST programs would be altered (see Recommendation B-6); and ERIC would be incorporated in a national electronic information system (see Recommendation B-7).

The RAD would also establish outreach, liaison, and collaboration with parents, professional development institutions, professional education associations, commercial publishers, employers, and policy makers. Each group has important roles to play in the reform of education in the United States. OERI should have at least one professional staff member assigned primarily to each group. Those people would be responsible for bringing the relevant needs and contributions of these groups to the attention of appropriate persons and units in OERI, as well as bringing to the attention of these groups the various resources and contributions of OERI.

NCES would remain a separate unit, operating much as it does currently. There would, however be corrections to the severe staffing shortage (see Recommendation B-8).

Better linkages are needed among all the directorates and NCES than has previously been the case among the offices in OERI (and NIE). Likewise, measures should be taken to improve linkages between OERI and the institutions it funds and among those institutions. This is an important administrative challenge that must be met by the agency.

The committee believes that this and following organizational recommendations will better coordinate disparate research activities, better focus the efforts on solving major education problems, better apply the expertise of researchers, teachers and administrators to these problems, and improve the technical assistance offered in support of education reform. The goal is to build an R&D system based on a new conceptualization of the relationship between research and practice, so that practice seeks the wisdom of research, and research effectively contributes to practice.

As with any organizational structure, this one has potential disadvantages. One is that evolving problems that do not fit into the established R&D directorates may go unaddressed. A second is that the Reform Assistance Directorate will have to serve, in effect, many masters, which is never easy.

Most aspects of this recommendation are elaborated in subsequent recommendations, and the consequences for OERI's staff and budget are discussed there. Approximately nine additional staff (including clerical help) would be needed in order to assign one staff member for liaison with each of the following group: parents, teacher development institutions, professional associations of educators, commercial publishers, employers, and policy makers.

The agency probably would benefit from the services of an organizational consultant when planning and executing the reorganization. We have not estimated that one-time cost.

B-2 Each of OERI's R&D directorates should allocate substantial resources to support field-initiated research for both basic and applied work.

OERI invests much less of its R&D budget in field-initiated research than other federal agencies with major research responsibilities. It funded only 12 new field-initiated proposals in each of the last 2 years. The lack of support for field-initiated research deprives the field of the ideas and efforts of many of the best and brightest researchers throughout the country. Those who are not on the winning team for a center have little opportunity for research support from OERI.

Each R&D directorate should operate a substantial program of field-initiated research that is consistent with its focus and coordinated with its other R&D activities. The program would support both basic and applied research, emphasizing sustained efforts. Embedding the field-initiated research in the directorates should focus the work on national priorities, help accumulate findings across studies, and bring findings to bear on practice.

The committee suggests that about 250 new field-initiated studies be funded by OERI each year. They should generally be supported for 3 years, at an average of about $200,000 per year, with opportunities for renewal when further meritorious work is likely. The committee believes OERI would have no problem attracting several hundred promising proposals if it makes substantial funding available for multiyear periods and if it actively solicits proposals from scholars in all relevant disciplines.

This recommendation would require about 22 additional staff members to administer the expanded field-initiated research programs. Since OERI currently has only $1.3 million for field-initiated research, an additional $148.7 million would be required annually, after a 3-year phase-in period.

B-3 Each R&D directorate should support national R&D centers for pursuing coherent and sustained programs of basic research, applied research, and development.

The centers were created to assemble a critical mass of multidisciplinary investigators to engage in large-scale, long-term, cumulative efforts to improve education. The centers have always varied in the activities undertaken. Some have conducted considerable basic research; others have focused on applied research. Some have done development work; others have not. A few have carried their development work into demonstration and evaluation phases; most have not. Over the past decade, as support for the centers has declined dramatically, their activities have shifted primarily to small-scale 2-4 year studies on related topics. The centers' past history has produced some major contributions, and it is important to build on those successes.

The committee recommends several changes to expand their contributions in the future. First, the centers should undertake considerable more basic research than they currently do. Second, the centers should engage in more sustained efforts of applied research, development, and demonstration, aimed at nurturing new methods, approaches, and tools to full maturity. Such efforts require long-term institutional support. Third, innovative methods, programs, and processes developed by the centers should be subject to a quality assurance process before wide-scale distribution. One possible mechanism is provided through the Program Evaluation Panel (see below). In the past the centers and laboratories have been allowed to engage in widespread dissemination of their innovations without any outside assessment of their merit. The Reform Assistance Directorate would be responsible for nationwide dissemination of the centers' completed innovative developments, to help ensure that dissemination of the innovations is coordinated with other reform assistance efforts.

Most of the centers now receive less than $1 million in annual support from OERI. The committee cannot imagine a robust R&D center operating at much less than \$3 million annually in core funding. Without that level of support, there will not be the critical mass, diversity of expertise, and scale of operation that are needed to tackle the difficult research problems and development efforts that confront the nation's schools. Some of the proposed R&D directorates in OERI might have only one large center. Others would have several. A center might engage in both research and development or might focus exclusively on one or the other.

The committee is concerned about the current practice of the centers' having to compete every 5 years, regardless of the importance and quality of their work. In several respects the competitions have been a success, but the 5-year cycles are inconsistent with the need for the repeated iterations of research, development, demonstration, and evaluation, which often require a decade or more.

The centers generally did not compete until the 1980s, and there is ample precedent in other federal agencies for negotiated renewals. One option would be to have competitions only every 10 or 15 years. During the interim period, accountability would be achieved by continuous monitoring and feedback, by periodic formal evaluations, and by basing a portion of the federal contribution at each 5-year renewal on the evaluations. A panel of researchers, developers, teachers, and administrators could be assembled in the fourth year to review internal and external evaluations of all the centers and judge their performance. OERI would adjust its contribution to each in response to the judgments; termination would be used only in cases of inadequate performance.

This recommendation would require an increase in the budget of OERI, but no increase in staffing. Assuming OERI has four R&D directorates, each with one to five centers and average funding levels of \$4 million per center, the annual cost would be at least \$48 million, or \$26.4 million more than current funding for centers. (The fiscal year 1991 appropriation provides \$20.6 million for centers, and an additional \$1.0 million of other money is used to fund one center.)

B-4 OERI's regionally governed laboratories should be administered by the Reform Assistance Directorate and converted to Reform Assistance Laboratories (RALs) with liaison and assistance staff assigned to each state in their respective regions.

Like the centers, the laboratories have varied in the activities they have undertaken. A few laboratories have conducted substantial applied research, but most have performed only a limited amount. Some have engaged in ambitious and sustained development efforts, while others have not, and only a few have vigorously conducted evaluations.

Research on change processes and experience with those processes repeatedly has shown that personal contacts are important in facilitating complex change. School reform is seldom achieved merely by the adoption of a new curriculum or teaching approach; rather, it involves a process of organizational development, including needs assessment, goal setting, the adoption of an integrated set of changes, continuous monitoring, and subsequent adaptation.

The laboratories are in a good position, with some modifications, to facilitate school reform. Laboratories have established contacts with most state education agencies, they are well known and respected by many of the school districts in their regions, and most have considerable experience in providing technical assistance. Although much assistance has been provided through the adoption of a discrete curriculum or approach, laboratories have increasingly assisted schools in achieving broad-based changes.

In fostering reforms, the RALs should also strive to help state education agencies, intermediate education agencies, school districts and schools to become learning communities, with the desire and skills needed to incorporate research findings and practitioner wisdom into improvements. Whatever the success in meeting today's reform needs, new challenges will always arise in the future.

The committee foresees at least five modes of operation by which the RALs would foster education reform and the creation of self-sustained learning communities. First, RALs would conduct a wide range of activities: applied research, development, demonstrations, evaluations, dissemination, state policy assistance, and technical assistance for the purposes of facilitating school reform. As with the centers, the RALs' innovative methods, programs, and processes should be subject to a quality assurance review—such as those conducted by the Program Evaluation Panel—before wide-scale distribution. Second, the RALs would assign a few liaison and assistance staff to each state in their respective regions. These staff would apprise state and intermediate service agency officials of the resources available through all of OERI, inform the RALs of the states' needs and interests, and provide some direct services with the support of the full RAL staff. Third, the RALs would scout for exemplary practices developed in the field by teachers and administrators and help them in further refinements, evaluations, and preparation of applications for PEP certification. Fourth, the RALs would provide short- and intermediate-term technical assistance to districts and schools through various of means, including personal visits by RAL staff, training of trainers, telephone assistance, and mailed materials. In this mode they would subsume the responsibilities of the NDN state facilitators. Fifth, the RALs would conduct long-term assistance at a few sites, with a RAL staff member, backed by the full RAL, spending 1 year or more providing intensive technical assistance.

The committee believes that direct services by RALS to the states, intermediate service agencies, and local school districts should be partially reimbursed, on a sliding scale (adjusted for the ability to pay). Partial reimbursement signifies a partnership between the federal government, the states, and the local districts that is important for the RALs' success. It will help to remind the RAL staff that they must address both local and regional concerns, allow the RALs to provide more services than otherwise possible, and help ensure that the recipients of RAL services make good use of them. The extent of cost sharing might be phased in, starting at a relatively low percentage while the RALs establish a track record that builds up demand for their services.

The committee questions the advisability of competitions for RALs. The laboratories competed in 1985 and 1990, and only one of the 19 incumbents was unseated in those two rounds of competitive bidding. (In 1985 OERI awarded planning grants to 21 institutions to encourage new bidders; no incumbent was unseated.) The competitions require considerable time from both the OERI staff and the laboratory personnel. Competition for the renewals of the laboratory contracts was a reasonable idea, but it resulted in only one new provider and it is not clear that it improved the performance of the incumbents.

An alternative way to try to ensure accountability from RALs would be for OERI to monitor them regularly and provide feedback, periodically evaluate them formally with expert consultants, and base a portion of the federal contribution to each RAL on these reviews. Assuming the RALs operate with 5-year contracts, a panel of researchers, developers, teachers, and administrators could be assembled in the fourth year to review internal and external evaluations of all RALs and judge their performance. OERI would adjust its contribution to each RAL in response to the judgments; termination would be used for significant noncompliance with the contractual terms.

This recommendation would require additions to OERI's staffing and budget. OERI currently assigns a staff member to monitor each laboratory. The monitors devote only about 50 percent of their time to these responsibilities. With state liaison and assistance responsibilities added to the RALS, the monitoring duties would expand, requiring almost full-time effort; this would require about seven additional staff (including clerical support).

The needed increase in budget depends on the number of state liaison and assistance staff and the extent of cost sharing with the state. Assuming one to four RAL staff are assigned to each state, depending on its geographic size and population, and assuming that the states would pay one-third of staff salaries for the first 5 years, the extra salaries and benefits would cost OERI approximately $5 million. If the states provided the office space and basic support services, the cost to OERI for the travel, communications, and other direct expenses would be about $4.5 million. The core functions of the RALs would probably cost about the same as the laboratories' current activities, and a modest expansion would be possible from the cost-sharing provisions.

B-5 The Reform Assistance Directorate should support the research-based refinement and rigorous evaluation of innovative programs and processes that have the greatest potential for use in school reform and help schools in using these programs and processes. This recommendation represents an expansion of the functions currently carried out by the Program Effectiveness Panel (PEP) and the National Diffusion Network (NDN).

PEP certifies the effectiveness of innovative programs and processes. NDN provides the developers of certified programs and processes with grants for dissemination activities and funds state facilitators to assist local schools in choosing and adopting these innovations. PEP and NDN have provided useful services, but those services have been limited (see Chapter 3). PEP's certifications standards are flawed, and NDN does not support refinements and evaluations of promising programs and processes. In addition, NDN has focused on facilitating the adoption of innovations, but the reform of schools requires far more.

The initial PEP certification process has been criticized by some as being too lenient and by others as being too rigid. Innovations that gain initial certification have often been field tested in only a few sites, assessed on only a few outcomes, and judged with no follow-up after termination of the "treatment." PEP makes little effort to assess possible disadvantages of innovations, and lower standards are used for recertification 6 years later. Yet developers find the process expensive, difficult, and time consuming.

The committee concludes that the PEP standards are reasonable for identifying an innovation as "promising," with the exception of their current failure to require reporting of identified program weaknesses. But for recertification, the standards should be more stringent. The evaluation should include a sample of dissemination sites to document broad generality of the innovation. It should require follow-up assessment of effects at least 2 years after completion of the "treatment," to ensure that the effects are not fleeting. And it should be conducted or monitored by PEP, or another competent body that is independent of the developers, to further assure high quality evaluation.

Such evaluations will be expensive and are not likely to be undertaken without new sources of funding. Schools that adopt innovations are often uninterested in externally managed assessments, identifying appropriate control groups can be difficult, and following a mobile student population for several years is never easy. But without high-quality and credible evaluations, school districts will never be able to choose wisely among available innovations.

Many NDN innovations have been the subject of a limited development process and rushed into dissemination. This is understandable because of the widespread lack of sustained support for education R&D activities, but it is dysfunctional. Given what is well known about the commercialization of technology, many of these programs could benefit from further cycles of research, development, testing, and refinement, aimed at maximizing their impact, expanding their effectiveness in a wide range of settings, improving their potential for dissemination and adoption, and minimizing their costs.

To meet the needs for further R&D and rigorous evaluation of promising innovations, every year NDN would identify five or ten NDN innovations that seem to have the most promise of improving education in the United States. Each would be funded for long-term additional research and development and for evaluation in accordance with the standards proposed above for PEP recertification.

An important part of NDN is the provision of funding to the developers of innovations so that they can disseminate the programs and provide training to adopting schools. These grants now average about $75,000 per year, for a 4-year period, with a good chance of renewal for another 4-year period. This level of funding is substantially less than is needed to make new programs widely known across the country and to support their adoption. In addition, because the original PEP certification is good for 6 years, decisions about NDN renewal are made before recertification, which deprives NDN of a reassessment of the merit of the program or process before making those decisions. The committee concludes that the average dissemination grants should be twice the current annual level and awarded for 5-year periods and that recertification should be required before awarding renewal grants for another 3-year period.

New curricula, teaching approaches, and technology can be important for school reform, but they are seldom sufficient by themselves. Effective reform requires coordinated changes across subject areas and grade levels and in the organization, management, and operations of schools. A few of the innovative processes disseminated by NDN are aimed at facilitating such changes, but most of the disseminated innovations have a much narrower focus. As a consequence, the committee suggests above that the duties of the NDN state facilitators be assumed by the state liaison and assistance staff of the Reform Assistance Laboratories. Because the NDN state facilitators have already generally forged good linkages with schools throughout the state, the RALs might well want to incorporate these people into their new state staffs.

This recommendation will require an increase in the NDN budget and staff. Assuming that seven innovations are selected each year to receive extra R&D and evaluation assistance and that the support is for 5-year periods with an average of $200,000 per year, after 5 years of phasing in the annual cost would be $7.0 million. Doubling the dissemination grants to developers would require an additional $7 million annually and should be implemented immediately. Elimination of the NDN state facilitators would yield annual savings of $6.4 million, so the net increase would be about $7.6 million annually. Only about two additional staff persons would be needed to administer this program because the staff who currently administer the state facilitator program could be reassigned.

B-6   The Fund for the Improvement and Reform of Schools and Teaching (FIRST) programs that support local school-based reforms should be administered by the Reform Assistance Directorate, should be modified to require utilization of research in development of the improvements, should involve teachers and principals in the development process, and should provide sustained support for these efforts.

The FIRST office manages a number of individually authorized programs designed to support local school-based reforms that are expected to have national significance (see Chapter 3). The committee finds the goals of these programs commendable, but the means used to achieve them inadequate. FIRST projects have been funded for 1- to 3-year periods and for total amounts generally between $50,000 and $150,000; "reforms of national significance" simply cannot be developed and adequately evaluated under these conditions. In addition, most of the activities supported by these programs are not education R&D. Using the NSF definitions, only $3.5 million of the $46 million budget supports research or research-based development. Neither the legislation nor the administrative guidelines specify that the proposals under these programs make use of relevant research.

The committee does not intend to imply that good reform ideas are derived only from research. We do believe, however, that the federal government should only sponsor the development of ideas that have been tested against applicable bodies of research and use the research to guide the development and refinement phases. The FIRST office's field-initiated improvement programs should exemplify collaboration between research and practice. These programs should be research based and involve teachers and principals in the development process. In turn, funding for these programs should be sustained at levels that are adequate for the tasks. The committee suggests that they be funded for 3- to 6-year periods, at levels of $100,000 to $300,000 per year.

This recommendation would not require additional expenditures because the committee proposes that the current level of funding be used to support fewer projects at higher levels of support. A reduction in staff by one or two would be possible because of the smaller number of projects, reducing monitoring responsibilities.

B-7 The Reform Assistance Directorate should foster development of a national electronic network that allows all concerned with education to access research and exemplary practice information. The system should incorporate an enhanced ERIC.

Electronic communication technologies offer new opportunities for linking research to practice that should be promoted by OERI. Many of them require only that users have access to a $800 microcomputer, with a modem and a telephone line. A national electronic network could serve at least three purposes: expand access to information and data resources, facilitate input by practitioners into the research process, and foster sharing of resources and expertise among practitioners.

Such a network would allow researchers, teachers, administrators, and parents to have access to the major resources of the federal education research enterprise. Those resources could include not only ERIC, but the electronic card catalog of the Department of Education's Research Library; information on the research, development, dissemination, and technical assistance activities of the laboratories and centers; the applications and other descriptive materials on all NDN programs; the databases of NCES; NSF's forthcoming database on its mathematics and science education projects; and similar resources of other federal agencies involved in education research and development. Computerized "expert systems" might also be developed to provide advice to researchers and practitioners on various matters.

Such a network would also facilitate practitioners' participation in the research enterprise. "E-mail," "file transfers," and "a synchronous computer conferencing" would allow geographically dispersed teachers to assist in planning studies, reviewing proposals, and discussion of preliminary results—without having to travel. Outstanding teachers and administrators are often reluctant to engage in national activities when school is in session because of the burdens caused by their absences.

Electronic networking would also allow teachers and school administrators to share ideas and feedback among themselves through "electronic bulletin boards." For instance, a bulletin board might be established for each NDN program, allowing users and potential users of the program to post queries, tips, and warnings, and to answer the posted queries.

The Reform Assistance Directorate should foster development of a national electronic network in several ways. NSF's National Research and Education Network, which currently serves universities, and commercial networks should be explored as the telecommunications backbone of the network. Resources that would be of substantial use to researchers, teachers, administrators, and parents should be identified and prepared for access through the network. Standardized information infrastructures, good documentation, and user-friendly "interfaces" should be developed so that even occasional users can have access the network and its resources. Demonstration grants should be provided to schools to purchase needed equipment, train staff in use of the network, and provide assistance to the end users. Library Programs funds should be used for demonstrations in public libraries so that the network resources will be readily available to all concerned with education.

ERIC would be one of the resources available through the network. Several modest enhancements should be made to ERIC even before the proposed network could be operational. ERIC should better coordinate the selection of journals to be indexed and assure that key journals in the social sciences are covered. Most of the major social science journals publish important research on education issues, and some of them are not currently being indexed. ERIC should continue efforts to flag key documents, publicize the presence of flags more widely, and take steps to assure that the flagging process is not politicized. Many users are overwhelmed by the large number of citations they receive in response to a search, and they need help in identifying those that represent the most thorough and objective treatments of the subject. Current efforts to provide full-text coverage of key documents and articles should also be expanded: currently, the results of ERIC searches are citations with brief abstracts, and these are of very limited to use to all except those with access to a university or other large library. Lastly, ERIC's efforts to provide access to the international literature should be augmented so that U.S. scholars and educators can benefit from the research and practice in other countries.

This recommendation will require an increase in the staffing and budget of OERI. Over the next 2 or 3 years, approximately three staff and $1 million will be needed to explore alternative options for the electronic network. The implementation phase will undoubtedly require additional staff and funding. The suggested enhancements to ERIC will require about six additional staff and $1.0 million more annually. The staff positions would allow four coordinators—for journal indexing, the flagging of key documents and articles, full-text initiatives, and international acquisitions and collaborations—and two clerical support persons. The budget increase would permit clearinghouse indexing of all key social science journals, expanded and more careful flagging of key documents and articles, the purchase of rights to the full text of key materials, and the augmented international efforts.

B-8 The National Center for Educational Statistics (NCES) should remain as a separate office in OERI with careful attention to pre-

serving its scientific independence. Staffing levels should be approximately doubled as soon as practical to be commensurate with the expanded responsibilities NCES has been given over the past 5 years.

The recent history of NCES is a story of success. In 1986 the National Research Council concluded that the center's operations and products suffered from so many problems that the center should be abolished unless several specified improvements were undertaken. The administration, Congress, the center administrator, and the field all faced the challenge head on. Five years later, NCES is widely perceived as a scientifically responsible agency, responsive to many needs, and an important source of statistics and assessment data.

Recent legislation mandated that NCES be headed by a commissioner appointed by the President, with the advice and consent of the Senate, for a 4-year term. NCES also has complete control over its reports. The committee commends these arrangements, which it believes will permit the center to maintain its independence and integrity.

The committee is gravely concerned, however, about the staffing levels of the center. Over the past few years the budgets and the number of projects have tripled, while staff levels have remained essentially unchanged. NCES now has a much lower rate of staff to program dollars than comparable federal statistics agencies (see Chapter 4). With many new data collection projects mandated in the past 3 years, staff have been focusing most of their time on starting these activities; the monitoring of contracts, verification of data, and preparation of reports have all been delayed. Delays in the release of NCES data and reports have begun, and they are likely to become much more severe in the near future.

The committee has not undertaken a detailed staffing analysis of NCES, but it believes that the available data suggest the need for a large and prompt increase in staffing. The exact number could easily be disputed. Our best guess is that current staff should be about doubled to carry out all new responsibilities added over the past few years. This recommendation would require approximately 138 additional staff positions.

B-9 OERI should work with teacher and administrator education programs, state agencies, and local districts to help practitioners and researchers create learning communities that use research findings, practitioners' craft wisdom, and pursue new inquiry in the quest for educational reform.

The committee is convinced that widespread school reform will require partnerships between researchers and practitioners. Each has much to contribute to the quest. Researchers can provide breadth and depth of inquiry and rigor of investigation: elaborate new theories, conduct carefully controlled experiments, study programs and practices in multiple sites, and prepare national indicators of educational progress. Practitioners have an intimate and holistic understanding of the realities of schooling: they accumulate craft wisdom from daily experiences. Among their ranks are exemplars of good practice and effectiveness whose "magic" needs to be understood and conveyed to others. Practitioners are also the ultimate implementers of most reform strategies.

Successful school reform usually depends on involving teachers and principals in defining needs, analyzing options, planning and coordinating changes, and monitoring their implementation. Good teaching is a complex activity that does not lend itself to compulsory or mechanical adoption. New curricula, teaching approaches, and technology can be valuable, but only in the hands of enthusiastic, coordinated, and committed teachers.

There are several important roles OERI can play in assisting local school reform. One role is through support of research and development efforts that will inform school improvement efforts and provide useful tools for them. Another is to ensure that the results are known by those who might use them. These have been the traditional roles pursued by OERI and NIE for the past two decades. There is, however, a need for another role in which OERI encourages and fosters partnerships among researchers, practitioners, and policy makers, where each becomes involved in disciplined inquiry and each contributes to the learning of the others, so that all come to understand education better and be more effective in contributing to its improvement.

OERI could encourage such partnerships in several ways. It could fund new approaches to conveying each group's needs to the other. It could support development of ways to better share the expertise of each group with the other. And it could support innovative collaborations where each group works with the other on their respective responsibilities.

OERI's efforts will have to be supported with leadership at the national, state, and local levels. For instance, school districts will have to provide release-time for teachers; teacher education institutions will have to experiment with substantial changes in their programs; and policy makers and researchers will have to take the time to listen and communicate with practitioners much more effectively than they have in the past.

This recommendation will require more staff and funding for OERI. We suggest a program of R&D and demonstration with perhaps 100 new awards a year, in amounts ranging from $25,000 to $300,000 a year, for 2- to 6-year periods. This program would require approximately $65 million dollars a year (after a 6-year phase-in period). About 15 additional staff would be needed. We propose a higher staff ratio for this program because it involves lending support to teachers, administrators, and researchers in seldom-undertaken activities.

B-10 OERI should develop research, training, and fellowship programs to attract high-quality personnel into education research, with particular efforts to recruit underrepresented minorities and scholars in disciplines other than education.

The long-term prospects for any field of research depend critically on long-range capacity building. NSF and NIH maintain vigorous programs for building human resources for science; OERI has rarely supported such efforts.

Some progress can be made in this direction if the committee's other recommendations are implemented. Revitalized programs of R&D at OERI would foster intellectual excitement and provide expanded opportunities. For example, a decade ago there were no AIDS researchers; today there are thousands, including many of the best biomedical researchers in the country. They were attracted by the importance of the problem, the intellectual challenge, and the financial support that became available. When established researchers entered a new field, students followed, and a new research area quickly became the focus of intense investigation.

Scholars from other disciplines who do not see how their work might be relevant to education research must be persuaded that OERI welcomes their insights and input: economists, sociologists, anthropologists, and political scientists have tools and lines of inquiry that are directly applicable to problems in education, as do neurobiologists studying the development and functioning of the brain; and mathematicians, natural scientists, and scholars in the humanities and arts obviously have a wealth of knowledge about the subjects taught in school. OERI needs to actively solicit proposals for research from them, as well as offer dissertation funds for graduate students in the sciences, humanities, and arts who choose to do research on education issues.

Twenty percent of school-age youth are racial or ethnic minorities, and they suffer disproportionately from the severest educational problems. Fourteen percent of U.S. adults are minorities. Only 10 percent of the U.S. members of the American Educational Research Association, who report their major responsibilities to be research, evaluation, or development, are minorities (Patricia Majors, personnel communication, 1992). In addition, only 10 percent of social scientists, and 6 percent of psychologists in the United States are minority (National Science Board, 1989). People hold many different views about the importance of race in the conduct of science and education. This committee believes it is important to have more minorities trained to participate fully in education R&D activities. OERI and NIE used to have modest minority fellowship programs, but none was offered from 1983 to 1990. In 1991 OERI funded a small program at one institution, with $150,000 to support up to 10 graduate student internships.

Both NIH and NSF support programs aimed at developing more minority and women researchers. As women now earn 58 percent of the doctorates in education and 46 percent of the doctorates in the social sciences and now comprise 49 percent of the membership of the American Educational Research Association, the training of racial and ethnic minority researchers should be given priority.

A solid program of dissertation grants for graduate students in all the social sciences would provide about 100 2-year grants of $10,000 per year, requiring about three additional staff and $2 million annually, phased in over 2 years. These grants would be incentives for dissertation research on issues relevant to education and therefore not have to cover the full expenses of graduate students. A viable program of minority fellowships would provide about 100 3-year grants, averaging $23,000 per year, to cover living expenses at the same level provided by major NSF and Department of Education fellowship programs, plus full payment of tuition and fees. This program would require another five staff members and $6.9 million annually, phased in over 3 years.

OPERATIONS

OERI depends on the Department of Education for hiring and other personnel matters, for procurement, and for report clearance, and OERI has experienced various problems with all three. It has had limited success in recruiting highly qualified personnel. Its proposal review process has commendably involved both researchers and practitioners, but they have been allowed to make decisions in areas outside of their respective expertise. And despite its research and development in areas of considerable dispute, OERI has rarely used a formal process for developing consensus.

The four recommendations in this section address these problems. They would give OERI its own personnel authority, its own contracts and grants office, and sole responsibility for its publications; encourage the agency to recruit top-flight personnel and create an intellectually attractive work environment for them; modify the peer review of proposals for grants and contracts; and have the agency use a consensus development process to determine the implications of important and controversial bodies of research and evaluation. Each of these should help the agency better fulfill its mission.

C-1 OERI should have independent authority for staffing, contracts, grants, and reporting.

Many individuals and institutions that have dealt with the Department of Education's contracts and grants office report inordinate delays, a lack of responsiveness to legitimate needs, and incompetence. Several OERI staff have echoed those complaints and voiced similar ones about the Department's personnel office. Such complaints are not uncommon at other federal agencies, but the vehemence of the criticism of OERI does appear unusual. In addition, many of the critics have had the benefit of experience with other federal agencies and claim the problems are more severe at the Department of Education. Providing OERI with its own contracts and grants office would not guarantee improved service, but it would put that possibility within the control of the agency.

Similar complaints of delays and nonresponsiveness have been frequently voiced about the Department of Education's personnel office. In addition, independent staffing authority would give OERI its own salary and expenses budget as well as its own personnel office. NCES has had its budget and number of projects tripled over the past 5 years with virtually no increase in its staffing slots. That represents a serious failure of the current salaries and expense budget process. Independent staffing authority will not guarantee avoidance of this in the future, but it will make disparities between staffing levels and agency responsibilities more obvious to those involved in the budget process.

There is at least one disadvantage in giving OERI its own personnel and procurement offices. As a small organization, OERI will not be able to acquire the depth or breadth of expertise that is possible at the departmental level. Indeed, because of this, one knowledgeable administrator in OERI has expressed doubts that the quality of service would be markedly improved. All things considered, however, the committee believes OERI should have its own authority for staffing, contracts, and grants.

All OERI reports, except those of NCES, must now be cleared by each assistant secretary of the Department of Education who has jurisdiction over matters discussed in the report. They also must be cleared by the Editorial Policy Division of the department's Office of Public Affairs. The criteria for approval include "consistency with ED's mission and goals" and "conformity with legislation, regulations, and policy" (see Chapter 3), and there have been many allegations of ideologically motivated delays and modifications, resulting from this review process. The committee has not attempted to verify these allegations, but thinks that the current clearance procedures are inappropriate for a research agency, whose work should be characterized by the highest standards of objectivity.

In place of the Department of Education's clearance procedure, OERI should establish a rigorous review and revision process for all reports that are formally issued under its imprimatur. The report review procedures currently used by NCES might be a good model for the rest of OERI to follow.

Independent staffing authority, contracts and grants authority, and reports authority are common among the larger research agencies, such as the Agriculture Research Service, NSF and NIH (with a few exceptions for reports) and have been granted to some relatively small federal statistics units. The Bureau of Labor Statistics within the Department of Labor has all three authorities. Recent legislation offered the former two for NCES, but the then Secretary of Education decided against implementation.

This recommendation will require additional staff for OERI, but there could be some offsetting reductions in departmental staff. No budget increase would be needed. The committee cannot estimate the number of staff needed for the personnel office and the contracts and grants office; the Office of Personnel Management should do that. OERI would need about four additional staff for its own rigorous report clearance process. OERI currently issues about 160 reports a year, and staff also prepare many other professional papers and speeches in their official capacities.

C-2   OERI should actively recruit highly qualified personnel from various disciplines for OERI staff positions and should create an intellectually stimulating working environment.

OERI can provide effective leadership in education R&D only if it is staffed with high-quality personnel. A cadre of professionals whose qualifications are known and respected is essential to develop a partnership between the agency and the field. NIE recruited many outstanding researchers during its first years, but many left as its budget dwindled, and for years OERI and NIE have held little attraction for top scholars. Although OERI has retained some excellent staff members and recruited some others, many observers within the agency and outside believe it does not have enough.

If this committee's various recommendations are implemented, OERI should have a better chance of attracting the kind of personnel needed. It is particularly important to secure excellence at the top levels—the director and associate directors—both because of the responsibilities of those positions and because such persons serve as magnets for attracting outstanding mid-level professionals.

Another mechanism that would help bring top talent to OERI is to implement a "rotators" program, bringing top researchers, developers, teachers, and administrators to the agency, for significant periods of time, involving them in the planning and the execution of OERI's work. Such a program would strengthen the agency, make it less parochial, enrich the intellectual environment, and improve OERI's relationships with the fields of research and practice.

There is widespread opinion in OERI, by staff and several managers, that the agency has provided very limited opportunities for staff to engage in professional activities such as attendance at professional meetings and advanced training seminars. This is a serious problem in a research agency. Staff need to be on the cutting edge of new developments when helping to develop the research agendas, soliciting research proposals, evaluating proposals, monitoring the work, and assessing its importance after completion. A perennially tight salaries and expenses budget is blamed for the problem.

This recommendation will not require additional staff positions or program budget. The rotators would fill existing staff slots.

C-3 OERI's contract and grant application review process should provide an appropriate balance between expertise in research and in practice for all proposals, with technical research merit judged by research experts and programmatic relevance judged by program experts.

NIE relied primarily on researchers to review proposals. OERI has considerably increased the use of teachers, administrators, policy makers, and others. The inclusion of practitioners as reviewers is commendable— and not unprecedented in federal agencies—but changes should be made in the procedures.

Administrators and teachers are generally not qualified to judge the technical adequacy of proposed research or evaluations. Similarly, researchers are generally not qualified to judge the programmatic promise of proposals, except those in their areas of substantive expertise. OERI has had both types of experts judge both the technical and programmatic merit of proposals, and all their ratings have been averaged. Proposals for basic research should be reviewed only by researchers, because, by definition, basic research is directed at probing fundamental understandings and is not expected to have direct programmatic application. Proposals for applied research, development, and technical assistance should be reviewed by panels with a broad range of expertise. Even then, however, given the nature of OERI's work, we think a minimum of one-third should be researchers—and a higher proportion when the proposed activities primarily involve research.

In addition, the review process should be structured to ensure that only reviewers with technical research expertise make judgments about scientific and technical merit, that only reviewers with the appropriate programmatic expertise make judgments about those matters, and that proposals that are judged to be technically *or* programmatically inadequate are not recommended for funding.

This recommendation would not affect the staffing or budget needed by OERI.

C-4 OERI should implement a consensus development process involving distinguished experts to review and report on the quality and implications of potentially important bodies of research and evaluations that appear to have unclear or conflicting results.

There are disputes over many education issues, including the interpretation of research results. Teachers, administrators, parents, journalists, and policy makers repeatedly state they have difficulty determining what is true in a large body of literature with apparently conflicting results. Is bilingual education or English as a second language (ESL) instruction most effective for students with limited English proficiency? For which students and under what conditions? Is the phonics or the whole-language approach superior for teaching beginning reading skills? Superior in what respects and inferior in what respects? Is homogeneous or heterogeneous grouping best— for the slower students and for the faster students? These and other contested issues have been subject to considerable research, but few practitioners know, or could themselves assess, what the weight of evidence says about each.

Although OERI (and NIE) has long sponsored and conducted reviews of research and evaluation literature—some of which have been high-quality scholarly works—reviews differ from the consensus process that we are advocating. Reviews are usually the product of one or two people; a consensus process typically relies on a panel of 10-15 people with diverse expertise and perspectives, who can be expected to raise more questions, apply a wider spectrum of knowledge and skill, and arrive at a broader set of insights. After considering the available evidence, they reach agreements about what is known from the evidence and what is not yet well established and issue a public statement reporting their judgments and rationales. Sometimes they also indicate needed lines of future research. The findings of a consensus development process are likely to be more credible to teachers and administrators than a review because a substantial number of prominent people must agree on the findings.

This recommendation would require some additional staffing and funding. If contracted out, each consensus development process would require about $400,000-$900,000 and perhaps 0.2 staff for liaison and monitoring over 12-24 months. If conducted in house, each would require about 1.5-2.5 full-time staff for 12-24 months and about $100,000 of program expenses. Given all the controversy in education, there could easily be two or three topics a year that would benefit from this scrutiny.

FUNDING

OERI's budget was $380 million dollars in fiscal 1991, of which most was spent on Library Programs and development work that is not based on research. Under the narrow definition of R&D used by NSF and OMB, the agency invested only an estimated $58 million in research and development work. By a broader definition that includes routine statistics collection and dissemination of R&D, the agency spent $126 million. Neither of these amounts is adequate for the mission of OERI and the education needs of the country.

The committee recommends increases in OERI's budget for more basic and applied research, more research-based development, laboratory staff with state liaison responsibilities, a minority fellowship program, more extensive refinement and evaluation of promising innovations, and consensus conferences to reach findings about important and contested bodies of research and evaluation. If that increase is not forthcoming, the mission and activities of the agency should be significantly narrowed.

D-1 To implement the committee's recommendations, OERI should be given substantial, phased-in, increases in its budgets and staffing levels.

The funding of OERI (and NIE) declined dramatically over the past two decades while its mission remained largely unchanged. As a consequence, the agency has carried on a broad array of activities with little depth and little chance of making substantial contributions. Over the same period, the need for significant reform of the nation's schools has gained prominence. There is now major public support for the six National Education Goals, but little agreement about how to achieve them. Other needs for research and development have long gone unfilled. Basic research on many education issues is almost nonexistent. Promising innovations have gone without rigorous evaluation. And there has been little effort to help teachers be full partners in the quest for school change.

A substantial increase in the budget and staffing of OERI is required if it is to play an important role in filling these needs and assisting the nation with effective education reform. In trying to determine how much money is needed for a given field of research, three lines of analysis are often brought to bear: a comparison of R&D investment in various fields; computation of likely rates of return on investments; and examination of what activities are important to undertake.

Federal expenditures for education R&D are much lower than federal expenditures for R&D in agriculture, transportation, health, and other major fields, not only in terms of dollars expended but also as a percentage of all federal expenditures in each field and as a percentage of national expenditures in each field (see Chapter 3). By this line of analysis, education R&D is significantly underfunded by the federal government.

In 1986 the Office of Technology Assessment completed a review of the return-on-investment approach for guiding scientific research and concluded that, "while valid conceptually, [it] does not provide a useful practical guide to improving Federal research decision making (U.S. Office of Technology Assessment, 1986:9)." The applicable return on investment is not dollars, but rather a broad spectrum of social benefits that are difficult to measure and assign dollar values.

The social benefits of improved education include both the personal satisfactions of a good education and the social contribution of education to "human capital." The productivity of any economy depends on its human capital—the knowledge, skills, and habits that employees bring to their jobs. If education R&D improves education's contributions to human capital, the returns to society will be in the form of increased economic productivity, improved competitiveness in world trade, and a heightened standard of living in the United States. Although it is not possible to apply returns-on-investment analysis to research investments, it is obvious that a small percentage increase in the productivity of the nation's $350 billion education enterprise could yield substantial cost savings, or alternatively, increased outputs in thousands of schools, and the benefits are likely to be reaped for many years.

The third line of analysis for deciding on the level of investment in a field of R&D is to list all the things that are considered important to do and price them. This report has noted many serious problems in the nation's schools for which the nation should be diligently seeking solutions, as well as needs and opportunities for R&D that have resulted from recent work. For example, progress in understanding reading difficulties is incomplete; there is much dissatisfaction with traditional means of measuring student learning, and several proposed alternatives need careful exploration; international comparisons have yielded attention-getting results but require several refinements to be fair gauges; intriguing new teaching approaches are in early stages of development and need much more work; several promising curriculum innovations have not yet been rigorously evaluated; and efforts to restructure schools offer the promise of large and sustained gains, but need further development and evaluation.

Another need for education R&D results from the current ferment in educational policy at both the state and federal level. New ideas are being advanced and implemented with little or no research foundation, such as proposals about school choice, national testing, and student mentors. There is a need for these ideas to be rigorously studied so that their full potential can be realized and assessed. Without well-designed and careful evaluation, new ideas will be judged by press releases and public opinion, rather than on the basis of rigorous evidence.

The committee's prior recommendations are based on the problems and opportunities identified in this report. For most we have estimated the cost and number of additional staff needed. Together our recommendations will require an addition of about $267 million annually for OERI's program budget. About 214 more staff will be needed for expanded program operations, several more for OERI's own personnel and procurement offices, and whatever additional number is required to provide support services for the enlarged staff (accounting and payroll, supplies, mail, computer support, etc.). Some of the additional staff will have considerable liaison or monitoring responsibilities, which require more travel and communications costs than those for other employees; therefore, the OERI staff and expenses budget will need to be increased somewhat more than would be expected by the number of added staff.

Several of the above recommendations could be implemented within 1 year; others will have to be phased in over 3-6 years. The new governance, agenda setting, and organizational changes should be implemented soon. Funding of the new multiyear grant programs should be phased in over the number of years for which the grants are to be awarded. A large portion of the additional staff should be brought on board as quickly as practical to meet the critical needs of NCES and the forthcoming needs of the reorganization.

The committee recognizes that its funding recommendations would require a large expenditure. Some people will simply dismiss it as too expensive. The committee sees it as a critical investment in the nation's future. Without the investment, and concomitant efforts at state and local levels, the country is not likely to come close to meeting the national education goals.

Over the first 6 years, our recommendations will cost the nation approximately $1.3 billion in additional expenditures. Over the same period, the nation will spend about $1,500 billion on elementary and secondary education in this country. It is clear that this added investment in R&D will be paid back many times over if it improves the effectiveness or efficiency of our education system by even 1 percent. It also should be noted that even with full implementation of all our recommendations, federal investment in education R&D will still be significantly less than federal investment in agriculture, transportation, or health.

Our committee cannot address the future of OERI much beyond the next 5 or 6 years. Recommendations A-4, A-5, and A-6 establish a mechanism for monitoring the health and needs of OERI's R&D and that of the entire federal government. This monitoring should be supplemented with a strategic planning process that anticipates the needs for education R&D 5, 10, and 15 years into the future and develops a strategy for effectively meeting those needs.

It should be noted that any research enterprise is much like an airplane accelerating down a runway. In the early stages, there is much noise and vibration, but the plane just rolls along the tarmac. Only when it has gained enough speed do the aerodynamic forces exceed the gravitational ones, allowing the plane to lift off. The committee believes that its recommendations, if implemented, will accelerate the education R&D enterprise in this country, but lift-off, moving the enterprise into a new mode of functioning, is several years away.

D-2 Unless OERI's budget is substantially increased in the near future, the mission and activities of the agency should be significantly narrowed.

Some of our recommendations require little, if any, additional funding. Given the federal budget difficulties, there will be the temptation to implement those and postpone the others requiring larger expenditures. We believe that would be a serious mistake.

The past and present strategy of sprinkling NIE's and OERI's limited funds across an enormous array of disparate activities has not proven to be an effective national strategy for education R&D. Basic research has almost dried up. The sustained efforts that are so important for progress in science and technology have been limited. Promising innovations are disseminated without the iterations of R&D that are needed to maximize results and minimize costs across diverse situations, and without evaluation of their long-term effects.

Important successes have been achieved, but for every accomplishment of OERI and NIE, teachers, researchers, and policy makers can cite at least ten unfulfilled needs that are fully within the agency's mission. And even if all the problems in organization and functioning identified in this report are remedied, the agency could not possibly fulfill its responsibilities with its current funding levels.

There are at least two alternatives for paring back the breadth of the agency's activities. First, OERI could focus exclusively on dissemination and technical assistance activities. Some people suggest that the biggest bang for the buck, at least in terms of school improvement in the short term, would come from putting the existing research knowledge base into wider use through enhanced dissemination and technical assistance. This approach, however is like eating one's seed corn, and would become self-defeating within a few years.

Second, the agency could invest the entire amount of its limited funds in research and statistics and a few highly targeted development activities, eliminating all dissemination and technical assistance. Several programs of high-quality research can be pursued at much less expense than widespread programs of dissemination and improvement. As these programs bear fruit, there would be increased motivation for dissemination, and perhaps the states or for-profit companies would move to meet the need, although history does not suggest this is very likely.

On several occasions OERI and NIE have tried to concentrate their limited resources, but they have always come under heavy pressure to do the opposite—from researchers of all the excluded fields of inquiry, from curriculum associations of all the excluded subject areas, and from policy makers concerned with all the excluded issues. Only an act of Congress would be likely to ensure a narrowing of focus. And such legislation would alienate so many participants in education that the travails of the agency might well worsen.

We emphasize that neither of these reductions to OERI's activities is consistent with the widespread, pressing, and diverse needs for education reform. They are not in the best interest of the agency, the federal government, or the nation's education system. Yet it would be more honest to drastically cut OERI's mission than to pretend that it can fulfill that mission without significant increases in funding.

CONCLUSION

OERI needs to be rebuilt for its complex and difficult mission. The agency has made some valuable contributions, but it has been seriously compromised by governance, organizational, operational, and funding difficulties.

Our study has led us to conclude that the agency can best fulfill its mission by strengthening its traditional roles and by supporting a research enterprise that is a powerful and enduring partner for learning communities—communities comprised of researchers, teachers, administrators, policy makers and parents.

School reform is rarely achieved by mechanically plugging in innovations. Rather it is a developmental and systemic process that requires new learning on the part of both researchers, practitioners, and policy makers.

We recommend major changes in the governance of OERI to improve the agenda setting of the agency, balance its portfolio of work, and bring stability to the top management. Our recommendations for reorganization would expand, focus, and integrate much of the research and development work; strengthen PEP and NDN; correct a critical shortage of staff in NCES; coordinate, extend and supplement the various dissemination and technical assistance efforts; strengthen quality assurance; and initiate efforts to encourage and foster the above mentioned learning communities. Our recommendations about operations would give OERI more control over staffing, contracts, grants and reporting; strengthen its peer review process; and enhance the quality of the staff.

We think these changes will make a difference, an important difference, if they are sustained for a substantial period of time. The story of OERI and its predecessor does not offer much hope for implementation and maintenance of these changes, but conditions are changing. Never before has education received so much attention simultaneously from the administration, Congress, and the governors. Despite the differences of opinion on many issues, there is widespread agreement that business cannot continue as usual in most of the nation's schools, that more than marginal improvements are needed, and that the nation's diverse resources must be mobilized to meet this challenge. Our recommendations for OERI are in full accord with that agreement.

Our recommendations will not be easy to implement, they will not be painless, and they will not yield immediate results. But we think they are a wise long-term investment in the future of the country.

References

Adams, M.J.
   1990   *Beginning to Read: Thinking and Learning about Print.* Center for the Study of Reading, The Reading Research and Education Center. Urbana-Champaign, Ill.: University of Illinois.

Alkin, M., ed.
   1992   *Encyclopedia of Educational Research, 6th Edition.* New York: MacMillan.

Alexander, L.
   1991   *America 2000: An Education Strategy.* Washington, D.C.: U.S. Department of Education

Anderson, J.
   1980   *Cognitive Psychology and Its Implications.* San Francisco, Calif.: W.H. Freeman.

Anderson, R.C., E.H. Hiebert, J.A. Scott, and I.A.G. Wilkinson
   1985   *Becoming a Nation of Readers: The Report of the Commission on Reading.* Washington, D.C.: The National Institute of Education.

Banks, J.
   1982   Educating minority youths: an inventory of current theory. *Education and Urban Society* November 15(1):88-103.

Bartlett, F.C.
   1932   *Remembering: A Study in Experimental and Social Psychology.* Cambridge, England: Cambridge University Press.

BCMA Associates, Inc.
   1977   *Relationships Among the National Institute of Education, Federally-Funded Educational Research and Development Agencies, and Commerical Publishers.* New York: BCMA Associates, Inc.

Becker, H.J.
   1990   How Computers Are Used in United States Schools: Basic Data from the 1989 I.E.A. Computers in Education Survey. Unpublished paper, Center for Social Organization of Schools, Johns Hopkins University.
Bennett, W.J.
   1985   Memo to the Honorable Augustus F. Hawkins. U.S. Department of Education, Washington, D.C.
Benton, S.L., and K.A. Kiewra
   1987   The assessment of cognitive factors in academic abilities. Pp. 145-189 In R.R. Ronning, J.A. Glover, J.C. Conoley, and J.C. Witt, eds., *The Influence of Cognitive Psychology on Testing*. Hillsdale, N.J.: Lawrence Erlbaum Associates, Inc.
Berman, P., and M. McLaughlin
   1975   *Federal Programs Supporting Educational Change. Vol. 1-5*. Santa Monica, Calif.: The Rand Corporation.
   1977   *Federal Programs Supporting Educational Change. Vols. 6-8*. Santa Monica, Calif.: The Rand Corporation.
Billups, L., and M. Rauth
   1987   Teachers and research. In V. Richardson-Koehler, ed., *Educator's Handbook*. White Plains, N.Y.: Longman.
Brophy, J., and T. Good
   1974   *Teacher-Pupil Relationships*. New York: Holt, Rinehart and Winston.
Brown, A., and A. Palinscar
   1989   Guided, cooperative learning and individual knowledge acquisition. Chapter 13 in *Knowing, Learning, and Instruction*. Hillsdale, N.J.: Lawrence Erlbaum Associates, Inc.
Brown, A.L., and S.M. Martin
   1987   Peer interaction in reading comprehension instruction. *Educational Psychologist* 22(3&4): 231-253.
Brown, J.S., and K. VanLehn
   1983   Towards a generative theory of "bugs." Pp. 117-136 in T.P. Carpenter, J.M. Moser, and T.A. Romberg, eds., *Addition and Subtraction: A Cognitive Perspective*. Hillsdale, N.J.: Lawrence Erlbaum Associates Inc.
Campbell, R.
   1975   *R&D Funding Policies of the National Institute of Education: Review and Recommendations*. National Institute of Education. Washington, D.C.: U.S. Department of Health, Education, and Welfare.
Campione, J.C., A.L. Brown, and M.L. Connell
   1988   Metacogntion: on the importance of understanding what you are doing. Pp. 93-113 in R. Charles and E. Silver, eds., *The Teaching and Assessing of Mathematical Problem Solving*. National Council of Teachers of Mathematics. Hillsdale, N.J.: Lawrence Erlbaum Associates, Inc.
Carpenter, T., and E. Fennema
   in   Cognitively guided instruction: building on the knowledge of students
   press   and teachers. In W. Secada, ed., *The Reform of School Mathematics in the United States*. Special issue of *The International Journal of Education*.

Carpenter, T., E. Fennema, P. Peterson, C. Chiang, and M. Loef
  1989   Using knowledge of children's mathematics thinking in classroom teach-
         ing: an experimental study. *American Education Research Journal* 26(4):499-
         531.
Castle, S.
  1988   Empowering Teachers Through Knowledge. Unpublished paper present-
         ed at the Annual Meeting of the Ameircan Educational Research Associ-
         ation, New Orleans, Louisiana.
Chalker, N.
  1990   Answers to Frequently Asked Questions, Information for Prospective
         Applicants, 1990.   National Education Research and Development Cen-
         ter Programs.   Office of Educational Research and Improvement, U.S.
         Department of Education, Washington, D.C.
Chall, J.S.
  1983   *Learning to Read: The Great Depate.* New York: McGraw-Hill.
Chase, F.S.
  1967   The Educational Laboratories: How Do They Fit Into the Future of
         American Education? Paper presented at the meeting of Laboratory Di-
         rectors, New Orleans.
  1968   The National Program of Educational Laboratories: Report of a Study of
         Twenty Educational Laboratories and Nine University Research and De-
         velopment Center.   Department of Health Education and Welfare, Wash-
         ington, D.C.
  1970   R&D in the remodeling of education. *Phi Delta Kappan* 52(4):299-304.
Chi, M., P. Feltovich, and R. Glaser
  1981   Categorization and representation of physics problems by experts and
         novices. *Cognitive Science* 5:121-152.
Chipman, S.F., J.W. Segal, and R. Glaser, eds.
  1985   *Thinking and Learning Skills. Volume 2: Research and Open Questions.*
         Hillsdale, N.J.: Lawrence Erlbaum Associates, Inc.
Chubin, D.E., and E.J. Hackett
  1990   *Peerless Science: Peer Review and U.S. Science Policy.* Albany, N.Y.:
         State University of New York Press.
Clay, M.M.
  1985   *The Early Detection of Reading Difficulties.* Portsmouth, N.H: Heine-
         mann Educational Books.
Clay, M.M., and C.B. Cazden
  1990   A Vygotskian interpretation of Reading Recovery. Pp. 207-222 in L.C.
         Moll, ed., *Vygotsky and Education Instructional Implications and Appli-
         cations of Sociohistorical Psychology.* New York: Cambridge Universi-
         ty Press.
Cohen, D.
  1987   Educational technology, policy, and practice. *Educational Evaluation and
         Policy Analysis* 9(2):153-170.
Cohen, D.K., and D.L. Ball
  1990   Policy and practice: an overview. *Educational Evaluation and Policy
         Analysis* 12(3):233-239.

Cohen, E.
   1986   *Designing Groupwork: Strategies for the Heterogeneous Classroom.* New
          York: Teachers College Press.
Colorado, R.
   1988   Computer-assisted instruction research: a critical assessment. *Journal of
          Research on Computing in Education* Spring:226-233.
Comer, J.P.
   1980   *School Power: Implications of Intervention Project.* New York: Free
          Press.
   1988   Educating poor minority children. *Scientific American* 259(5):42-48.
Comer, J.P., N.M. Haynes, and M. Hamilton-Lee
   1989   School power: a model for improving black student achievement. Pp.
          187-200 in Willy DeMarcell Smith and Eva Wells Chunn, eds., *Black
          Education: A Quest for Equity and Excellence.* New Brunswick, N.J.:
          Transaction Books.
Congressional Research Service
   1991   U.S. Department of Education: Major Program Trends, FY 1980-1991.
          U.S. Library of Congress, Washington, D.C.
Cross, C.T.
   1989   Report of the Laboratory Review Panel on the Pending Laboratory Rec-
          ompetition. Macro Systems, Inc., Silver Spring, Md.
Cox, P.L., K.A. Kahn, and L.C. French
   1985   *Making the Match for Use of Educational Information: Volume III, A
          Study of Clients of Information Service Providers and Their Use of ERIC-
          based Resources and Services.* Andover, Mass.: The NETWORK.
Crandall, D., and associates
   1982   *People, Policies and Practices: Examining the Chain of School Improve-
          ment. Vol. 1-10.* Andover, Mass.: The NETWORK.
Crandall, D., and S. Loucks
   1982   *Preparing Facilitators for Implementation: Mirroring the School Im-
          provement Process.* Andover, Mass.: The NETWORK.
Cuban, L.
   1990   Reforming again, again, and again. *Educational Researcher* 19(1):3-13.
Darling-Hammond, L.W., E. Wise, and S.R. Pease
   1983   Teacher evaluation in the organizational context: a review of the litera-
          ture. *Review of Educational Research* 53(3):285-328.
Dole, J., G. Duffy, L. Roehler, and P. Pearson
   1991   Moving from the old to the new: research on reading comprehension
          instruction. *Review of Educational Research* 61(2):239-264.
Doyle, W.
   1976   *The Birth, Nurturance and Transformation of an Educational Reform.*
          Portland, Ore.: Northwest Regional Educational Lab.
Elam, S.M.
   1990   The 22nd annual Gallup Poll of the public's attitudes toward the public
          schools. *Phi Delta Kappan* September:41-55.
Elam, S., L. Rose, and A. Gallup
   1991   The 23rd annual Gallup Poll of the public's attitudes toward the public
          schools. *Phi Delta Kappan* September:41-56.

Elmore, R.F., and M. McLaughlin
  1988   *Steady Work: Policy, Practice and the Reform of American Education.*
          Santa Monica, Calif.: The Rand Corporation.
Emrick, J., S. Peterson, S., Agarwala, and R. Rogers
  1977   *Evaluation of the National Diffusion Network Volume I: Findings and
          Recommendations.* Menlo Park, Calif.: Stanford Research Institute.
Federation of American Societies for Experimental Biology
  1977   Evaluation of health aspects of GRAS food ingredients: lessons learned
          and questions unanswered. Select Committee on GRAS Substances. *Fed-
          eration Proceedings* 36(11):25-28.
  1985   *The Reexamination of the GRAS Statues of Selfiting Agents.* Life Scienc-
          es Research Office. Washington, D.C.: Federation of American Societ-
          ies for Experimental Biology.
Fennema, E., T. Carpenter, and P. Peterson
  1989   Learning mathematics with understanding: cognitively guided instruc-
          tion. Pp. 193-220 in J.E. Brophy, ed., *Advances in Research on Teach-
          ing, Vol. 1.* Greenwich, Conn.: JAI Press Inc.
Finn, C.
  1986   Strengths (and weaknesses) of peer review. *Educational Researcher* Au-
          gust/September:14-15.
Fischer, K., and D. Bullock
  1984   Cognitive development in school-age children: conclusions and new di-
          rections. Chapter 3 in A. Collins, ed., *Development During Middle Childhood.*
          Washington, D.C.: National Academy Press.
Fox, J.
  1990   The Impact of Research on Education Policy. Working paper prepared for
          the Office of Research, U.S. Department of Education, Washington, D.C.
Fullan, M.B.
  1991   *The New Meaning of Educational Change.* New York: Teachers College
          Press.
Fuson, K., J. Stigler, and K. Bartsch
  1988   Grade placement of addition and subtraction topics in Japan, Mainland
          China, the Soviet Union, Taiwan, and the United States. *Journal for
          Research in Mathematics Education* 19:449-456.
Garduque, L., and D.C. Berliner
  1986   Beyond the competition. *Educational Researcher* 15(6):19-20.
Gallagher, J.J.
  1969   *Educational Research and Development in the United States.* National
          Center for Educational Research and Development. Document No.
          HE5.212:12049. Washington, D.C.: U.S. Department of Health, Educa-
          tion, and Welfare.
Glaser, R.
  1984   Education and thinking: the role of knowledge. *American Psychologist*
          39:93-104.
Glaser, R., A. Lesgold, and S. Gott
  1991   Implications of cognitive psychology for measuring job performance. Pp.
          1-16 in A. Wigdor, and B.F. Green, Jr., eds., *Performance Assessment for*

the Workplace, Vol. II. Committee on the Performance of Military Personnel, Commission on Behavioral and Social Sciences and Education. National Research Council. Washington, D.C.: National Academy Press.

Glass, G.
1976   Primary, secondary, and meta-analysis of research. *Educational Researcher*
        5:3-8.

Goodlad, J.I.
1984   *A Place Called School: Prospects for the Future*. New York: McGraw-
        Hill.
1990   *Teachers for Our Nation's Schools*. San Francisco, Calif.: Jossey-Bass.

Graves, D.
1983   *Writing: Teachers and Children at Work*. Portsmouth, N.H.: Heine-
        mann.

Griffin, G., and S. Barnes
1986   Using research findings to change school and classroom practices: re-
        sults of an experimental study. *American Educational Research Journal*
        23(4):572-586.

Gross, N., J. Giacquinta, and M. Bernstein
1971   *Implementing Organizational Innovations: A Sociological Analysis of
        Planned Educational Change*. New York: Basic Books.

Guthrie, J.
1989   Regional Educational Laboratories: History and Prospect. Report pre-
        pared for the Office of Educational Research and Improvement, U.S.
        Department of Education, Washington, D.C.

Hall, D., and S. Alford
1978   *Evaluation of the National Diffusion Network: Evolution of the Network
        and Overview of the Research Literature on Diffusion of Educational
        Innovations*. Menlo Park, Calif.: Stanford Research Institute.

Hauser, R.
1991   What happens to youth after high school? *Focus* 13(3):1-13.

Heidema, C.
1991   Comprehensive School Mathematics Program. Application to the Pro-
        gram Effectiveness Panel, U.S. Department of Education, Washington,
        D.C.

Herriott, R.E., and N.G. Gross, eds.
1979   *The Dynamics of Planned Educational Change: Case Studies and Analy-
        ses*. Berkeley, Calif.: McCutchan Publishing Corp.

Hodgkinson, H.
1991   Reform versus reality. *Phi Delta Kappan* September:9-16.

Hopkins, D.
1990   Integrating staff development and school improvement: a study of teach-
        er personality and school climate. In *Changing School Culture Through
        Staff Development*. Alexandria, Va.: Association for Supervision and
        Curriculum Development.

Howey, K.R., and N.L. Zimpher
1989   *Profiles of Preservice Teacher Education: Inquiry Into the Nature of
        Programs*. Albany, N.Y.: SUNY Press.

Huberman, A., and D. Crandall
  1982 *People, Policies, and Practices: Examining the Chain of School Improvement, Volume IX: Implications for Action.* Andover, Mass.: The NETWORK.
Huberman, M.
  1984 The role of teacher education in the improvement of educational practice: a linkage model. *European Journal of Teacher Education* 6(1):17-29.
Hunter, J., and F. Schmidt
  1990 *Methods of Meta-Analysis Correcting Error and Bias in Research Findings.* Newbury Park, Calif.: Sage Publications.
Hutchins, C.L.
  1989 A brief review of federal dissemination activities: 1958-1983. *Knowledge: Creation, Diffusion, Utilization* 11(1):10-26.
Ianni, F.
  1965 The emerging role of the Bureau of Research. In *Transcript of Proceedings: Conference on the Status of Educational Research Activities.* San Francisco, Calif. Washington, D.C.: U.S. Department of Health, Education, and Welfare.
Institute of Medicine
  1990 *Consensus Development at the NIH: Improving the Program.* Washington, D.C.: National Academy Press.
Jackson, P.
  1968 *Life in Classrooms.* New York: Holt, Rinehart & Winston.
Jasanoff, S.
  1990 *The Fifth Branch.* Cambridge, Mass.: Harvard University Press.
Jencks, C.
  1991 Is the American underclass growing? In C. Jencks and P. Peterson, eds., *The Urban Underclass.* Washington, D.C.: Brookings Institution.
Jennings, J.
  1991 Congressional intent: the House's legal expert on vocational education explains what Congress wants the Perkins Act to do. *Vocational Education Journal* 66(2):18-19.
Johnson, D., and R. Johnson
  1990 *Learning Together and Alone.* New York: Printice Hall.
Johnston, W.B., and A.B. Packer
  1987 *Workforce 2000: Work and Workers for the 21st Century.* Indianapolis, Ind.: Hudson Institute.
Kaestle, C.
  1991 Everybody's Been To Fourth Grade, An Oral History of Federal R&D in Education. Unpublished paper, prepared for the Committee on the Federal Role in Education Research, Commission on Behavioral and Social Sciences and Education, National Research Council. Department of History, University of Wisconsin, Madison.
Knepper, P.
  1989 *Student Progress in College: NLS-72 Postsecondary Education Transcript, 1984.* CS 89-411. National Center for Education Statistics. Washington, D.C.: U.S. Department of Education.

Kulik, C., and J. Kulik
  1986   Effectiveness of computer-based education in colleges. *AEDS Journal*
          Winter/Spring:81-197.
  1987   Review of recent research literature on computer-based instruction. *Con-
          temporary Educational Psychology* 12:222-230.
Kulik, J., C. Kulik, and R. Bangert-Drowns
  1985   Effectiveness of computer-based education in elementary schools. *Com-
          puters in Human Behavior* 1:59-74.
Levin, H., G. Glass, and G. Meister
  1987   Cost-effectiveness of computer-assisted instruction. *Evaluation Review*
          11(1):50-72.
Lieberman, M.
  1991   Research and the renewal of education: a critical review. *Education
          Week* June 19:33.
Light, R., and D. Pillemer
  1984   *Summing Up the Science of Reviewing Research.*   Cambridge, Mass.:
          Harvard University Press.
Little, J.W.
  1982   Norms of collegiality and experimentation: workplace conditions of school
          success. *American Educational Research Journal* 19(3):325-340.
Lortie, D.
  1975   *Schoolteacher: A Sociological Study.* Chicago: University of Chicago
          Press.
Louis, K.S., and M.B. Miles
  1990   *Improving the Urban High School: What Works and Why.* New York:
          Teachers College Press.
Louis, K.S., R.A. Dentler and D.G. Kell
  1984   *Putting Knowledge to Work: Issues in Educational Dissemination.* Bos-
          ton, Mass.: Abt Associates, Inc., and the Center for Survey Research,
          University of Massachusetts.
Louis, K. S., S. Rosenblum, and J.A. Molitor
  1981   *Strategies for Knowledge Use and School Improvement.* Washington,
          D.C.: National Institute of Education.
McCarthy, M.
  1990   University-based policy centers: new actors in the education policy are-
          na. *Educational Researcher* November:25-29.
McLaughlin, M.
  1990   The Rand change agent study revisited: macro perspectives and micro
          realities. *Educational Researcher* December:11-16.
Miller, G., ed.
  1973   *Linguistic Communication: Perspectives for Research.* Report of the
          Study Group on Linguistic Communication to the National Institute of
          Education. Newark, Del.: International Reading Association.
Moorman, H.N., and T.G. Carroll
  1986   Peer review and the NIE/OERI competition for regional educational labo-
          ratories and national R&D centers. *Educational Researcher* August/Sep-
          tember:16-18.

Murnane, R.J., and D.K. Cohen
   1986   Merit pay and the evaluation problem: why most merit pay plans fail and a few survive. *Harvard Educational Review* 56(1):1-17.

National Academy of Education
   1991   *Research and the Renewal of Education.* Stanford, Calif.: National Academy of Education, Stanford University.

National Advisory Council on Educational Research and Improvement
   1989   *Fourteenth Annual Report.* Washington, D.C.: National Advisory Council on Educational Research and Improvement.

National Assessment Governing Board
   1991   *The Levels of Mathematics Achievement*, Vol. 1, National and State Summaries. Washington, D.C.: National Assessment Governing Board.

National Center for Education Statistics
   1990   *Use of Educational Research and Development Resources by Public School Districts.* Document no. NCES 90-084, Office of Educational Research and Improvement. Washington, D.C.: U.S. Department of Education.
   1991a *The Condition of Education 1991. Vol. 1, Elementary and Secondary Education.* Washington, D.C.: U.S. Department of Education.
   1991b *Digest of Education Statistics 1991.* Document no. NCES 91-697, Office of Educational Research and Improvement. Washington, D.C.: U.S. Department of Education.
   1991c *Programs and Plans.* Washington, D.C.: U.S. Department of Education.
   1991d *Trends in Academic Progress: Achievement of American Students in Science, 1970-90, Mathematics, 1973-90, Reading, 1971-90, and Writing, 1984-90.* Prepared by the Educational Testing Service. NCES 90-1294. Washington, D.C.: U.S. Department of Education.

National Commission on Excellence in Education
   1983   *A Nation At Risk.* Washington, D.C.: U.S. Government Printing Office.

National Council of Teachers of Mathematics
   1989   *Curriculum and Evaluation Standards for School Mathematics.* Reston, Va.: National Council of Teachers of Mathematics.

National Dissemination Study Group
   1990   *Educational Programs That Work.* Edition 16. Longmont, Colo.: Sopris West, Inc.

National Education Goals Panel
   1991   *The National Education Goals Report: Building a Nation of Learners.* Washington, D.C.: National Education Goals Panel.

National Institute of Education (NIE)
   1973a *A Brief Outline of Its History, Status, and Tentative Plans.* NIE 73-25000. Washington, D.C.: National Institute of Education.
   1973b NIE Task Force on Resource Planning and Analysis. Washington, D.C.
   1976   *The 1976 Databook: The Status of Education Research and Development in the United States.* Washington, D.C.: U.S. Department of Health, Education, and Welfare.
   1977a *Violent Schools, Safe Schools: The Safe School Study Report to the Congress.* National Institute of Education. Washington, D.C.: U.S. Department of Health, Education, and Welfare.

1977b *Women and Mathematics: Research Perspectives for Change.* Washington, D.C.: U.S. Department of Health, Education, and Welfare.

1983a *Expanding and Strengthening NIE's Regional Laboratory Services: Needs, Issues, and Options.* Final Report of the NIE Laboratory Study Group. Washington, D.C.: U.S. Department of Education.

1983b Laboratory Purposes and Functions: Issues for the National Study Group on Regional Laboratories. Unpublished paper. U.S. Department of Health, Education, and Welfare, Washington, D.C.

1984   Regional educational laboratory institutional operations. Request for proposal. RFP No. NIE-R-85-0003. U.S. Department of Eduction, Washington, D.C.

National Research Council

1958   *A Proposed Organization for Research in Education.* Washington, D.C.: National Academy of Sciences.

1977a *Decision Making in the Environmental Protection Agency, Vol. II.* Committee on Environmental Decision Making. Washington, D.C.: National Academy of Sciences.

1977b *Fundamental Research and the Process of Education.* Committee on Fundamental Research Relevant to Education, Assembly of Behavioral and Social Sciences, National Research Council. Washington, D.C.: National Academy of Sciences.

1986   *Creating a Center for Education Statistics: A Time for Action.* Committee on National Statistics, Commission on Behavioral and Social Science and Education. Washington, D.C.: National Academy Press.

1990   *Reshaping School Mathematics: A Philosophy and Framework for Curriculum.* Mathematical Sciences Education Board. Washington, D.C.: National Academy Press.

National Science Board

1989   *Science and Engineering Indicators—1989.* Washington, D.C.: National Science Foundation.

National Science Foundation

1990   *Research and Development Expenditures of State Government Agencies: Fiscal Years 1987 and 1988.* NSF 90-309. Washington, D.C.: National Science Foundation.

1991a *Federal Funds for Research and Development: Fiscal Years 1989, 1990, and 1991.* Vol. XXXIX, NSF 90-327. Washington, D.C.: National Science Foundation.

1991b *Selected Data on Federal R&D Funding by Budget Function: Fiscal Years 1990-92.* NSF 91-319. Washington, D.C.: National Science Foundation.

Nestlehutt, M. Bruce

1991   Management Improvement Report No. 91-10: Technical Assistance Centers and Clearinghouses. Atlanta, Ga: Office of Inspector General, U.S. Department of Education.

New American Schools Development Corporation

1991   *Designs For a New Generation of American Schools.* New American Schools Development Corporation, Arlington, Va.

Newell, A., and H. Simon

1972   *Human Problem Solving.* Englewood Cliffs, N.J.: Prentice-Hall.

Newmann, F.M.
   1990   Proposal for Center on Organization and Restructuring of Schools. Wis-
           consin Center for Education Research, Madison, Wisc.
Niemiec, R., G. Samson, T. Weinstein, and H. Walberg
   1987   The effects of computer based instruction in elementary schools: a quan-
           titative synthesis. *Journal of Research on Computing in Education* Win-
           ter:85-103.
Office of Educational Research and Improvement
   1986   *Good Secondary Schools: What Makes them Tick?*   Washington, D.C.:
           U.S. Department of Education.
   1989a   *Becoming a Nation of Readers: What Principals Can Do.* Alexandria,
           Va.: National Association of Elementary School Principals. U.S. De-
           partment of Education.
   1989b   Publication and Audiovisual Review System. Departmental directive (A:MIS:1-
           110). U.S. Department of Education, Washington, D.C.
   1990a   *Dealing with Dropouts: The Urban Superintendents' Call to Action.*
           Washington, D.C.: U.S. Department of Education.
   1990b   *Guide to Department of Education Programs.* Washington, D.C: U.S.
           Department of Education.
   1990c   *Increasing Achievement of At-Risk Students at Each Grade Level.* Wash-
           ington, D.C.: U.S. Department of Education
   1990d   *Profiles of Successful Drug Prevention Programs.* Programs for the Im-
           provement of Practice. Washington, D.C.: U.S. Department of Educa-
           tion.
   1990e   *Science Education Programs that Work: A Collection of Proven Exem-
           plary Educational Programs and Practices in the National Diffusion Net-
           work.* Washington, D.C.: U.S. Department of Education.
   1991   *ERIC Annual Report: Summarizing the Accomplishment of the Educa-
           tional Resources Information Center.* Washington, D.C.: U.S. Depart-
           ment of Education.
Palincsar, A., and A. Brown
   1984   *Reciprocal Teaching of Comprehension Fostering and Comprehension
           Monitoring Activities.* Center for the Study of Reading, University of
           Illinois. Hillsdale, N.J.: Lawrence Erlbaum Associates, Inc.
Panel for the Review of Laboratory and Center Operations
   1979   *Research and Development Centers and Regional Educational Laborato-
           ries: Strengthening and Stabilizing a National Resource.* Final report,
           National Institute of Education. Washington, D.C.: U.S. Department of
           Education.
Peterson, P.E.
   1991   The urban underclass and the poverty paradox. In C. Jencks and P.
           Peterson, eds., *The Urban Underclass.* Washington, D.C.: Brookings
           Institution.
Peterson, P.E., and B.G. Rabe
   1983   The role of interest groups in the formation of educational policy: past
           practice and future trends. *Teachers College Record* 84(3):709-729.

Pinnell, G., C. Lyons, and D. DeFord
  1991   Studying the Effectiveness of Early Intervention Approaches for First
          Grade Children Having Difficulty in Reading. Educational Report No.
          16. Martin L. King Literacy Center, Early Literacy Research Project.
          The Ohio State University, Columbus, Ohio.
Porter, A.
  1989   A curriculum out of balance: the case of elementary school mathematics.
          Educational Researcher 18(5):9-15.
Porter, A., D. Archbald, and A. Tyree, Jr.
  1991   Reforming the curriculum: will empowerment policies replace control?
          Pp. 22-36 in S. Fuhrman, ed., *The Politics of Curriculum and Testing*.
          London: Taylor and Francis, Ltd.
Porter, A., and J. Brophy
  1988   Synthesis of research on good teaching: insights from the work of the
          institute for research on teaching. *Educational Leadership* May:74-85.
President's Task Force on Education
  1964   Report of the President's Task Force on Education. Unpublished report.
          Department of Health, Education, and Welfare, Washington, D.C.
Rackliffe, G.
  1988   Obstacles To Teacher Use of The Knowledge Base For School Reform.
          Paper presented at the symposium, "Teacher Empowerment Through Knowl-
          edge: Linking Research and Practice for School Reform," at the annual
          conference of the American Educational Research Association, New Or-
          leans, La.
Ralph, J., and M.C. Dwyer
  1988   *Making the Case: Evidence of Program Effectiveness in Schools and
          Classrooms*. Washington, D.C.: U.S. Department of Education.
Ravitch, D.S.
  1974   *The Great School Wars*. New York City: Basic Books.
Resnick, L.
  1987a *Education and Learning to Think*. Commission on Behavioral and Social
          Sciences and Education, National Research Council. Washington, D.C.:
          National Academy Press.
  1987b Learning in school and out. *Educational Researcher* 16(9):13-20.
  1989   Introduction. Pp. 1-24 in L.B. Resnick, ed., *Knowing, Learning, and
          Instruction: Essays in Honor of Robert Glaser*. Hillsdale, N.J.: Lawrence
          Erlbaum Associates, Inc.
Rogoff, B., and H. Lave, eds.
  1984   *Everyday Cognition: Its Development in Social Context*. Cambridge,
          Mass.: Harvard University Press.
Rosenholtz, S.
  1989   *Teachers' Workplace: The Social Organization of Schools*. New York:
          Longman.
Rudner, L., C. Corry, L. Pike, and D. Antonoplos
  No   Impact of NIE Funded Research on Testing and Methodology 1977-1983.
  date   Unpublished paper, National Institute of Education. U.S. Department of
          Education, Washington, D.C.

Sarason, S.B.
  1971   *The Culture of the School and the Problem of Change.* Boston: Allyn
         and Bacon.
  1990   *The Predictable Failure of Educational Reform: Can We Change Course
         Before It's Too Late?* San Francisco, Calif.: Jossey-Bass.
Sawyer, R.
  1987   Roadblocks to Use of the Knowledge Base in MILP Schools. Unpub-
         lished working paper, Mastery in Learning Project, National Education
         Association, Washington, D.C.
Schmidt, P.
  1991   New Jersey to implement Comer program in urban districts. *Education
         Week* September 18:20.
Schon, D.A.
  1983   *The Reflective Practitioner.* New York: Basic Books.
Shanker, A.
  1988   Statement to Subcommittee on Select Education, Committee on Educa-
         tion and Labor, U.S. House of Representatives, April 20.
Simon, H.A.
  1974   How big is a chunk? *Science* 183:482-488.
Skrtic, T.
  1991   The special education paradox: equity as the way to excellence. *Har-
         vard Educational Review* 61(2):148-206.
Slavin, R.
  1986   *Using Student Team Learning, 3rd Edition.* Johns Hopkins Team Learn-
         ing Project, Center for Research on Elementary and Middle Schools.
         Baltimore, Md.: Johns Hopkins Universtiy.
  1990   *Cooperative Learning: Theory, Research, and Practice.* Englewood Cliffs,
         N.J.: Prentice-Hall.
Smith, M., and J. O'Day
  1990   Systemic School Reform. Unpublished paper, School of Education, Stan-
         ford University.
Sproull, L., S. Weiner, and D. Wolf
  1978   *Organizing an Anarchy: Belief, Bureaucracy, and Politics in the Nation-
         al Institute of Education.* Chicago: University of Chicago Press.
Sroufe, G.
  1991   Educational enterprise zones: the new national research centers. *Educa-
         tional Researcher.* 20(4):24-29.
Svenson, E.
  1969   Observations on Emerging Relationships Between Regional Educational
         Laboratories and State Departments of Education. Unpublished paper,
         CEMREL, Inc., St. Louis, Missouri.
Tenopir, C.
  1991   The most popular databases. *Library Journal* April 1:96-98.
Tikunoff, W., and B. Ward
  1983   Collaborative research on teaching. *The Elementary School Journal* 83(4):453-
         468.

Timpane, P.
  1982   Federal progress in educational research. *Harvard Educational Review*
         52(4):540-548.
Trester, D.
  1981   *ERIC—the First Fifteen Years*. Columbus, Ohio: SMEAC Information
         Reference Center.
Turnbull, B.
  1991   Research Knowledge and School Improvement: Can This Marriage Be
         Saved? Unpublished paper prepared for the Committee on the Federal
         Role in Education Research, Commission on Behavioral and Social Sci-
         ences and Education, National Research Council. Policy Studies Associ-
         ates, Washington, D.C.
U.S. Department of Education
  1989   Publication and Audiovisual Review System. Unpublished manuscript.
         U.S. Department of Education, Washington, D.C.
  1990   *Guide to Department of Education Programs*. Washington, D.C.: U.S.
         Department of Education.
U.S. Department of Health, Education and Welfare
  1969a *Educational Research and Development in the United States*. Washing-
         ton, D.C.: U.S. Department of Health, Education, and Welfare.
  1969b *Office of Education: Support for Research and Related Activities*. OE-
         12025-B. Washington, D.C.: U.S. Department of Health, Education and
         Welfare.
U.S. Department of Health and Human Services
  1991   *NIH Data Book 1991*. NIH Publication No. 91-1261, September. Na-
         tional Institutes of Health. Washington, D.C.: U.S. Department of Health
         and Human Services.
U.S. General Accounting Office
  1981   *Greater Use of Exemplary Education Programs Could Improve Educa-
         tion for Disadvantaged Children: Report to the Congress of the United
         States*. Washington, D.C.: U.S. Government Printing Office.
  1987   *Changes in Funds and Priorities Have Affected Production and Quality*.
         GAO/PEMD-88-4. Washington, D.C.: U.S. Government Printing Of-
         fice.
  1988   *R&D Funding: The Department of Education in Perspective*. Report to
         the Chairman, Subcommittee on Select Education, Committee on Educa-
         tion and Labor, House of Representatives. Washington, D.C.: U.S. Gen-
         eral Accounting Office.
U.S. Office of Management and Budget
  1990   Preparation and Submission of Budget Estimates. Circular no. A-11,
         revised transmittal memorandum no. 61. Office of Management and
         Budget, Washington, D.C.
  1991   *Budget of the United States Government: Fiscal Year 1992*. Executive
         Office of the President of the United States. Washington, D.C.: U.S.
         Government Printing Office.
U.S. Office of Technology Assessment
  1986   *Research Funding As An Investment: Can We Measure the Returns?*

Background Report No. 12 transmitted to the Task Force on Science Policy Committee on Science and Technology, U.S. House of Representatives. Washington, D.C.: U.S. Government Printing Office.

1988 *Power On! New Tools for Teaching and Learning.* OTA-SET-379. Washington, D.C.: U.S. Government Printing Office.

Vellutino, F.R.
1991 Introduction to three studies on reading acquisition: convergent findings on theoretical foundations of code-oriented versus whole-language approaches to reading instruction. *Journal of Educational Psychology* 83(4):437-443.

Vygotsky, L.
1978 *Mind in Society: The Development of Higher Psychological Processor.* Cambridge, Mass: Harvard University Press.

Wade, S., B. Marenus, and E. Reuben
1982 Regional Educational Laboratories: A Service Delivery Assessment. Division of Performance Management Systems, Office of Management, U.S. Department of Education, Washington, D.C.

Weiss, C.
1980 Knowledge creep and decision accretion. *Knowledge: Creation, Diffusion, Utilization* 1(3):381-404.

1989 Congressional Committees as Users of Analysis. In *Journal of Policy Analysis and Management* 8(3):411-431.

Winocur, S.
1983 Improve Minimal Proficiencies by Activating Critical Thinking. Project IMPACT, Santa Anna, California.

1987 Improve Minimal Proficiencies by Activating Critical Thinking. Project IMPACT, Santa Anna, California.

Wirt, J., L. Muraskin, R. Meyer, and D. Goodwin
1989 National assessment of vocational education: testimony before the House Education and Labor Committee. *Economics of Education Review* 8(4):383-392.

Wirtenberg, J.
1982 Compendium of Accomplishments for the Teaching and Learning Program of the National Institute of Education. Unpublished paper, National Institute of Education, U.S. Department of Education, Washington, D.C.

Appendix

Biographical Sketches of Committee Members and Staff

RICHARD C. ATKINSON (*Chair*) is chancellor of the University of California at San Diego and professor of cognitive science and psychology. He formerly served as director of the National Science Foundation and president of the American Association for the Advancement of Science. His research on problems of memory and cognition has been used to develop computer-controlled systems for instruction in the primary grades. Atkinson is a member of the National Academy of Sciences, the Institute of Medicine, the National Academy of Education, and the American Philosophical Society. He obtained a Ph.B. degree from the University of Chicago and a Ph.D. degree from Indiana University.

LAWRENCE BADAR is assistant dean of the Department of Mathematics and Natural Science at Case Western University. His responsibilities include supervising in-service training programs for elementary and secondary teachers, directing the high school science olympics, and coordinating the university's programs for gifted and talented precollege students. He received a Presidential Award for Excellence in Science and Mathematic Teaching in 1985 for his work as a high school physics teacher, and he subsequently served 2 years at the National Science Foundation supervising that award program and another grants program designed for the enhancement of teaching.

G. CARL BALL is chairman of the board of George J. Ball, Inc., one of the largest agriculture and horticulture producers in the country. For two decades he served as president of Ball, Inc. Ball is president of the Ball Foundation, which does research on human ability and education issues. He also provides major support to a consortium organized by Teachers College at Columbia University that is exploring productivity in U.S. education. Ball serves on the boards of the Corridor Partnership for Excellence in Education, the Illinois Math and Science Academy (IMSA), the IMSA Alliance, and the Illinois Institute of Technology, West.

JAMES A. BANKS is professor of education and director of the Center for Multicultural Education at the University of Washington, Seattle. A former classroom teacher, Banks is a frequent lecturer and consultant to school districts and universities. In 1986 he was named Distinguished Scholar/ Researcher on Minority Education by the American Educational Research Association. He has received fellowships from the National Academy of Education, the Kellogg Foundation, and the Rockefeller Foundation. Banks has written or edited 14 books on multicultural education and social studies including *Teaching Strategies for Ethnic Studies* (5th Ed.), *Multiethnic Education: Theory and Practice* (2nd Ed.) and *Teaching Strategies for the Social Studies*, (4th Ed.). He has also written more than 100 articles and contributions to books.

KATHERINE L. BICK is the U.S. scientific liaison for Centro SMID Firenze, the Italian research group studying Alzheimer's disease and other dementias in association with the World Health Organization and other organizations. A neurobiologist, she was previously Deputy Director for Extramural Research at the National Institutes of Health (NIH). During her career at NIH, she developed new programs in brain research and framed policies that guided federal sponsorship of biomedical research. Prior to her government service, she was a faculty member at the University of California at Los Angeles; California State University, Northridge; and Georgetown University. In addition to research reports, she edited *Alzheimer's Disease: Senile Dementia and Related Disorders* and published translations of early European works in *The Early Story of Alzheimer's Disease*. She received B.Sc. and M.Sc. degrees from Acadia University, Nova Scotia, Canada, and a Ph.D. degree from Brown University.

C. L. HUTCHINS is the executive director of the Mid-continent Regional Educational Laboratory (McREL) and the McREL Institute. He was formerly an assistant director at the National Institute of Education (NIE). Hutchins's work has focused on dissemination of educational research and development products. He has served as chair of the Council for Educational Development and Research (CEDaR), and he is currently a program chair for the International Society for the Systems Sciences (ISSS), focusing attention on education as a system.

GREGG B. JACKSON is the study director for the Committee on the Federal Role in Education Research and a senior staff officer at the National Research Council. Formerly, he was director of research for the International City Management Association, a project director at the Center for the Study of Services, and a senior scientist at the George Washington University. His research and writing has been in the areas of program evaluation, meta-analysis, postsecondary and adult education, and the education of minority youth. He has a B.A. degree in economics from the University of Hawaii and a Ph.D. degree in education planning and policy from the University of California at Berkeley.

BEVERLY JIMENEZ is the consulting principal for the Collaboration for Educational Excellence, a San Francisco-based school restructuring project aimed at significantly improving educational opportunities for children of poverty. During her 22 years with the San Francisco Unified School District, she has served as a classroom teacher and elementary school principal and as founder and head teacher of a collaboratively administered elementary school. Her work has centered on issues of organizational development and change, collaborative leadership development, and child-centered instructional strategies. She currently serves on the advisory board to the International Network of Principals Centers and on the planning board of the San Francisco Principals' Center. She has a B.A. degree in english literature from Ohio University and an M.A. degree in educational administration from San Francisco State University.

CHARLES F. MANSKI is Wolfowitz professor of economics at the University of Wisconsin-Madison. His research spans econometric theory, the economics of education, and the empirical analysis of individual behavior. He is presently editor of the *Journal of Human Resources* and recently completed a term as director of the Institute for Research on Poverty. He is fellow of the Econometric Society and of the American Association for the Advancement of Science. Manski received a Ph.D. degree in economics from Massachusetts Institute of Technology.

ANNE S. MAVOR is a senior research associate for the Committee on the Federal Role in Education Research. She joined the National Research Council in 1989 as associate study director for the Committee on Performance Appraisal for Merit Pay and is currently serving as study director for the Committee on Military Enlistment Standards. Her work has been concentrated in the areas of testing, training, decision making, and information system design for The College Board and other private organizations. She has a master's degree in experimental psychology from Purdue University.

PAUL E. PETERSON is Henry Lee Shattuck professor of government and director of the Center for American Political Studies at Harvard University.

Formerly, he was professor of public policy at Johns Hopkins University and director of government studies at the Bookings Institution. He is the author or coauthor of *When Federalism Works, The Politics of School Reform, 1870—1940, School Politics Chicago Style, City Limits*, and numerous articles on education, urban affairs, and welfare policy. Two of his books have received awards from the American Political Science Association. Peterson received a B.A. degree from Concordia College and a Ph.D. degree from the University of Chicago.

ANDREW C. PORTER is a professor of educational psychology and director of the Wisconsin Center for Education Research at the University of Wisconsin-Madison. He has also served on the faculty at Michigan State University, where he was associate dean for research and graduate study and codirector of the Institute for Research on Teaching. He was a visiting scholar and an associate director of basic skills research at the National Institute of Education. Porter has published on psychometrics, student and teacher assessment, teaching research, and education policy. He has served on the editorial boards of eight professional journals including, currently, the *American Journal of Education* and *Educational Evaluation and Policy Analysis*. Porter has a B.S. degree in education from Indiana State University and master's and Ph.D degrees in educational psychology from the University of Wisconsin-Madison.

ALBERT H. QUIE is president emeritus and a member of the board of Prison Fellowship Ministries. He also serves on the boards of several corporations and other nonprofit organizations. Formerly, he was governor of Minnesota and a U.S. Representative from that state. In the latter position he served on the House Education and Labor Committee and played key roles in the passage of the Higher Education Act—Student Aid Act, the Education of All Handicapped Children Act, and the Vocational Education Act. He has received nine honorary doctorate degrees and several awards for his contributions to education and to the disabled.

MARILEE RIST is a senior editor for *The American School Board Journal* and *The Executive Educator* magazines, both published by the National School Boards Association. As a long-time education journalist, she has visited school districts across the nation and written on a wide range of education topics. She has received numerous awards from the Education Writers' Association and from the Society of National Association Publications and was a finalist in the National Magazine Awards competition for her article on merit pay for teachers.

SUSAN M. ROGERS served as research associate for the Committee on the Federal Role in Education Research and is currently working as a program officer at the Institute of Medicine. Previously, she served on the staff of the National Research Council's Committee on Population and the Committee on AIDS Research and the Social, Behavioral, and Statistical Sciences. She received a B.A. degree in biology from the University of North Carolina at Chapel Hill and an M.A. degree in demography from Georgetown University.

CAROL WEISS is a professor at the Harvard University Graduate School of Education. She has published eight books on the route from research to decisions: methods of evaluation research, the influences of research on policy, and channels through which research and other forms of information reach decision-making arenas. Weiss has been a congressional fellow, a guest scholar at the Brookings Institution, visiting professor at Arizona State University, and senior fellow with the Department of Education. She has been a consultant to the National Science Foundation, the U.S. General Accounting Office, the U.S. Agency for International Development, the U.S. Department of Education, and other governmental and voluntary organizations. She holds a Ph.D. degree in sociology from Columbia University.

KENNETH WILSON is Hazel C. Youngberg Trustees distinguished professor of physics at Ohio State University and coprincipal investigator for Ohio's Project Discovery, one of the National Science Foundation's statewide systemic science and mathematics reform initiatives. Previously, he served as professor of physics and director of the supercomputer center at Cornell University. Wilson's research has been in elementary particle theory, condensed matter physics, quantum chemistry, and computer science. He has received several awards for his contributions, including the Nobel Prize in Physics (1982). He is member of the National Academy of Sciences, the American Academy of Arts and Sciences, and the American Philosophical Society. Wilson received an undergraduate degree from Harvard and a Ph.D. degree from the California Institute of Technology.